RETHINKING RAPE

Rethinking
RAPE

ANN J. CAHILL

Cornell University Press | ITHACA AND LONDON

First published 2001 by Cornell University Press
First printing, Cornell Paperbacks, 2001

Library of Congress Cataloging-in-Publication Data

Cahill, Ann J.
    Rethinking rape/Ann J. Cahill.
        p. cm.
    Includes bibliographical references and index.
    ISBN 0-8014-3794-6 (cloth : acid-free paper); ISBN 0-8014-8718-8 (pbk.)
    1. Rape. 2. Feminist theory. I. Title.
    HV6558 .C34 2001
    364.15′32—dc21

                            00-011504

Printed in the United States of America

Cornell University Press strives to use environmentally responsible suppliers and materials to the fullest extent possible in the publishing of its books. Such materials include vegetable-based, low-VOC inks and acid-free papers that are either recycled, totally chlorine-free, or partly composed of nonwood fibers. Books that bear the logo of the FSC (Forest Stewardship Council) use paper taken from forests that have been inspected and certified as meeting the highest standards for environmental and social responsibility. For further information, visit our website at www.cornellpress.cornell.edu.

Cloth printing   10 9 8 7 6 5 4 3 2 1
Paperback printing   10 9 8 7 6 5 4 3 2 1

FSC FSC Trademark © 1996 Forest Stewardship Council A.C
     SW-COC-098

to my Weirdo
in grief, defiance, and hope
with love

Contents

Acknowledgments

Like any major project, *Rethinking Rape* came about with the help of a variety of institutions and individuals. I am thankful for the philosophy department at SUNY Stony Brook, a rigorous and encouraging environment within which to explore feminist theory. The American Association of University Women supported my final year of dissertation writing with an American Fellowship; I am in their debt. A Summer Fellowship from Elon College allowed me the time necessary to complete the final revisions to the manuscript. Many thanks to Sarah J. Cahill for her diligent preparation of the index.

I bow deeply to my colleagues in the philosophy department of Elon College: Nim Batchelor, Martin Fowler, Yoram Lubling, John Sullivan, and Anthony Weston. They provide me with a philosophical home rich in camaraderie and intellectual stimulation, and it is my great fortune to think and be with them.

I thank my teachers, especially Susan Kinder, Joanne Harder, Ailsa Steinert, Joseph Lawrence, Mary Rawlinson, Ed Casey, and Eva Feder Kittay, for that ineffable combination of challenge and guidance that marks teaching at its best. I thank my students for their courage in grappling with uncomfortable ideas and their willingness to listen to my stories. My friends are a constant source of insight and humor. I am particularly fortunate to have the pleasure of discussing philosophy with the generous and razor-sharp minds of Jennifer Hansen and Janine Jones. It doesn't hurt that I love to cook for both of them!

No words can express the appreciation I have for the strength, humor, and resourcefulness of the members of my family. I am grateful to my mother for her presence, my siblings and siblings-in-law for their diversity of talents, my nieces and nephews for their overwhelmingly charming ways, and my parents-in-law for their unflinching support. I have been truly blessed.

I reserve my deepest gratitude for my husband, Neil Koehler Swenson, and his persistent, dynamic, and steadfast love. He is my truest home.

ANN J. CAHILL

Greensboro, North Carolina

RETHINKING RAPE

The Problem of Rape

The threat of rape in contemporary U.S. society constitutes a persistent and pervasive element in women's lives. So constant is this threat that it becomes assumed as a basic consideration in the daily choices women face. Although I myself have not been a victim of rape, the threat of rape has had a profound effect on the structure and quality of my life. The possibility of rape shapes the space I inhabit, designating certain hours and places as dangerous to me while to men they remain open prospects. It makes me think twice as I walk to my car late in the night; it discouraged me from joining a male college friend as he spent two weeks of spring break living on the streets with homeless people. Because of the possibility of sexual violence, I did not invite a new male friend, later one of my best friends, to my room for coffee when I had only had one or two conversations with him. I was rapable, and therefore I had to be careful.

Like many women who have not been raped, I have had various, more indirect encounters with sexual violence. I had a friend who charged her father with the rapes he inflicted on her since her childhood, and I witnessed parts of the three trials that she endured. A college acquaintance whose room was several doors down from mine was raped on an early spring morning as I slept in. While I was working on the final version of this manuscript, a woman dear to my heart was drugged and date-raped. All these experiences, but especially the last one, inspired in me emotions of despair, white-hot anger, and fear. Rape has never been far from my experiences.

As my undergraduate and then graduate work continued, I began to read a few pieces on the theory of rape, Susan Brownmiller's *Against Our Will: Men, Women, and Rape* (1975) being among the first. Most of what I read seemed strangely dissatisfying. When I read Michel Foucault's suggestion that rape be considered legally merely an act of assault, with no significance given to the sexual nature of the crime (see chapter 5), I began to investigate the theoretical significance of rape with regard to feminine subjectivity, agency, and embodiment. This volume is the culmination of that investigation.

Rape in Feminist Thought

Rape is, for many feminists, the ultimate expression of a patriarchal order, a crime that epitomizes women's oppressed status by proclaiming, in the loudest possible voice, the most degrading truths about women that a hostile world has to offer. In much of feminist theory and discussion, then, rape has functioned as the outer limit of the oppression of women, that indisputable act of violence and loathing. Rape has also presented feminism with some of its most difficult problems. Some stem from its sheer frequency: how do we explain why so many men rape? Others involve rape's ethical significance: what exactly is wrong in the wrong of rape? The application of force? The lack of consent? Still others concentrate on the implications of the feminist concern with violence against women: by stressing the extent of that violence, do we risk defining women primarily as victims? How does one resist the phenomenon of rape, and how is it implicated in larger discourses of sex, gender, race, class, nationalism, and "ethnic cleansing"? How are we to understand what rape does and can do to women?

I have located two distinct schools of feminist philosophy concerning rape, both of which are taken up in detail in the ensuing chapters. The first is exemplified best by Brownmiller and can generally be summed up in the pithy formulation that rape is "violence, not sex." This position held considerable sway in the 1970s, especially among liberal feminists, and emphasized that the motivations behind an act of rape were not primarily sexual, that is, did not arise out of a sexual need, but rather were primarily violent, such that rape was an act of power that sought to dominate and degrade the victim. The second strand, exemplified by Catharine MacKinnon, argued somewhat to the contrary that, given the compulsory nature of heterosexuality and the eroticization of masculine dominance, rape was in fact continuous with most heterosexual sex and could not be distinguished from it by mere reference to coercion or violence. This position held that given women's inferior status with regard to sexual freedom, their social and economic dependence on men, and the social constraints on their sexuality, rape was not an exception to heterosexual sexuality as presently constructed and organized, but rather its logical extension. It was not the case, then, that rape was violent and therefore not sexual, but rather that rape was violent precisely due to its (hetero)sexual content and meaning.

As the chapters below demonstrate, I find both theories sorely lacking. Most telling, they are at odds with what I understand to be a significant portion of women's experiences of rape. Defining rape as primarily violence, not sex, implied that rape was significantly similar to other types of assault, and that its sexual nature was relatively irrelevant to the experience. Yet few women would agree that being raped is essentially equivalent to being hit in the face or otherwise physically assaulted. Likewise, contrary to MacKinnon's theory, most women can generally and with relative ease distinguish between acts of rape and consensual, mutually desired heterosexual sex.

The problems with these theories, however, are deeper than even these contradictions suggest. Both fail to account sufficiently for the intricate interplay of social and political power, sexual hierarchization, and embodiment. Brownmiller's thesis assumes that it is possible to distinguish strictly between sex and violence (that is, the imposition of power), such that if rape is primarily about power, it is not about sexuality. Moreover, by understanding violence as essentially political and sex as essentially natural, Brownmiller approaches the body as wholly biological and therefore unmarked by social forces, to the extent that she accepts the female body as inherently rapable and the male body as inherently capable of rape. Her argument therefore rests on an understanding of the body as a natural, rather than social, entity, and an assumption of sexuality as a biological matter. Assuming a dichotomous relationship between nature and culture allows Brownmiller to assume a similarly dichotomous relationship between sex and violence. Following in large part the insights of contemporary feminist theories of the body, I find these dichotomies to be flawed and ultimately ill suited for illuminating the complex phenomenon of rape.

MacKinnon's position presupposes that the patriarchal social structure that renders heterosexuality compulsory and feminine sexuality derivative of masculine sexuality is not only powerful, but omnipotent, such that it makes impossible any true exercise of feminine (sexual) agency. From this perspective, women, qua women, are constituted by their inferior social status. To speak of women's consent with regard to sexuality is to ignore the fact that women's sexuality is in large part, and perhaps entirely, shaped not by the desires of women themselves, but by a social structure centered around the needs and desires of men. MacKinnon asserts that given a patriarchal social environment, women have virtually no free choice when it comes to matters sexual, and that therefore rape is much more similar to "normal" heterosexual sex than the liberal feminist position (such as that of Brownmiller) allows. Where Brownmiller emphasizes the coercion and force—that is, the violence—of rape, MacKinnon insists not only that sexuality and violence are not mutually exclusive, but that for women in a patriarchal culture, they are mutually defined. Here too I disagree with MacKinnon regarding the implication of individual feminine bodies in an overall power structure. While MacKinnon assumes women to be wholly constituted by the power structure that imposes their inferiority, I argue that such a model ignores the possibility of resistance as well as the degree to which women themselves are implicated in that structure. Patriarchy holds enormous sway over the lives of women, their possibilities and their choices, but its power is neither unidirectional nor omnipotent. If we understand the body as a central site for both the production of power and the possibility of resistance, women's agency—and therefore the validity and efficacy of their choices with regard to sexuality—becomes possible.

    Both Brownmiller and MacKinnon rely theoretically on philosophical dichotomies—nature/culture, self/society, violence/sex—that are ultimately untenable. The abdication of these dichotomies is not an easy one, for it involves not only a rethinking of such concepts as agency, force, and power, but also a serious exploration of the intricate ways the individual and the larger society mesh, interact, and define each other. If we live in what some have termed a "rape culture" (Buchwald, Fletcher, and Roth 1993), a social environment where the crime of rape is not only assumed, but necessary for the perpetuation of other, more subtle forms of gender inequity, then we must be careful to remember that women are not only victims of that culture, but members of it (albeit secondary members, in many ways). Social contract theory defined women primarily as property, and in doing so excluded them from the possibility of subjectivity; but if we understand women as not merely acted upon, but acting—that is, if we understand power as producing possibilities, abilities, and identities—then women are not fundamentally outside culture, but implicated in it. As a moment in that culture, rape needs to be rethought as a pervasive, sustained, and repetitive, but not ultimately defining, element of the development of women's experience; as something that is taken up and experienced differently by different women but also holds some common aspects; as a factor that marks women as different from men; as an experience that perhaps begins with the body but whose significance does not end there.

The Significance of Embodiment

Recent years have witnessed a rediscovery of the body and its significance in feminist theory. This burgeoning branch of scholarship has challenged the traditional philosophical dichotomy between body and mind, arguing often for a more fluid, complex model of self. It has noted the traditional association of the feminine with the body, in contrast to the male realm of mind, theory, and abstract thought. While refusing the hierarchy that resulted in such gender ghettoes, it has insisted that the realms traditionally identified as feminine not be abandoned or ignored.

The body, however, is also somewhat of a stumbling block for feminism. It highlights the difficulty of the very categories (male/female, masculine/feminine) that constitute the cornerstones of feminist inquiry, though many feminisms are committed to annihilating these categories. Ostensibly, and traditionally, it is the body that determines who is male and who is female. The sex/gender distinction prevalent in 1970s liberal feminism allowed feminists to declare much of what constituted femininity "unnatural," that is, cultural, and not biologically determined. What was of culture could be changed, and there the revolution lay. What was of nature—the sheer existence of different reproductive organs, for example, and the various biological truths concerning them—was fact, and beyond the tainting influence of a patriarchal culture.

This innocence of biology (and, in a larger sense, science) did not persist for long. Closer examination of the sexes challenged the naturalness of the sexed body and the opposition between male and female. Feminist critics of science noted that the cultural messages concerning men and women often found their way into the supposedly unbiased claims of biology; moreover, it became more and more difficult to determine, definitively, the line between the sexes on the basis of the body alone. This realization provided as many questions as it did answers, for while it demonstrated the inefficacy of the nature/culture opposition, it also threatened the coherence of the category of "woman," a category that had been threatened (more implicitly, perhaps) before when charges of racism and heterosexism were brought against feminism. If feminism is to be, in any sense, "for women," then it would seem provident to have some understanding of the delineations of that category. Culture, in its constantly shifting practices, could provide no such certainty, and now it appeared that nature was similarly inept.

Yet as feminist theory turned its gaze to the body, it became less interested in solidifying the category of "woman"—well aware that such solidification could as easily be used for less honorable purposes than its own—than in understanding the (female) body as a site where the traditional philosophical oppositions of self/other, society/self, and emotion/intellect reveal themselves not as opposites, but as mutually defining reversibilities whose elements adhere to each other even—and precisely—as they differ from each other. The models that reduce self to society or demand the control of the emotions by the intellect fail in their attempts to isolate one element over another. The details of the (female) body and its fluid, indeterminate nature undermine patriarchy's demand for unity and static truth, and call into question both the nature of subjectivity and the nature of sexual difference.

To consider the body in this light has not, however, been to toll the necessary death of either gender or sex as politically and philosophically relevant realities. That gender cannot be easily mapped onto specific bodies does not mean that there is no relation between the two; that women should not be utterly defined by the specifics that mark their bodies does not mean that sexually specific bodily experiences (such as pregnancy and menstruation) do not warrant attention. Rather, as feminist theory begins to look seriously at the body and its role in producing and sustaining a gendered system, it has discovered that the body's fluid nature allows us to challenge and celebrate both female and feminine bodily experiences.

Specifically, recent scholarship has insisted that the woman referred to in feminist theory be understood as embodied. This emphasis on the bodily, material facets of women's experiences is in direct contrast to a philosophical tradition where the person/subject/agent (purportedly unsexed, notoriously masculine in its pertinent characteristics) is marked not by physical attributes but by intellectual ones: the abilities to think abstractly, to make rational decisions, to remain unaffected by emotional or material concerns. Such a person, feminist theory asserts, is not only clearly masculine, but deeply splintered by the categorical imposition of the public/private split, an imposition that renders entire areas of experience irrelevant, both philosophically and politically. To consider persons as necessarily embodied, and to understand the body as the site of multiple boundaries, dynamics, and forces, is to avoid the pitfall of treating individuals as mere abstractions and to attribute appropriate significance to their material, emotional, and psychical attributes.

In addition, it is primarily through embodiment that persons become sexed. Therefore, the emphasis on embodiment precludes the denial of the significance of sexual difference. We may follow many feminist theorists of the body in contending that the body is that place where cultural truths concerning men and women are written (Butler 1990, 1993; Bartky 1988; Bordo 1991, 1993; Young 1990; Frye 1983); thus, we are able to recognize such things as feminine bodily comportment and experience as culturally specific whose details are not, in any sense of the words, natural or given. Nevertheless, in the contemporary world, women exist as sexed bodies. As Carol Bigwood argues

> In affirming a link between gender and the body, however, we need not resort to fixed, biological differences that dictate innate ahistorical differences and inflexible cross-cultural categories. We need a new model of the body that leads neither to biological determinism nor to gender skepticism and cultural relativism. The body must be understood as culturally and historically contextualized, on the one hand, and yet as part of our embodied givenness, on the other. (1991, 57)

For Rosi Braidotti, the development of a "female corporeal materialism" (1994, 52) and an understanding of the nomadic subject rescue the importance of sexual difference and therefore the importance of a variety of differences:

> [T]he decline of the universal in the age of modernity, marks the opportunity for the definition of a nomadic standpoint that is based on differences while not being merely relativistic. . . . In other words, gender is a notion that allows us to think the interdependence of sexual identity and other variables of oppression such as race, age, culture, class, and lifestyle. (98–99)

To begin with embodiment is, almost paradoxically, to begin with difference (and is thus, importantly, to follow Irigaray). For if embodiment is perhaps the one element of human experience that exists universally, it is precisely the one most marked by difference, sexual or otherwise. We are all embodied; we are all, perhaps, embodied differently in certain basic ways. Recognizing the differences inherent in embodiment allows us to avoid the mistake of universalism, while emphasizing the givenness of embodiment precludes the mistake of radical relativism. Feminist theorists, often calling on the work of Foucault, Derrida, Deleuze, and Merleau-Ponty, seek to articulate a model—or many models—of the (female) body that emphasizes its very elasticity. This branch of feminist theory refuses any definitive demarcation of the category of "woman," while still seeking to retain gender meanings.

It is, therefore, the perfect tool with which to reinvestigate the area of rape. For where previous theories of rape risked defining women solely by their victimization, ignoring women's experience, or resorting to theoretical dichotomies that no longer hold, contemporary feminist theories of the body resist those problems. Moreover, the emphasis on embodiment—not as a simple, biological fact but as a complex, sexually marked element of human experience—would serve to begin the theory of rape at the level of women's experience. If we understand embodiment as the possibility condition for all human activity, as well as the site of both sexual difference and the inscription of power, we can recognize the bodily ramifications of the threat and the fact of rape, the different ways the presence of rape functions for men and women, and the different ways the various truths concerning rape are expressed.

Legally speaking, the "wrongness" of rape has been defined in a myriad of ways: as an affront to women's sexual honor, as the theft of a man's property, as an assault on civil rights. Likewise, the actions that constitute rape have been controversial, as various legal bodies have broadened the definition of the crime to include penetration by objects other than body parts. By locating the body as central to a woman's identity, while not demanding that such identity be unified or determined, contemporary feminist theories of the body will approach rape as a crime not limited to an assault on a woman's sexuality, but as an assault on various but fundamental aspects of her embodied selfhood. At the same time, the understanding of the sexually differentiated nature of a woman's bodily experience and the sexually differentiated nature of rape itself will serve as a defense against that branch of theory that seeks to define rape as merely another type of assault.

By using the insights of contemporary feminist theories of the body, namely, the work of Judith Butler, Elizabeth Grosz, Rosi Braidotti, and others, I develop an analysis of rape as an embodied experience, an analysis that sheds considerable light on the phenomenon of rape, its gendered and sexual meanings, and its role in the production of gender hierarchies. By emphasizing the significance and nature of embodiment while refusing any determinate model of the body itself (that is, by understanding the body as primarily a field of possibilities, which are then concretized in individual bodies), my theory does not reduce rape to either violence or sexuality, but presents it as an assault that includes both elements. More particularly, my theory will blur those lines by arguing that the particular violence of rape is sexual, and that the sexuality inherent in it is violent.

One of the great difficulties presented by previous feminist theories of rape is that they tended to define rape in a certain way, not always allowing for differences of experiences among individual rape victims. This indeterminacy of the phenomenon of rape can often be confusing, even paralyzing: if we can't say what rape "is," how can we struggle against it? Embodiment provides a way out of this puzzle. It accounts for the multiplicity of experiences of rape by acknowledging that rape occurs only to individual bodies, and that individual bodies are marked and constructed by larger discourses (although never in a wholly determinate way). By recognizing those discourses, we are able to construct the scope of harms that rape as an embodied experience may include. Every rape experience is unique, but each is bodily; therefore, we are capable of locating the various axes of bodily meanings that rape affects.

Another difficulty in feminist theories of rape, often repeated by so-called antifeminist feminists, is that they risk constructing women solely as victims. To speak at some length of the sexual violence imposed on women in contemporary western society is, this argument claims, actually to increase women's powerlessness. Yet it would seem foolhardy to ignore sexual violence, as if the refusal to name it will allow women to pretend that it doesn't exist. The challenge is to be able to name rape and other forms of sexual violence as persistent realities in women's lives without constructing them as all-powerful or necessary. Again, the particular quality of the embodiment as theorized by these feminist thinkers proves to be useful. The intersubjectivity of embodiment allows us to understand that the embodied self is significantly affected, even constructed, in relation to others and to the actions of others. In this way, the horrific destructiveness of rape becomes obvious: if a being chooses to victimize another in a particularly sexually violent way, then the embodied being of the victim is going to be deeply, even fundamentally affected. However, embodied intersubjectivity is not static. It is an ongoing process; therefore, the violent actions of a rapist, while profoundly destructive to the victim's being and intersubjective personhood, need not be the final word. The being of the rape victim is transformed by the experience (and women who have not been the victims of sexual violence have themselves been affected by the pervasive threat of such violence), but that transformation is not necessarily that self's final development. Intersubjectivity allows for the possibility of understanding the rape victim as not only a victim, but as a person whose experience of victimization is a crucial element, among many crucial elements, of her being.

By approaching rape in terms of women's bodily experience, as well as in terms of the various, culturally specific ways the feminine body is organized and defined, we will elucidate the particular and unique wrongness of rape, a wrongness that has always eluded any legal definitions. We need no longer understand rape as a "theft," because we will no longer understand feminine sexuality as something that is possessed by the feminine subject, to be doled out on appropriate occasions. We need no longer understand it as mere battery, because we will begin with an acknowledgment of sexual difference that will mark it as significantly distinct from other assaults. We need no longer understand it as a mere extension of compulsory heterosexuality, because we will refuse any determining definitions of "woman," including those that deny her any and all agency. We will, instead, understand rape as an act charged with political and bodily meanings, as a threat to the possibility of the bodily integrity of women, and therefore as a threat to her status as a person.

If the nature of feminine embodiment will provide a ground for determining the wrongness of rape, the pervasive threat of rape will likewise provide insight into the specifics of feminine embodiment. The wrong that rape presents in contemporary society is not limited to an individual's experience of being raped, nor even to the imposition of persistent fear on women. It is also to be found in the specific ways women experience their bodies and the internalization and materialization of the belief in feminine culpability. It is no coincidence that many measures women take against the prospect of being raped involve the limitation of their mobility, and indeed, the rendering small of their bodies. The effects of rape, then, can be found in the details of feminine bodily comportment, which, although not shared by each and every woman, nevertheless carry powerful and damning messages concerning women's responsibility for their own victimization. Thus, although my analysis of rape will begin at the body, I will not assume that the latter exists prior to the former. Rather, women's bodily experience in contemporary society already includes the fact of rape, a fact that is no less significant for not being naturally or biologically necessary.

Defining Rape

Defining rape has been a persistent problem in both legal and philosophical thought. Stephen J. Schulhofer notes that

In common thought and common parlance, rape is the imposition of intercourse by force. . . . At common law rape was "unlawful sexual intercourse with a female person without her consent." The common law definition was both broader and narrower than that of everyday usage: some instances of forcibly compelled intercourse were not legally rape, and some instances of rape in the legal sense involved no force. With the proliferation of modern statutes, some disparities between ordinary and legal meaning have been eliminated, others have expanded. The basic gulf remains wide. (1992, 59–60)

Linda Brookover Bourque has argued that there is a diversity of definitions of rape functioning in contemporary society, and that "this diversity has ramifications for reporting, preventing, intervening in, and treating rape, as well as for conducting research on the topic" (1989, 285). Some definitions of rape include a criterion of actual or threatened force; some demand a lack of consent; others assume that rape always includes vaginal penetration by a penis. In many cases, legal reform concerning the definition of rape has resulted in the replacement of the category of rape with the more general term of "sexual assault" (see Berger, Searles, and Neuman 1995), a reconfiguration that serves to place rape on a continuum of sexual violence but ultimately refuses its specificity.

These contrasting criteria for the act of rape will constitute an implied but not central aspect of the discussion to follow. For the purposes of my analysis, I take rape generally to be the imposition of a sexually penetrating act on an unwilling person. While much of my analysis of rape as an embodied experience will have bearing on other acts of sexual assault, I choose to distinguish rape from other acts of sexual assault primarily by the act of penetration. However, I diverge from traditional definitions of rape by acknowledging that an act of rape need not involve the penetration of the vagina (it can occur through other orifices), nor need it involve the use of the penis (other objects, bodily and otherwise, can perform the penetration).

This privileging of penetration is not without its drawbacks. To a certain extent, it could be perceived as an example of a particularly phallocentric model of sex that does not recognize nonpenetrating sexual acts as properly sexual. However, in emphasizing the significance of penetration, I am not claiming that non-penetrating acts are not sexual. These acts may well constitute sexual assault, but not rape. In my view, to penetrate the body of an unwilling other is by definition a more invasive, more destructive act than any that stops at the surface of the body. This in no way diminishes the horrific ramifications of other types of sexual assault. It is, however, to recognize that rape constitutes a significantly different position on the continuum of sexual violence than other acts. In general, my definition of rape shares much with the conclusion reached by Rosemarie Tong, namely, that "*all* jurisdictions should follow the lead of states that have ruled that rape can be oral or anal as well as vaginal, and that penetration need not be by a penis, but can be accomplished by tongue, fingers, toes, or artificial instruments" (1984, 94).

Summary of Chapters

The first chapter consists of a survey and criticism of the two major schools of feminist thought on rape. While noting the valuable contributions of the theories of Susan Brownmiller and others, I hold that they ultimately fail to describe the phenomenon of rape sufficiently, and that their failure can be attributed to a mistaken (and politically significant) understanding of the body. I then turn my attention to the branch of feminist theory represented by Catharine MacKinnon and Andrea Dworkin. In my analysis, the problem with these theories is not that they are mistaken in their questioning of the possibility of feminine autonomy and consent, but rather that they overstate their case by rendering such autonomy and consent impossible. Both schools of feminist thought on rape fail on the basis of misunderstandings about power and the body, and importantly, the interaction of the two. To define rape as primarily violent is to fail to address the particular sexual meanings that rape holds for women; to define rape as primarily sexual is to adopt a totalizing theory of power and to understand the feminine body and subject not only as constructed, but as *only* constructed. To arrive at a more complex and accurate understanding of the phenomenon of rape demands a more subtle and nuanced analysis of the phenomenon of feminine embodiment.

Chapter 2 considers the historical significance of the body with regard to subjectivity and, more importantly, with regard to the exclusion of women from modern conceptions of personhood. The problem of the universal yet masculinized generic subject—by which the male functions as the norm and the female is automatically constructed as inferior and lacking in the very characteristics that define the human being—urges feminist theory to arrive at an understanding of subjectivity that both recognizes the importance of the body and accounts for sexual difference without the hierarchization that marks the theories of modernity. Such an understanding of subjectivity is crucial to any understanding of the phenomenon of rape.

The feminist theorists of the body discussed in chapter 3 provide a spectrum of different approaches to the problem of the body and its relation to subjectivity. The theories of Elizabeth Grosz, Rosi Braidotti, Moira Gatens, Judith Butler, and Luce Irigaray differ significantly, yet all insist on understanding the feminist subject as material and embodied, and on understanding embodiment as central to agency. As I explore the significance of sexual difference in the context of theories of the body, relying heavily on Irigaray's thought, I assert that the sex neutrality often sought after in the fields of law and morality (not only, but significantly, in those areas that address the problem of rape), insofar as it fails to recognize the significances of sexual difference and embodiment, also fails to address the specific parameters of women's experience.

The fourth chapter applies the insights gained from contemporary feminist theories of the body to the problem of rape. Rape must be understood fundamentally as an embodied experience, as an affront to an embodied subject. If we understand the feminine body both as a site for the inscription of patriarchal and misogynist truths and as a fluid, indeterminate set of possibilities, we can address the complexity of rape without overdetermining women as victims or insisting that it is no different from any other kind of assault. To define rape primarily as assault (the legal version of understanding it as fundamentally or primarily violent) is to ignore the sexually specific meanings and sexually differentiated social functions of rape. If we understand it as an embodied experience, the relevance of sexual difference is preserved, while the complexities of feminist theories of the body prevent the overdetermination of women as sexual. Rape cannot be defined or understood as theft, mere assault, or virtually identical to other forms of heterosexual intercourse. Rather, it is a sexually specific act that destroys (if only temporarily) the intersubjective, embodied agency and therefore personhood of a woman.

Chapter 5 explores the details of feminine bodily comportment, calling on the work of, among others, Sandra Bartky, Iris Marion Young, and Michel Foucault. If the preceding chapter considered rape as an experience that occurs to the embodied subject, here I explore the role of rape in the construction of the particularly feminine body. Beginning with those behaviors and mannerisms associated with the feminine, I hold that the threat of rape is fundamental to the development of such habits. Insofar as the threat of rape is ineluctably associated with the development of feminine bodily comportment (although not determinately so; to say that rape has a fundamental influence on the construction of feminine behavior is not to say that it is the only effect, or that it impacts all women in identical ways), the fact of rape, or of being raped, holds a host of specific bodily meanings. Although my theory of rape begins with a recognition of the significance of embodiment, women's bodily experiences are already marked by the threat of rape.

Finally, chapter 6 considers the ethical aspects of the crime of rape. Before I approach the ethical significance of a theory that understands rape primarily as an embodied experience, I survey in detail a variety of ways the wrongness of rape has been framed. Unlike previous ethical theories of rape, the specific tools of feminist theories of the body will not demand that we understand rape as the theft of sexuality, as if sexuality is something possessed by the subject (or, more traditionally still, possessed by the male who owns the woman: the husband or the father). Departing from a discourse of property will allow for an ethical understanding of rape that does not privilege sexuality per se as a seat of identity, but rather acknowledges the (sexually differentiated) necessity of bodily integrity to the constitution of a subject. Subjects do not have bodies; subjects are bodies, and they are sexed bodies. To violate the sexed body of a woman in a way that is laden with political and sexual meanings is to attack the integrity of her person—not because, as in traditional theory, a woman is worthless without the honor of an intact sex, but rather because identity and integrity are necessarily connected to embodiment, and embodiment is marked by sexual difference.

I conclude my analysis of rape by looking to some of its possible implications with regard to the possibility of resistance. Legal reform concerning rape would benefit from an increased awareness of the significance of embodiment, and specifically the relevance of sexual difference. Most important, the best possibility for resistance against the discourses that make rape a possibility is to be found in the recodification of women's bodies themselves. Women's self-defense training holds remarkable potential not only for reducing the prevalence of rape and other types of sexual violence, but also for questioning the assumptions that make such violence both conceivable and likely. Amid the depressing facts and statistics about rape, such training constitutes a feasible and powerful means of change.

Feminist Theories of Rape

Sex or Violence?

W here feminism and feminist theory have approached the
problem of rape, it has almost always been described as paradigmatic of
women's larger oppression. That is, the crime of rape has been understood not primarily as a specific, singular crime, but rather as the most blatant example of systematic misogyny and masculine dominance. According to Andrea Dworkin, "The celebration of rape in story, song, and
science is the paradigmatic articulation of male sexual power as a cultural
absolute" (1989, 23). Robin Morgan describes rape as "the perfected act
of male sexuality in a patriarchal culture—it is the ultimate metaphor for
domination, violence, subjugation, and possession" (1977, 163–164), and
in one of the very first attempts to analyze the social phenomenon of rape,
Susan Griffin claimed that "[a]s the symbolic expression of the white male
hierarchy, rape is the quintessential act of our civilization" (1977, 332).

To describe in detail a paradigm, a metaphor, a quintessential act, is a
proposition that tends to inspire claims bordering on the certain and the
absolute. The function of a limit is to define that which exists within it,
and many analyses of rape relied on its unquestionably horrific nature to
demonstrate by extension other aspects of the oppression of women. Pay-
ing women less than men for identical work, the injustice of marriage
laws, reproductive choice: if feminists found it difficult at times to inspire
political outrage at these and other social manifestations of women's inferior status, rape was a phenomenon that all members of society ostensibly

[15]

decried. As an unequivocally unjust act, rape functioned as an effectively disruptive lever that had the potential to reveal the systematic discrimination against and devaluation of women.

The following discussion will describe and analyze two distinct feminist approaches to the problem of rape. While neither approach will prove ultimately satisfactory, it is important to recognize that both achieved important feminist insights. They brought to light the social and political nature of rape at a time when it was assumed to be not the symptom of a larger pattern of oppression, but a mere aberration among the normally pleasant interactions of the sexes. They raised sexual violence as a political and philosophical question, and in doing so they affirmed and highlighted aspects of women's oppression that had remained veiled and mystified. They spoke the unspeakable, and their efforts encouraged women to be more open and less self-blaming about the violence that had been so unjustly imposed upon them.

Susan Brownmiller and the Second Wave

The first school of feminist thought regarding rape developed in the second wave of U.S. feminism. In many ways, this aspect of liberal feminism, best represented by the work of Susan Brownmiller, is often perceived as *the* feminist perspective on rape and so has been influential in the development of reforms concerning rape law.[1]

In Brownmiller's book *Against Our Will: Men, Women, and Rape* (1975), she seeks, as she claims in the work's penultimate sentence, "to give rape its history" (404). Brownmiller endeavors to place the phenomenon of rape within the context of social and biological realities, to unveil its political purposes, and to counter the persistent myths surrounding it. Above all, she seeks to counter the perception that rape is a sexual act. Until now, Brownmiller claims, rape has been understood as an act that serves primarily sexual (that is, natural and biological) needs and is a response to sexual stimuli. To the contrary, rape is inspired not by sexual stimuli, but by political motivations to dominate and degrade. Moreover, in refusing the primacy of sexuality in the phenomenon of rape, Brownmiller denies its individualistic nature. The meaning of rape cannot be elucidated by mere reference to individual cases, because rape is, in her startling phrase, "nothing more or less than a conscious process of intimidation by which *all men* keep *all women* in a state of fear" (15).[2]

Although Brownmiller does not distinguish them clearly in her work, it would appear that for her, rape has two primary political functions. First, it ensures the continued and necessary protection of women by men. Hampered by the fear of rape—not a paranoia, but a reasonable fear grounded in empirical reality—women are incapable of moving in the social and political world without the accompanying arm of a male. Such vulnerability has produced, among other things, the institution of marriage:

> Female fear of an open season of rape, and not a natural inclination toward monogamy, motherhood or love, was probably the single causative factor in the original subjugation of woman by man, the most important key to her historic dependence, her domestication by protective mating. . . . The earliest form of permanent, protective conjugal relationship, the accommodation called mating that we now know as marriage, appears to have been institutionalized by the male's forcible abduction and rape of the female. (Brownmiller 1975, 16–17)

In the institution of marriage, as codified by patriarchal law, the woman abdicates any possibility of an independent being; one symbol of this abdication is the fact that the wife takes her husband's name.[3] The married woman's social status and being are thereby rendered solely derivative of her husband's; she adopts his name, prestige, and, most importantly, his protection. William Blackstone, in his 1765 *Commentaries on the Laws of England,* notes that "[b]y marriage, the husband and the wife are one person in law; that is, the very being or legal existence of the woman is suspended during the marriage, or at least is incorporated and consolidated into that of the husband: under whose wing, protection, and *cover,* she performs everything" (Blackstone [1765] 1979, 430).

If Rousseau insists on the absurdity of any contract that would involve slavery, noting that such a contract necessarily contradicts the self-interest of one of the parties ([1762] 1968, chap. 4), a similar criticism may be made of this contract of marriage. Who would sign away their self to accept a life of dependence? As Brownmiller describes, given the threat of rape, it is only by such a contract that women can hope to keep their persons safe. In addition, women's fundamental dependence on men for their physical safety justified their socially inferior status by presenting them as a priori lesser beings, as, in fact, beings who are profoundly incomplete by themselves (in a way that men are not). In Brownmiller's analysis, the very social existence of a woman, as well as her economic survival, was directly linked to her institutionalized relationship to a man, whether father or husband. Women's vulnerability, along with the fact that they do not *in and of themselves* have the power to retaliate or resist, translates into a consistently inferior social status. The fact of rape, according to Brownmiller, inspired a host of social institutions that render women necessarily derivative of men, dependent in the most profound ways, and lacking any sense of independent value or self-worth.

The second function of rape, although linked importantly to the first, considers the role of women in the context of conflicts among men. Brownmiller cites act after act of rape in the context of political strife, from world wars to urban racial violence. In every instance, she notes, the particular physical appearance of the victim was utterly irrelevant. What mattered was her status as the property of the enemy:

> It is worth noting the similarity of experience, as far as women were concerned, between such disparate events in time and place as the Ukrainian pogroms and, for example, the Mormon persecutions in this country and the periodic outbreaks of white mob violence against blacks. In each historic interlude a mob of men, sometimes an official militia, armed itself with an ideology that offered a moral justification—"for the public good"—to commit acts of degradation upon women. In each interlude a campaign of terror, and a goal that included the annihilation of a people, provided a license to rape. In each interlude the symbol of the man's hatred and contempt became its exuberant destruction of *other men's property*, be it furniture, cattle, or women. Further, it mattered little to the rapists acting under the cover of a mob whether or not their victims were "attractive." This, too, is significant, since it argues that sexual appeal, as we understand it, has little to do with the act of rape. A mob turns to rape as an expression of power and dominance. Women are used almost as inanimate objects, to prove a point among men. (Brownmiller 1975, 124–25)

Here women are used as political pawns, as symbols of the potency of the men to whom they belong. To rape a woman in the context of war or other violent conflicts, Brownmiller suggests, is not (according to the ultimate intention and motivation of the rapist) an act against the woman herself. Indeed, such a formulation would demand that the woman is someone *herself*, which she clearly is not. Rather, the act is a direct threat to the ownership of the man who is the rapist's enemy. This model too can account for the phenomenon of rape during slavery, where the forcible taking of slave women as sexual partners was an assertion of the slave owner's power as well as a demonstration of the powerlessness of the male slave. Under this rubric, the *male* slave is emasculated (and therefore dehumanized, rendered powerless) by being denied sole access to the slave women.

Brownmiller asserts that rape in all its forms is primarily political. The political motivation of rape predominant in contemporary society is directly linked with the first political purpose. Given a context wherein the institutions by which men dominate women are well established, rape is an act that expresses a political dominance that is already, by and large, accepted. It is an act by which individual men can enact and personally impose the dominant status that society has endowed on them.

> Today's young rapist has no thought of capturing a wife or securing an inheritance or estate. His is an act of impermanent conquest, not a practical approach to ownership and control. . . . The economic advantage of rape is a forgotten concept. What remains is the basic male-female struggle, a hit-and-run attack, a brief expression of physical power, a conscious process of intimidation, a blunt, ugly sexual invasion with possible lasting psychological effects on all women. (Brownmiller 1975, 377)

Rape is thus "a deliberate, hostile, violent act of degradation and possession on the part of a would-be conqueror, designed to intimidate and inspire fear" (391). By raping a woman, the rapist degrades and denies her being and her autonomy and in doing so (thinks he) elevates his own. The act therefore becomes an echo and an imposition of a social structure by which the full personhood of women is not recognized. Yet Brownmiller's point here is that, even in the context of an individual case, the meaning of rape is never individualistic. Rapists do not rape individuals, but members of a class; the act of rape, then, becomes a reminder to both assailant and victim that membership in one of these classes is the defining element of identity. To be a man is to be a member of the dominant class and thus to have nearly limitless power, or at least power extensive enough to include the power over the bodies of women; to be a woman is to be constantly subject to that dominant power and unable to protect oneself from its reach.

This motivation to rape allows Brownmiller to claim so persuasively that the attractiveness of the rape victim is utterly irrelevant to the rapist's motives, contrary to societal myths of a male sexuality that cannot help but respond to the stimulus of a beautiful woman. The claim that a rape makes is generic: men in general (whether attractive or not, wealthy or not, educated or not) have power over women in general (whether attractive or not, etc.). Rape is not inspired by the shapely leg or the exposed cleavage of the victim, but by the desire for power and dominance of the assailant. Rape is not primarily sexual, but violent.

Separating rape from sexuality was a crucial step in developing a particularly feminist analysis of rape. As long as rape remained associated in the common consciousness with other, allegedly consensual sexual encounters, rape victims were assumed to be at least partially responsible for their own victimization. The sexual connotations of rape had made its brutality, its sheer violence and destructiveness, virtually invisible. Victims of rape were immediately interrogated regarding their sexual behavior, history, and preferences. Rather than being constructed as sympathy-worthy persons who had been viciously brutalized, they were assumed to be sexually voracious, manipulative, untrustworthy women who lied about sexual encounters that they came to regret. Since "everyone" knew how dangerous feminine sexuality was, this story made a great deal of sense. Brownmiller's theory provided a means by which the violence and cruelty of rape could be articulated without reference to the victim's sexuality, a reference that had only served to obscure the reality of women's experiences of rape.

Brownmiller's account of rape represented a significant leap forward in feminist thought and politics. However, it also contained some significant gaps and difficulties. For example, neither of the two political functions of rape that Brownmiller describes (to ensure the continued dependence of women on men by necessitating male protection, and to allow men to express their dominance and hatred of each other through the bodies of women) can sufficiently account for the pervasive phenomenon of rape in present-day Western culture.[4] Despite Brownmiller's questionable claim that the process of intimidation is "conscious," one can hardly presume that individual men rape so that men as a class will retain their protective roles and so that those institutions dependent on women's social inferiority will remain impervious to claims of women's autonomy. While Brownmiller clearly states that the combined actions of individual rapists have precisely those effects ("Rather than society's aberrants or 'spoilers of purity,' men who commit rape have served in effect as front-line masculine shock troops, terrorist guerrillas in the longest sustained battle the world has ever known" [1975, 209]), she does not claim that those effects provide the individual motivation for rape. Nor is the present-day United States engaged in a full-out war; unless, as the above quote suggests, one chooses to perceive everyday Western culture as literally in a state of war, gender pitted against gender. However, even in such an extreme model, the conflict would be between men and women, and thus the model discussed above—where women are precisely denied a participatory role in the conflict, but are rather mute, powerless representations of the warring factions—would be inaccurate. Even more strikingly, Brownmiller does not address, with the exception of a discussion concerning the legal status of marital rape, the phenomenon of rape within the context of familial and/or sexual relationships. Yet the majority of women raped in the United States know their attacker in a social context (almost 75 percent, according to the latest numbers from the Department of Justice; see Greenfeld 1997, iii).

The political functions of rape and the resulting definition of rape as primarily violent describe the social meanings of rape and its role with regard to existing political structures. However, they cannot sufficiently account for the origins of rape itself, that is, the specificity of rape as a particularly sexual and violent means of domination. How did this particular technique of intimidation and degradation come about? The beginnings of rape, which Brownmiller speculatively describes in her introduction, are to be found not in a specific political structure, but in the fateful accidents of biology:

> Our call to sex occurs in the head, and the act is not necessarily linked, as it is with animals, to Mother Nature's pattern of procreation. Without a biologically determined mating season, a human male can evince sexual interest in a human female at any time he pleases, and his psychologic urge is not dependent in the slightest on her biological readiness or receptivity. What it all boils down to is that the human male can rape.
>
> Man's structural capacity to rape and women's corresponding structural vulnerability are as basic to the physiology of both our sexes as the primal act of sex itself. . . . When men discovered that they could rape, they proceeded to do it. (Brownmiller 1975, 13–14)

For Brownmiller, the very facts of the male and female bodies make rape a possibility, a possibility that is then exploited on behalf of male dominance. Women, incapable of retaliating in kind, have no suitable response to rape, no similar threat they can make in turn, no corresponding ability to wield.[5] They are marked only by a "structural vulnerability" that is undeniable and inescapable. They are—prior to the social structures that rape inspires and supports, prior to the wars and the laws and the institutions—rapable.

Brownmiller accepts this organization of male and female bodies as a fact of nature. This state of affairs (namely, that all men are, by definition, potential rapists and all women are, by definition, potential rape victims) is, as a biological reality, beyond politics. Moreover, it is a reality that is universally true. How this possibility is taken up, expressed, and utilized occurs within the realm of political and social action, but the *possibility* of rape is a biological one, inherent in the human bodily condition.

Brownmiller's argument has at least two assumptions here: that the body is biologically given and is therefore not a political entity; and that understanding rape correctly necessitates the eradication of the relevance of sexuality. Let us consider each of these assumptions in turn.

The Politics of Biology

In locating the possibility of rape in the specifics of the human genitals, both male and female, Brownmiller appeals to biology as a politically innocent field of knowledge. This was generally in keeping with the feminist theory of the day, which stressed the distinction between sex (biologically determined, hence natural, distinctions between men and women) and gender (socially specific expressions of masculinity and femininity that were not reducible to the biological distinction of sex). Brownmiller accepted the seemingly indisputable fact that men qua men were equipped with the tool necessary to rape. It would be unthinkable, and somewhat ridiculous, to define rape as political all the way down to its condition of possibility. That men have penises, which can penetrate, and that women have vaginas, which are penetrable, is for Brownmiller a fact beyond all specific political structures.

Alison Jaggar (1987), among other feminist theorists, has argued that biology is not the politically innocent discipline it was once believed to be.[6] In her consideration of the sex bias in scientific research, Jaggar writes,

> I no longer view investigations into sexual similarity and difference as value neutral scientific research, as resulting in *discoveries* that logically precede or constitute the basis in some way for philosophical *decisions* about sexual equality. On the contrary, I now believe that our decisions about sexual equality are at least as much the basis for our supposed discoveries about sexual similarity or sexual difference. Indeed, on both the practical and the symbolic level, I now think that social equality or inequality may be the major determinant of our scientific conclusions about sexual similarity or sexual difference. (1987, 30).

Jaggar continues to explore the social effects on such allegedly biological realities as menstruation, upper body strength, and childbirth. She con-

cludes that "the whole nature/nurture distinction is fundamentally mis-
leading when applied to human beings: we simply cannot identify any social phenomena that are independent of biological influence, nor any
human 'natural' or biological features that are independent of social influence" (1987, 36). In this relatively early questioning of the sex/gender
distinction that grounded much of the feminism of the second wave, Jaggar begins the process of approaching the body as socially constructed.
She issues a twofold warning to feminist thinkers: first, feminists of all disciplines must be wary of the claims emanating from the allegedly objective
sources of science and biology, for those disciplines too (even, or perhaps
especially, when those disciplines fix their inquisitive gaze on sex differences) are subject to the socially accepted assumptions concerning the
genders; second, an argument concerning sex equality should not rest
utterly on scientific or biological claims, which are neither certain nor politically innocent.

All of this is to say that to define men as potential rapists on the basis of
their physiology is not merely a biological claim, but also, and perhaps
more importantly, a social and political one. To view the penis as an in-
strument of rape is already to organize the male body in such a way as to
privilege the genitals as a grounding of sexuality and to understand heterosexuality as a process of conquest, wherein women are disadvantaged by
their inability to use force. Yet under different social and political rubrics,
men do not exist as potential rapists, nor are women constantly under the
threat of rape. Studies such as that by Schwendinger and Schwendinger
(1983) and Peggy Reeves Sanday (1981) demonstrate that the occurrence of rape varies widely from culture to culture, and that there exist
cultures in which it is virtually unknown.[7]

Similarly, we may imagine a different organizing model of human
bodies, for example, one that emphasizes the hands instead of the genitals. Under such a model, women may be understood as biologically capable of forcibly entering a man's anus. Technically speaking, of course,
women have this capability in present-day Western society, and yet it is a
capability that is rarely utilized. Note too that, given proper training, many
women are physically capable of overcoming an assault by a male. Such
training, however, is perceived as contrary to the feminine gender identity, and so the nearly intuitive response of passivity on the part of female
victims, as instinctive as it feels, is also related to the social structure. To return to our thought experiment: the capability on the part of women to
forcibly enter a man's anus cannot be understood as purely biological, for
it is only truly a possibility under a particular political structure. A radically
different political structure *and* model of the human body than those cur-

rently in force could, conceivably, produce a perception of women as biologically capable of committing this act of violation on men. However, the mere biological possibility is not sufficient to render such an act (and surely not the pervasive occurrence of such an act) possible. That men can rape does not explain why they do; and that we understand men as, by biological definition, rapists only reflects the extent to which rape has permeated our social environment.

Another significant drawback to Brownmiller's rooting of the phenomenon of rape in biological, ostensibly unquestionable claims is that it renders her hope of denying rape a future (1975, 404) rather weak. If, at the most basic level, men rape because they can—because the bodies of men can enter the bodies of women by force and without the women's consent—then the prospect of attempting to eradicate rape seems something close to futile. The only certain way, it would appear, is mass castration, or perhaps vigilant separatism. Yet if even the biological reality of the masculine ability to rape is itself political, then there exist other possible ways of understanding the male body. It is at least theoretically possible to understand the penis as other than a penetrating, violent tool, and indeed to rid it of such meaning entirely; and it is this theoretical possibility that affords room for hope.

The Politics of Sexuality

Brownmiller's defense of the essentially political, and therefore primarily violent, nature of rape is largely dependent on the irrelevance of the attractiveness of the victim. In this aspect of her work, she is responding directly to the prevalent understanding of rape as essentially a crime of passion. Men rape, so the theory went (and sadly, in some cases, still goes), because they find themselves at the mercy of their sexual desires. They view an attractive woman and find it difficult, if not impossible, to control themselves. This model implied that because of this hormonal reaction on the part of men, the women who provided the men with the stimuli that resulted in such a reaction were themselves responsible for the ensuing assault. Hence the socially accepted relevance of the "appropriateness" of the victim's attire.

Such an understanding of rape, Brownmiller avers, is utterly mistaken. The motivation for rape is not to be found in the goal of sexual satisfaction, nor can it be reduced to the visual stimuli that rape victims present. It is rather to be discovered in the will to dominate, to degrade, to possess: motivations that relate directly to a male-dominated culture. Brownmiller's motivations in redefining rape as primarily political (that is, as a matter of power and domination) are clear and certainly honorable, although the specifics of her argument are at times difficult to determine and therefore demand some interpolation. By locating rape in relation to political, social, and economic structures that define women as the property of men, she effectively renders moot the question of victim culpability that had, among other things, ably discouraged women from prosecuting rape cases. Because those political and social structures are developed contrary to the interests and in fact the very being of women, it is unthinkable that any result of those structures can be traced back causally to women themselves.

This is a somewhat implicit point in Brownmiller's analysis that demands careful attention. When rape was understood as primarily sexual, women were perceived as inciting the crime on the basis of their appearance. (Interestingly enough, despite the gender roles of victim and assailant, under this model of rape, the women are allegedly the active agents, and men the passive recipients of hopelessly tempting sensations that cause unstoppable actions.) In order to free women from this assumption of guilt, Brownmiller must eradicate sexuality as a motivation, or at the very least, render it subject to the political structure by which women are dominated by men. That feminism needed to answer the law's implicit assumption of the victim's guilt is obvious, and Brownmiller's theory achieved much to that end. However, Brownmiller's particular answer to this problem presents at least two difficulties.

First, this model of rape places women strictly over and against the political and social structures that underscore the phenomenon of rape, or at the very least understands women as merely objectified by them. In an attempt to undermine the prevailing assumption that women actively provoke the act of rape, Brownmiller paradoxically threatens the possibility of any female agency. She claims that women are acted on by these political dynamics, constructed as rape victims, and forbidden the freedom and mobility granted to men. Yet while all these claims are true, it is inaccurate to understand women as *only* acted on and never acting. In other words, to say that the political and social structure acts in such a way as to perpetuate rape and the threat of rape, and thus to construct women as rape victims by definition and training, is to assume that that same structure does not in some important way include women as acting subjects themselves. Political dynamics are set in direct opposition to women and are perceived as relentlessly hostile to the possibility of female autonomy, when in fact those dynamics are far more complex and are not immune to the influences of actual, particular women. Brownmiller here is hampered by the sheer urgency of her need to halt the assumption of victim culpability. Pushed by this urgency, she risks overdetermining women as victims and only victims, by definition and social convention utterly unequipped to affect the political order. While her final chapter suggests some ways women can "fight back" (the inclusion of women in law enforcement, and a "gender-free, non–activity-specific law governing all manner of sexual assaults" [Brownmiller 1975, 378]), those suggestions hardly seem up to the task of purging society of its fundamentally pervasive acceptance of rape, mainly because women, as she has defined them, have little or no power to invoke.

Second, Brownmiller's own work does not sufficiently take into account the complex interplay between sexuality and politics. In her claim that rape is not primarily sexual but political, she sets up a false distinction between the two domains. This tension is reflected in an important difference between her theory and some legal theories that were developed subsequent to Brownmiller's work and relied heavily on her insights. The latter tend to encourage the eradication of the specific category of rape in favor of including it under the definition of "assault," while Brownmiller herself maintains the specific category.[8] This distinct status implies that there is something about the crime of rape that distinguishes it from other political violence; and what can this distinction be but the sexual nature of rape? According to Brownmiller,

> When rape is placed where it truly belongs, within the context of modern criminal violence, and not within the purview of ancient masculine codes, the crime retains its unique dimensions, falling midway between robbery and assault. It is, in one act, both a blow to the body and a blow to the mind, and a "taking" of sex through the use or threat of force. Yet the differences between rape and an assault or a robbery are as distinctive as the obvious similarities. (1975, 377)

These differences, it turns out, are relevant only in a court of law (that is, unlike other physical assaults, rape does not always leave physical markings; unlike cases of theft, rape involves no tangible object that can be recovered). Brownmiller's own description of rape as primarily an act of violence does not sufficiently defend its particular status before the law, that is, its legal differentiation from types of assault. Indeed, according to her redefining of rape, such a defense would be impossible, because it would drag with it the sexual questions that Brownmiller is attempting to evade.

The problem is that when one is dealing with rape, such questions are unavoidable. They need not include the question of victim culpability; indeed, Brownmiller was quite correct to insist that the emphasis on such a perspective ignores, and in fact obscures, the larger political and social meanings of rape. It is striking that the feminine culpability often invoked in rape cases can be answered only by an eradication of any and all sexual significance. Yet the mere presence of sexual significance need not include the vilification and blame of women. It is both possible and necessary to understand rape as a particularly sexual crime as well as a politically and socially meaningful one.

The sexuality of rape differentiates it from other forms of violence and assault. The quality of the assault is marked indelibly by its invocation of not only the sexuality of the assailant, but also that of the victim. Simply put, it *matters* that sexuality is the medium of the power and violence that are imposed on the victim. It matters that the act of rape constructs male sexuality in a particular way such that it constitutes a way of imposing harm, pain, and powerlessness. It matters that the act of rape constructs female sexuality in terms of passivity, victimhood, and lack of agency.

It matters too that in the context of the assault, the rapist is sexually aroused. Brownmiller is correct to argue that the appearance of the victim is not to be blamed for the attack. However, that the rapist's actions are not an automatic, essentially understandable response to the sexualized appearance of the victim does not indicate the total absence of sexual stimuli. The rapist's sexuality *is* engaged: he experiences an erection and, frequently, orgasm. That these sexual experiences may be the result of the violence and the asymmetric power relations inherent in the assault makes them no less sexual in nature.[9]

Brownmiller's theory attempts to separate the effects of power (the violence, the victimization) from their means (sexuality), but such a separation seriously misrepresents the phenomenon. It is not only the case that, as Brownmiller's quotation above implies, a victim's body and mind are assaulted. Her sexuality is also assaulted, such that rape victims often find it difficult to return to the sexual behavior in which they engaged prior to the assault. To assume that the realms of sexuality and politics are easily demarcated and separable is to ignore that the violence of rape is peculiarly sexual, that the sexuality on which the phenomenon of rape feeds is peculiarly violent, and that the complex relationship between the two cannot be reduced to one factor.

Brownmiller herself is, perhaps dimly, aware of this problem, for even as she insists on defining rape as primarily political, she also continually defines it as "sexual assault." Nor, as mentioned above, would she appear to support the eradication of the particular criminal category of rape and a subsequent subsumption of such crimes under the general category of assault. Nowhere, however, does Brownmiller seriously address the question of the sexuality present within the act of rape. In stressing the political motivations of rapists—the desire to dominate, degrade, humiliate, and control—she at times seems to forget that the rapist usually also achieves a sexual climax. The crime of rape finds its source at the cross-section of these motivations.

Other Second Wave Views of Rape

For the most part, feminist theorists writing in the 1970s echoed and developed the insights of Brownmiller's *Against Our Will*. While some anticipated an alternative model, developed in more detail by Catharine MacKinnon, that emphasized the similarities between rape and "normal" heterosexual intercourse, most were concerned with expanding on the definition of rape as violence and aggression to the exclusion of sexual motivations. In one of the earliest volumes dedicated to the overlap of feminism and philosophy, *Feminism and Philosophy* (Vetterling-Braggin, Elliston, and English 1977), an entire section was devoted to the subject of rape, a striking demonstration of the centrality of the issue to feminist concerns of the day. Susan Griffin's contribution to the volume, a piece originally published in 1971 and thus predating Brownmiller's work by several years, introduces many themes similar to Brownmiller's. While she differs from Brownmiller in noting that the phenomenon of rape does not in fact occur prior to the imposition of social controls via the social contract (that is, she does not locate its possibility in the biologically determined structures of male and female genitalia), she too notes that the stereotype of the impulsive, sexually motivated rape is a false one, and she insists that rape should be understood as a culturally taught behavior (Griffin 1977, 315–16). Moreover, she finds the social acceptance of rape to be rooted in familiar gender stereotypes and a refusal to see things sexual as things political:

> That the basic elements of rape are involved in all heterosexual relationships may explain why men often identify with the offender in this crime. But to regard the rapist as the victim, a man driven by his inherent sexual needs to take what will not be given him, reveals a basic ignorance of sexual politics. For in our culture heterosexual love finds an erotic expression through male dominance and female submission. A man who derives pleasure from raping a woman clearly must enjoy force and dominance as much or more than the simple pleasures of the flesh. . . . If a man can achieve sexual pleasure after terrorizing and humiliating the

object of his passion, and in fact while inflicting pain upon her, one must assume he derives pleasure directly from terrorizing, humiliating, and harming a woman. (318)

Griffin here addresses what Brownmiller does not, the curious but fundamental interplay of pleasure and power of which rape consists. Yet her analysis too falls short. Although she later defines rape as "an act of aggression in which the victim is denied her self-determination. It is an act of violence" (331), the larger quotation above clearly describes the sexual moment inherent in rape. A rapist not only succeeds in physically harming a woman, in degrading and humiliating her, he also derives sexual satisfaction. Rape provides what the "simple pleasures of the flesh" cannot; but in turn, it also provides what a simple act of violence cannot. Griffin's explanation of the phenomenon of rape invokes a socially specific male sexuality that is based upon the erotic value of dominance, and as such it suggests the possibility of other ways of shaping masculinity such that dominance and degradation no longer hold erotic sway. However, her analysis still cannot account for this particular marriage of sexuality and dominance. Griffin can persist in defining rape as primarily violent only insofar as she defines culturally imposed heterosexuality itself as primarily violent (an argument that differs from that of MacKinnon in subtle but significant ways). That is, she is able to reduce the sexuality in rape to the violence in sexuality.

Note that Griffin is led to this conclusion by the exact same motivation that compels Brownmiller: the need to answer the image of the rapist as victim of his sexual desires, that is, as victim of the woman who incites those desires. In attempting to free women from the damning accusations that render the rape victim culpable, Griffin overstates the influence of compulsory heterosexuality and thus cannot sufficiently describe the distinction between rape and "normal" (here taken to mean consensual) heterosexual intercourse. For if masculine sexuality, as defined by contemporary culture, includes at its most basic level a celebration of the domination of the female, thus making the pervasive nature of rape understandable, then virtually any act of heterosexual sex could be perceived as contributing to the degradation of women. This conclusion, however, is clearly excessive.

Although Griffin claims that "heterosexual love finds an erotic expression through male dominance and female submission," we cannot infer from her analysis that the eroticization of male dominance and female submission is merely one among many moments that heterosexuality, as currently constructed, offers. The sexual politics that Griffin invokes is one that insists on the fundamental nature of this domination; that is, it takes the oppression of women by men as socially, and therefore sexually, necessary. Indeed, it is only insofar as this domination is largely accepted that the phenomenon of rape, despite ostensible public outrage at individual cases, is even possible.

The faults in Griffin's argument foreshadow the difficulties that the theories of Catharine MacKinnon and Andrea Dworkin faced some years later. However, the real difficulty for Griffin is not the mere overdetermination of compulsory heterosexuality or the valorization of masculine dominance, but rather the failure to articulate specifically the complexity of sexual politics. Given her analysis of the erotic role of masculine dominance, it is difficult to accept her ultimate definition of rape as violence. As much as Griffin appears at first glance to be in agreement with Brownmiller, her analysis does not, in fact, eradicate sexuality from rape; quite to the contrary, it places sexuality at the very root of the phenomenon. While Griffin does not make the mistake of assuming that sexuality is defined by biological realities, nevertheless she describes a patriarchal sexual politics so pervasive that it seems hardly less potent or fixed than the allegedly necessary biological facts that have justified women's social inferiority. Like Brownmiller, Griffin is aware of the inevitably oppressive effects of sexual politics on women; unlike Brownmiller, she cannot avoid defining rape in terms of sexuality, and so her conclusion that rape is primarily violent rings hollow.

Whereas Brownmiller's tactic risks defining women out of any and all agency, Griffin's strategy risks subsuming all that is sexual under the strict delineation of the political. This is not a necessary outcome of her analysis, which initially includes a recognition of both the sexual and the violent factors of rape. However, in choosing to define rape by its violent, rather than its sexual, content, she reduces the latter to the former. As a "classic act of domination," rape is essentially viewed by Griffin as yet another method of male supremacy, perhaps the most extreme tool in the patriarchal arsenal. But rape is not just another tool, and its significance in women's lives and experience cannot be exhausted by a reference to violence, precisely because its particular violence is so explicitly and indelibly sexualized.

The Sex-Neutral Solutions of the Second Wave

Perhaps the most telling downfall of the theories of rape that derived from the second wave of U.S. feminism is their acceptance of gender-neutral legal definitions and approaches to the crime of rape. Brownmiller claims that "a gender-free, non–activity-specific law governing all manner of sexual assaults would be but the first step toward legal reform" (1975, 378), and indeed many feminist attempts to reform rape law have supported the removal of the significance of gender from the definition of the crime. Such a pattern is consistent with the liberal feminism of the 1970s, which often assumed that it was the distinctions between men and women that oppressed the latter in favor of the former. Remove the distinction, and justice would be more easily achieved. Michael Davis argues for subsuming the crime of rape under the general category of assault and stripping it of any unique status (and invokes Brownmiller to support his conclusion):

> Feminists are probably right that judges and jurors have peculiar views about women and rapists. Indeed, feminists are probably right that our thinking about sex in general is often quite peculiar. There does not, however, seem to be similar peculiarities in our thinking about being threatened, beaten, choked, or the like. Rape-as-battery shifts the focus of proof away from the "sexual" moment to the first use of threat or force. Rape-as-battery tends to downplay the sex just as rape-as-forced-penetration tends to play it up. Our views about consent to battery are likely to be far more reliable than our views about consent to sexual intercourse. Everyone is supposed to like sex. . . . No one is supposed to like being threatened, beaten, choked, or the like (unless he is a masochist). (Davis 1984, 109)

Indeed, the method of subsuming rape under the category of assault is the most favored means of ridding rape of its sexual content in order to focus more directly on its more trenchant defining element, violence. In Davis's view, in fact, the sexual content of rape is relatively unimportant: "it is hard to see that the difference between a beaten man (or woman) and a raped women [*sic*] (or man) can be all that great" (78). Unlike the category of rape, the legal understanding of assault supposedly includes no emphasis on the genders of the parties involved. It is precisely the *gendered* assumptions concerning consent to intercourse that Davis is invoking, however implicitly, in the longer passage quoted above; it is not that we tend to assume that people in general often protest sexual advances even as those advances are desired, but that we expect such behavior from women in particular. Our assumptions concerning battery are perceived as more reliable *only insofar as they are free from the bias of gender;* only insofar, that is, as they do not take into account sexual difference.

I will ignore for the moment the claim that our biases concerning battery and other claims are indeed free from gender biases; a lack of gender specificity does not in fact denote gender neutrality, since claims about persons in general or average persons are often based on a male generic that is decidedly, if surreptitiously, gendered.[10] The main difficulty with this strategy is that the suggested legal definition of rape is contrary to the nature of rape as described by Brownmiller and others. That is, if the phenomenon of rape is directly linked to the oppressive structure by which women are dominated by men, if rape is a major tool of patriarchy, then a law that renders such sex-specific claims inaudible will not be able to take into account that very characteristic. Understanding rape solely in terms of violence, to the exclusion of its sex-specific meanings, will separate rape from that which defines it most deeply, that is, the sexual hierarchy by which men dominate women. Theorists such as Brownmiller articulate clearly the implication of rape in supporting such a hierarchy, but their solution of eradicating sex-specific elements of rape in the discourses of law and policy assumes that the factor of sex is irrelevant. One cannot have it both ways; either rape is merely another act of violence, with no specific relation to the sexes and sexual relations, or rape is part and parcel of a larger system of sexual domination, in which case sex remains as a significant element of the phenomenon itself.

It may perhaps be argued that the contradiction between the analysis of rape as a gendered act (that is, as implicated in and supportive of a gender hierarchy) and the ensuing legal definition of rape as a sex-neutral act of violence can be accounted for by the sex/gender distinction developed by liberal feminism. By distinguishing between the social organization of gender and the biological fact of sex, such that the former is understood as artificial and malleable while the latter is considered devoid of social content, one could argue that the phenomenon of rape has a place within the social construction of gender. Because that social construction is inimical to the interests and perspectives of real-life, biologically defined women, it should not be imposed on the victims themselves. From this perspective, simply because a victim is sexed female does not justify the relevance of that which is socially produced, namely, gendered meanings and significance; the just and right approach is to eradicate those gendered meanings from the process, so that the victim will be able to present her experience free from their oppressive effects.

The difficulty with such an argument is that the sex/gender distinction fails to hold, as will be discussed at length in the following chapter. For the purposes of this chapter, let us simply note that the fact that the gendered significances of rape are imposed as part of a larger sexual hierarchy (and are not, for example, "natural" or biologically necessary) does not indicate that they are any less meaningful for the victim, or indeed for the legal discourse representing the society at large. The gendered aspects of rape are fundamental to the phenomenon itself and are no less "real" than biological realities. Any attempt to excavate the true, sex-neutral meaning of rape (i.e., that it is "really" about "violence," and not about sex) by discarding the artificial, socially imposed, gender-specific meanings underestimates the depth of the significance of gender, as well as the various ways sex and gender are co-constituted. If rape is socially constructed as a gender-specific method of supporting, producing, and enforcing a gender hierarchy, then that construction will be basic and essential to (although not necessarily exhaustive of) any one instance of rape.

When the sex-specific elements of rape are denied, when it is perceived as merely another kind of violence, the patriarchal aspects of rape are lost. Consider for example the argument of Christina Hoff Sommers, a self-proclaimed "equity feminist," in support of a gender-free conception of rape:

> Equity feminists find it reasonable to approach the problem of violence against women by addressing the root causes of the general rise in violence and the decline in civility. To view rape as a crime of gender bias (encouraged by a patriarchy that looks with tolerance on the victimization of women) is perversely to miss its true nature. Rape is perpetuated by criminals, which is to say, it is perpetuated by people who are wont to gratify themselves in criminal ways and who care very little about the suffering they inflict on others. . . . Rape is just one variety of crime against the person, and rape of women is just one subvariety. The real challenge we face in our society is how to reverse the tide of violence. (1994, 225–26)

Note that Sommers's analysis of rape, in terms of the "root causes of the general rise in violence," has no need for or use of an overall analysis of patriarchy or structural misogyny. The problem is not men against women; the problem is violence *in general* (that, and a deplorable "decline in civility"—one wonders exactly what age Hoff Sommers is harking back to, and what opportunities such an earlier age would, or did, offer to women). Yet were Sommers's position to be applied to the law itself, it would be virtually indistinguishable from that of Davis, and perhaps that of Brownmiller, even as it seeks to disregard the very structural and gender-specific political role of rape that both Davis and Brownmiller elucidate.

The support of a gender-neutral legal approach to the problem of rape is a symptom of a problem that has haunted liberal feminism from its inception. Where the distinction between men and women was utilized in such a way as to hinder women's justice or advancement, the instinctive response was to remove the distinction itself. If juries or judges are not allowed to perceive a *man* accused of rape and a *woman* accusing him, then typical gender biases that would encourage the blaming of the woman and the pitying of the man will be undermined. Presenting the crime and its assailant and victim as simply that, free from gender identification, the argument goes, will ensure that the victim will receive just, unbiased treatment.

Yet sex neutrality does not, in and of itself, guarantee justice for women; often, it has precisely the opposite effect. As Zillah Eisenstein puts it, "Men are the norm, so women *are* different (from men). But for women to be treated as equal, they must be treated *as* men, *like* men, because equality is premised on men. . . . Requirements and standards are designed with men in mind" (1988, 54).[11] In her analysis and history of feminist attempts to achieve justice for women by means of the law, Deborah Rhode (1989) argues forcefully that precisely because the institutions to which women seek equal access were and are historically male-oriented, feminist goals must include the transformation of those institutions, that is, a critique of the assumptions that underlie them: "If we are to make significant progress toward a more humane and egalitarian social order our focus must be not simply on access to, but alteration of, existing structures. . . . For women to attain equality without relinquishing difference, to ascend the hierarchy without losing commitment to change it, remain central objectives" (Rhode 1989, 304). To judge a (woman) victim by the standards of justice that have been developed in a distinctly male-dominated tradition that assumes that the "normal" or "average" person has predominantly male characteristics is to judge her unfairly. More precisely, it is to construct the woman victim as necessarily outside the limits of "normal" behavior and expectations. Eisenstein claims that "woman is made absent by the presence of the male standard . . . which is supposedly sex neutral" (1988, 67).

The standards of consent, violence, threat, and force, while ostensibly gender-free, are riddled with masculinist bias. When the situation in question concerns a sexual interaction between a man and a woman, the question of consent is sexualized, in that it always focuses on the purported consent of the woman. Rarely, if ever, does one question whether the man consented to the encounter. Moreover, as will be discussed in chapter 6, the concept of consent itself is embedded in an understanding of the subject as autonomous, independent, and significantly masculine, such that women's consent holds very different social meanings—and is subject to different social standards—than that of men. Finally, the use or threat of violence and/or force is insistently sexed. Because of the persistent hierarchization of the sexes, such that men consistently wield more social *and* physical power than women, the threat of violence emanating from a male and aimed at a female is vastly different, and more trenchant, than it would be were the positions reversed. Robin L. West argues that the ways women and men experience pain (and therefore the threat of pain, or injury) are qualitatively different, and that unless legal theory addresses such differences, women's pain will continue to be dismissed or trivialized on the basis of its very incomprehensibility:

> Women's subjective, internal pain, because it is so silent and invisible— and because it is so different—is quite literally incomprehensible. To state the obvious—men do not understand, have not shared, have not heard, and have not felt, the pain—the numbing terror—of an unwanted pregnancy. They have not heard, shared or felt the tortuous violence of a stranger rape or the debilitating, disintegrating and destructive self-alienation of either violent or nonviolent marital rape. . . . [M]en have no conception of what "non-violent" forms of rape are even about, for the simple reason that they have no sense of what could possibly be painful about sex, when it is not accompanied by a threat of violence. This communication breakdown is not slight or incidental, it is total. Men's conception of pain—of what it is—is derived from a set of experience which *excludes* women's experience. (West 1991a, 133)

In its current social incarnation, rape is not a gender- or sex-neutral crime, and the particular victimization that it imposes on women of this society cannot be articulated by means of sex-neutral terms. While such terms would prohibit the questioning of the victim about her attire or her (perhaps supposedly irresponsible) whereabouts—questions that are not likely to arise in other cases of battery—they would also prohibit a legal understanding of, for example, the different reactions men and women have to being attacked. Although the theoretical analyses of rape address its role in terms of sexual hierarchy, their suggested legal applications would render invisible the pervasive threat of rape that marks women's daily experiences so indelibly, and the social failure to prepare women physically to fend off such attacks. Indeed, they would obfuscate the force of sexual politics entirely, and thus reduce rape only to a set of meanings that have currency in a masculinist field, and that are likely, perhaps certain, to be incapable of accurately describing women's experiences. Maria Los writes that "such a [gender-neutral] approach negates an argument which many women feel strongly about, namely that rape is a unique crime in that it involves predominately the victimization of members of one gender group by members of the other" (1994, 166). Rosemarie Tong argues more strongly against the redefinition of rape as assault, rather than as particularly sexual assault:

> [T]here is no more reason to deny that rape constitutes *sexual* assault (a specific type of assault directed against women on account of their sexuality) than there is to deny that repeatedly calling attention to a woman's body when she would prefer it to go unnoticed constitutes *sexual* harassment (a specific type of harassment directed against women on account of their sexuality). Those who wish to stress the assaultive, nonerotic nature of rape and sexual harassment are correct to the degree that rape and sexual harassment are power plays. Nevertheless, rape is also very much related to this culture's view of women as persons who exist to serve male sexual desires and interests no matter the cost to their own female sexual desires and interests. (1984, 119)

In other words, the violence and the power present in an act of rape are particularly sexualized; they gain, at least in part and perhaps entirely, their meaning from a particular sexual hierarchy. Considering rape free from its sexed and gendered meanings is to miss the mark entirely. While the play of gender biases served to silence women's experiences, an attempt at gender neutrality would almost certainly have similar results.

Catharine MacKinnon and the Radical Feminist Strategy

If the liberal feminist perspective on rape risked defining any and all terms of sexuality out of rape in favor of its violent characteristics, the arguments of radical feminists such as Catharine MacKinnon and Andrea Dworkin reverse the emphasis. The theoretical positions of MacKinnon and Dworkin place the phenomenon of rape squarely within the confines of so-called normal, but imposed, heterosexuality. Such a strategy raises important questions concerning the violence inherent in imposed heterosexuality, the erotic centrality of dominance to such an imposed heterosexuality, and the relation between what is perceived as "normal" heterosexual sex and rape. However, my analysis of MacKinnon and Dworkin will demonstrate that their position depends on a theory of power and social construction that does not allow for the possibility of female sexual agency. The radical feminist strategy is correct in drawing links between compulsory heterosexuality and rape, but as exemplified in the writings of MacKinnon and Dworkin, it overestimates the influence and coherence of the patriarchal construction of heterosexuality such that it identifies that construction with the impossibility of feminine agency.

MacKinnon approaches rape directly in a chapter from her work *Toward a Feminist Theory of the State* (1989). Her analysis questions the legal perspective on rape that defines it as nonconsensual, forced, and coerced sex. MacKinnon notes that it is not legally sufficient to define rape as merely forced, but that the crime must be marked by a distinct and proven lack of consent as well. Such a demand "assumes the sadomasochistic definition of sex: intercourse with force or coercion can be or become consensual" (172). In legal, political, and social realms, that is, a certain level of force or coercion can be expected in "normal" heterosexual sex, or at least the presence of force does not necessarily indicate a lack of consent. Thus the demonstration that force was used will not necessarily convince a judge or jury that rape occurred; because the scope of what is considered "normal" heterosexual sex includes the use of (only male) force, the judge or jury may well assume that the alleged (female) victim may have consented to the use of force.

Moreover, for MacKinnon it is not merely the case that heterosexuality as currently constructed allows for the possibility of the mutual coexistence of force and consent. What lies at the heart of the problem of rape is a construction of heterosexuality wherein the use of force is at the very least prevalent, and perhaps endemic. She notes that "rape is not less sexual for being violent. To the extent that coercion has become integral to male sexuality, rape may even be sexual to the degree that, and because, it is violent" (1989, 173). Given the central and privileged place that (male) force (utilized against females) has in the construction of compulsory heterosexuality, the question becomes not how to distinguish between rape and "normal" heterosexual intercourse, but whether the two are in any significant way distinguishable.

> The convergence of sexuality with violence, long used at law to deny the reality of women's violation, is recognized by rape survivors with a difference: where the legal system has seen the intercourse in rape, victims see the rape in intercourse. The uncoerced context for sexual expression becomes as elusive as the physical acts come to feel indistinguishable. Instead of asking what is the violation of rape, their experience suggests that the more relevant question is, what is the nonviolation of intercourse? To know what is wrong with rape, know what is right about sex. If

this, in turn, proves difficult, the difficulty is as instructive as the difficulty men have in telling the difference when women see one. Perhaps the wrong of rape has proved so difficult to define because the unquestionable starting point has been that rape is defined as distinct from intercourse, while for women it is difficult to distinguish the two under conditions of male dominance. (174)

Because women are hard pressed to describe sexual encounters that are not coerced, rape appears not as an exception to, but merely a variation on, normal heterosexual activity. This indicates that forced sex is not merely possible within the scope of women's experiences of heterosexual sex, but that, given male dominance and compulsory heterosexuality, intercourse is virtually always accompanied by a degree of coercion or force. "If sexuality is central to women's definition and forced sex is central to sexuality, rape is indigenous, not exceptional, to women's social condition" (172). Given the central nature of force to heterosexuality itself, women are already implicated in terms contrary to their interests (assuming those interests include physical well-being and the freedom from both rape and the fear of rape) as soon as they enter and participate in the heterosexual world.

The violence in rape, then, is virtually indistinguishable (that is to say, indistinguishable in kind) from the violent imposition of compulsory heterosexuality that serves the needs of male supremacy.[12] Indeed, MacKinnon suggests that it is precisely in rape's sexual meanings that one finds its violence embedded. To define rape solely or primarily by its violent characteristics to the exclusion of its sexual qualities, then, is paradoxically to miss the specific violence that rape represents. "Considering rape as violence not sex evades, at the moment it most seems to confront, the issue of who controls women's sexuality and the dominance/submission dynamic that has defined it" (1989, 178).

MacKinnon is making two distinct points about heterosexuality as currently constructed, although she does not always delineate the two explicitly. First, heterosexuality itself is forced, that is, socially compulsory. One cannot speak of women freely choosing a heterosexual identity (or, more poignantly yet, a "lifestyle") in a culture where alternative sexualities are not equally valued, accepted, or institutionalized. By means of social pressure, encouragement, and at times crass manipulation, women are both urged and expected to be heterosexual. If they respond positively to the various means of persuasion (which are themselves veiled and subtle, for compulsory heterosexuality must be portrayed as natural and inevitable), they receive social rewards that are barred to those who resist. When it comes to heterosexuality, there is no moment of "true choice."

Second, heterosexuality is defined primarily as a dynamic of masculine domination and feminine submission. Specifically, heterosexual intercourse and the social rituals and habits pertaining to it are constructed in such a way as to endow the male with the role of conqueror and the female with the role of the conquered. Women are properly courted, and they risk a loss of their feminine appeal should they appear overly aggressive or even active; men are properly the pursuers who seek to convince women, by whatever means necessary, to surrender the sought prize. Feminine sexuality is thus constructed as primarily reactive or derivative of masculine desire. It has no independent ontological status of its own, but is a means to an end (that end being, for women, among other things, social status and/or financial security). Feminine sexuality, MacKinnon writes, is "socially, a thing to be stolen, sold, bought, bartered, or exchanged by others. But women never own or possess it. . . . The moment women 'have' it—'have sex' in the dual gender/sexuality sense—it is lost as theirs" (1989, 172).

MacKinnon is here emphasizing the erotic role of the dominant/submissive structure. Given the twin and intertwined demands of compulsory heterosexuality and male privilege, domination itself must ground erotic experience. Women are implicated in the system of their own domination precisely as they participate in a constructed heterosexuality that assumes, even requires, that they respond erotically to masculine aggression. Indeed, the possibility of women's positive sexual response to sexually and otherwise physically aggressive men (a response that is socially expected and accepted) is directly linked to their inferior social status. Hence MacKinnon's claim, somewhat the inverse of that of Brownmiller, that "[a] feminist analysis suggests that assault by a man's fist is not so different from assault by a penis, not because both are violent but because both are sexual" (1989, 175).

For MacKinnon, then, if women inhabit a world where their (hetero) sexuality is already and always predicated on an assumption of the regular use of force and coercion, then to blithely invoke the omnipotence of consent in references to matters sexual is nothing short of farcical. Virtually every aspect of the heterosexual woman's experience is pervaded by a valorization of her submissive position. She has no true choice in becoming heterosexual; moreover, once constructed as heterosexual, she is automatically subject to a discourse that defines both her appeal and her desire in terms of her passivity and vulnerability (men, of course, are also subject to compulsory heterosexuality; however, in their case the imposed sexuality reiterates their socially endowed superiority over women by defining their desire in terms of control and activity). She cannot choose to redefine her sexuality according to some alternative paradigm without risking literal social nonexistence. A failure to accept her passive, submissive role is a sure indication of antisocial and perhaps pathological behavior, and at the very least it places her at odds with the dominant heterosexual institutions and behaviors.[13] Thus the consent that women believe they wield—the illusion that they actually have choices with regard to sexuality and sexual encounters—serves to obscure the extensive degree to which women's sexuality is imposed. Valid consent has no place in this model of constructed heterosexuality, where there are only various types of force and coercion, the most explicit and blatant being the pervasive phenomenon of rape.

According to MacKinnon, rape varies from normal heterosexual intercourse only in quantity (its violence is more palpable, its level of coercion more blatant and explicit), not in quality. The law's confusion in determining the difference between rape and consensual sex is due to its masculinist assumption that sex is, by definition, consensual, and that most women, most of the time, freely consent to heterosexual intercourse. That assumption reflects the expectation on the part of heterosexual men that women will, even as—and perhaps because—they desire sex, protest it. The more force, the sexier the encounter; hence, women's protests can easily, and sincerely, be read as implicit consent, and perhaps even encouragement:

> Many women are raped by men who know the meaning of their acts to their victims perfectly well and proceed anyway. But women are also violated every day by men who have no idea of the meaning of their acts to the women. To them it is sex. Therefore, to the law it is sex. . . . [T]he law assumes that, because the rapist did not perceive that the woman did not want him, she was not violated. She had sex. Sex itself cannot be an injury. Women have sex every day. Sex makes woman a woman. Sex is what women are for. (MacKinnon 1989, 180–81)

MacKinnon's response to this legal perspective is, in essence, a pithy one. The truth that the law and the institutions that produce and support compulsory heterosexuality and male dominance refuse to recognize is that sex itself can be an injury to women. In fact, virtually every detail surrounding the social construct of heterosexuality—its alleged naturalness, its assumption and celebration of masculine aggression, its institutional and social incarnations—is a blow to female autonomy. Until sex, as currently constructed, can be understood as contrary to women's social and political independence, the law will remain forever confused as to the line between heterosexual sex and rape.

MacKinnon's analysis indicates that it is not the violence surrounding a particular act of rape (the threatening weapon, the bodily weight that immobilizes the victim, or the threat of worse violence if the victim does not submit) that gives rape its peculiar character. Rather, the violence of rape is to be found in its (hetero)sexual characteristics. Rape is violent insofar as it is a moment on the continuum of heterosexual experience, which is pervaded through and through by the presence of coercion and force. Its sexual nature is not set against its violent nature, but the latter is equated with the former.

Andrea Dworkin too invokes the relentlessly coercive nature of socially constructed heterosexuality when she writes that "[a]ny so-called choice for [heterosexual] sex is a choice for prostitution" (Dworkin 1989, 151). Like MacKinnon, Dworkin defines the phenomenon of rape as predicated upon a wholly derivative feminine sexuality. Pornography, which Dworkin considers to be directly and causally linked to the occurrence of rape, serves to veil this derivative nature of feminine sexuality even as it is proclaiming it. That is, although pornography explicitly portrays women solely as sexual objects created for the consumption of masculine desire, at the same time it insists that the women it portrays voluntarily choose such a status, and that in fact, most women make identical choices. Although pornography demonstrates in the clearest way the dominance inherent in heterosexuality, its power demands that the agency of the women involved be assumed:

> The essence of rape, then, is in the conviction that no woman, however clearly degraded by what she does, is a victim. If the harlot nature of the female is her true nature, then nothing that signifies or reveals that nature is either violating or victimizing. The essence of rape is in the conviction that such [pornographic] photographs—in any way, to any degree—show a female sexuality independent of male power, outside the bounds of male supremacy, uncontaminated by male force. (138)

Dworkin asserts that the feminine sexual identity portrayed by pornography and assumed implicitly or explicitly in various defenses or understandings of the phenomenon of rape is not in fact independent of male power, but rather is the most blatant expression of the extent of masculine dominance. Not only do women not choose to be degraded or violated, but in fact, according to Dworkin, (heterosexual) women cannot choose anything when it comes to sexuality. The two concepts are mutually exclusive, for women's sexual experiences, the contexts in which those experiences occur, and the social meanings and ramifications produced by those experiences are all manifestations of and elaborations on women's social inferiority and powerlessness. Women cannot choose to have (heterosexual) sex for physical pleasure, as a demonstration of affection, or for any other reason. Their heterosexuality can only be used for other purposes, traded for social status, bartered for other, nonsexual goods; insofar as they are heterosexual, they are necessarily prostitutes.

The theories of MacKinnon and Dworkin effectively served to caution feminist thought against presuming that women's sexuality, sexual preferences, and sexual practices are somehow unconnected to, and therefore protected from, larger discourses of sexual inequality. They pushed the envelope of the insight that "the personal is political" by linking what seemed to be the most private and personally held desires to a political system so comprehensive as to be virtually transparent. In doing so, they encouraged feminists to challenge more deeply their assumptions concerning the criteria that must be met in order for women's sexual choices to be truly freely made. One of the strengths of compulsory heterosexuality as a political institution is its ability to conceal itself, such that women believe that their desire for marriage, for example, is authentically their own, untainted by coercive forces. MacKinnon and Dworkin undermine that concealment, and thus expand the scope of the visible effects of patriarchy. However, their theories tend to overstate the power of patriarchal discourse to such an extent that they actually serve to render impossible women's subjectivity. By defining rape as essentially similar to other heterosexual practices, their theories assume not only that women's sexual desires are affected by compulsory heterosexuality, but that they are wholly constituted by it.

For both MacKinnon and Dworkin, rape is virtually (or, at the very least, importantly) indistinguishable from "normal" heterosexual intercourse. MacKinnon has vehemently refuted those who interpret her theory as a claim that "all sex is rape" (1997). Clearly, to reduce her complex theory to such an oversimplified statement is inaccurate and perhaps ambiguous, as David Estlund notes (1997, 167). Yet it is clear that the theoretical perspectives of MacKinnon and Dworkin are compelled by the fundamental similarities between rape and consensual intercourse; those similarities are emphasized so strongly and are so central to the theories being developed that they render those theories incapable of accounting for a differentiation between the two phenomena. Perhaps more exactly, the theories cannot account for such a differentiation within the context of sexual inequality, and MacKinnon's analysis certainly states that such a context is pervasive in contemporary Western society. As Estlund remarks, "It is certainly possible that the view attributed to MacKinnon under the phrase 'all sex is rape' is the view that all intercourse under present conditions is rape. And that is pretty close to her view" (1997, 167).

In reducing the violence of rape to the violence inherent in compulsory heterosexuality, both MacKinnon and Dworkin fall prey to theoretical dichotomies that ultimately cannot hold. The first clue to the weakness of their position is that it renders virtually all heterosexuality misogynistic. While noting this implication does not in and of itself constitute a sufficient argument against their theory, it does ring some fairly serious warning bells. If we are to give women's experience any credence in a theory of rape, it must be acknowledged that for most women, in most cases, to be raped is a strikingly different experience than to engage in voluntary heterosexual sex. Even women who are involved in relationships that have consistently included forced sex can, for the most part, conceive of heterosexual encounters that are enjoyable and centered around their sexual pleasure. Some women, it is true, may learn to associate dominance with eroticism and may in fact eroticize their own submission and inferior status. But MacKinnon and Dworkin assert that such eroticization is fundamental to any and all heterosexual experiences on the part of women; it is just as theoretically significant that in fact, heterosexuality and women's heterosexual experiences are far more varied and complex than their account allows.

Moreover, such a theory of rape pits female sexuality and female agency strictly against each other. Given that, as MacKinnon herself notes, sexuality is integral to identity, the denial of the possibility of heterosexuality in favor of the possibility of autonomy seems a poor choice indeed. If MacKinnon is correct, if heterosexuality as currently constructed is hopelessly pervaded by notions of female inferiority and by the valorization of masculine dominance, it is impossible for women to be both actively heterosexual and actively pursuing their equality and autonomy. Nowhere in her account is there an emphasis on, or even the hope for, reconstructing heterosexuality in such a way as to rid it of its insistently misogynistic values. If we take her theory to its ultimate application, even assuming that such a reconfiguring of heterosexuality was possible, it is difficult to imagine how it would be undertaken, or, more significantly, who would undertake it. Women, insofar as their heterosexual identities were formed contrary to their own desires and interests (so much so that even their desires are not their own), could hardly be capable of envisioning an alternative, for they have virtually no capabilities outside those determined by the masculinist paradigms. Considering the privileges that accompany the present system of compulsory heterosexuality and male dominance, the possibility of a masculine undermining of the system is far-fetched indeed. It would appear that insofar as women participate in the heterosexual paradigm, they themselves are undermining the possibility of their own agency; and yet if that paradigm is as powerful and pervasive as MacKinnon and Dworkin imply, to exist outside it is not to exist socially at all.

Again, that such ramifications are merely distasteful or pessimistic does not, as some seem to think, in and of itself constitute a sufficient answer to the theories of MacKinnon and Dworkin. After all, it is theoretically possible that feminine agency is a literal impossibility. However, such implications should give us pause. Is the power of patriarchy unlimited? Where, in this model, is the possibility of resistance?

The theoretical structure outlined by MacKinnon and Dworkin cannot, ultimately, account sufficiently for the possibility of resistance precisely because it endows male dominance with a potency that is virtually infinite. It adopts a dichotomous model of power dynamics whereby, by definition, women are victims and men are oppressors. For this reason, Drucilla Cornell (1995, 104, 125) argues that MacKinnon's perspectives on male and female sexuality correspond to, rather than contradict, the rigid gender identities that mainstream heterosexual pornography portrays. For MacKinnon and Dworkin, power is a strictly straightforward matter, a means wielded by men to dominate women, a force that infuses all aspects of social interaction and is therefore inescapable. In this model of power, women are only acted on, not acting; they are at the whims of a society that studiously ignores their true desires and even goes so far as to construct those desires that women (perhaps foolishly) believe to be their own. Yet if women are so diligently constructed, how is it possible that some women end up questioning their own situations? How do we have a history of feminist consciousness existing within (even as it is sometimes opposed to) Western culture? As Cornell observes, "In MacKinnon's account . . . nothing of women's personhood is left over with which we could organize so as to begin the feminist process of becoming 'for ourselves.' There is in MacKinnon's account of silencing no space at all for the woman's aspiration to become a person. We have been effectively shut off from ourselves by the imposed fantasies of others" (1995, 144).

Carol Smart has pointed out that "there is a difference between saying that we should not call rape violence because this means we fail to face the larger and more difficult problem of phallocentric sex, and saying that we should not call rape violence because all (hetero)sex is violence" (1989, 44); continuing, and quoting the work of Kelly (1987), she notes that the fact that "normal" heterosexual intercourse and rape share some common elements does not indicate that they are identical (Smart 1989, 44). In the process of overstating their case, MacKinnon and Dworkin fall prey to some philosophically traditional dichotomies. Because power is, for MacKinnon and Dworkin, an essentially repressive force, with a single source (men) and a well-defined target (women), it is theoretically impossible to construct women as anything other than the victims of that power. The very existence of women, and certainly any possibility of feminine agency, will, or desire, is pitted directly against the overwhelming authority of society. Were a woman to insist on the validity of her heterosexual desires, for example, a theory such as MacKinnon's would dismiss such a defense on the basis of false consciousness. Robin L. West, in criticizing radical feminist legal theory, notes that

> to radical legalists generally, and to radical feminist legalists in particular, the extent to which the disempowered desire anything other than their own empowerment, and anything at odds with an equalitarian idea, is the extent to which the disempowered are victims of false consciousness. Phenomenological reports by the disempowered of pleasure and desire that counter the radical correlation of equality and subjective well-being thus reinforce, rather than cast in doubt, the radical's definitional assumptions. They reflect the permeating influence of our objective condition, not the limit, imposed by subjective pleasure and desire, of the normative ideal. (1991a, 125–26).

Such a dismissal of the empirical experience of the disempowered group, namely, women, is not identical to the patriarchal stereotype of the lying, untrustworthy woman, but it is uncomfortably close. Moreover, it rests upon a dichotomy of power versus powerlessness that is altogether too simple.

The point is not that MacKinnon and Dworkin are incorrect about the deep links between compulsory heterosexuality and masculine dominance. The point is rather that they assert that those links are bonds of identity, to the extent that heterosexuality (and therefore any participation in heterosexual activity) is *identified strictly* with misogyny. That heterosexuality is not constituted as a true choice (that is, an option among other equally valid options) in contemporary Western society is clear; however, the absence of absolute choice does not necessarily indicate the presence of totalizing coercion. West's (1991a) analysis of radical legal feminist theory notes that it shares with liberal feminism an essential belief in the possibility of autonomy, and indeed a view of the human being as essentially autonomous (given a just political structure). Indeed, the autonomy that the radical legal feminist position seeks is an all-or-nothing affair; hence MacKinnon's implicit claim that heterosexuality can be a valid, real choice or experience only in the context of the eradication of all sexual dominance and hierarchy. However, as West (1991a) points out, the concept of a profound autonomy, the ability to act in complete independence from the influence of others and of society as a whole, is faulty, not to mention deeply masculinist. A belief in profound autonomy or utterly free choice is an illusory one that ignores the real and complex matrix of relationships, social and political as well as familial, sexual, and so forth, that constitute the context of any decision. If autonomy and valid choice are not the all-or-nothing affairs that MacKinnon implies, then the choices and sexual experiences that women make and have, *even within the context of sexual hierarchies,* cannot be dismissed as invalid.

To claim that free choice, understood in an absolutist sense, is illusory is not to claim that any agency is impossible. Rather, it is to situate agency within a defining context; while I am not free to choose anything at any time (precisely because my context is specific, and therefore limited), nevertheless my context is never, or rarely, so limited as to preclude any options whatsoever. Compulsory heterosexuality does indicate that women especially do not have unmitigated choice in terms of their sexual orientation or experience, and MacKinnon and Dworkin are quite correct to articulate the various ways society imposes limitations on those choices. However, that women's choices are limited does not necessarily indicate that women are precluded from making any choices whatsoever; that particular extension of the argument assumes a polarity (choice versus coercion) that is more properly a continuum. Defending herself against critics, on both the left and the right, who claim that her analysis implies that all sex is rape, MacKinnon pithily sums up her position by stating that "sexuality occurs in a context of gender inequality" (MacKinnon 1997, 103), and indeed, that is an irrefutable claim. However, that sexuality takes place in such a context does not indicate that (hetero)sexuality and women's experiences of (hetero)sexuality are wholly derivative of or strictly reducible to that inequality.

In seeking to describe the very real ways women's experiences are formulated and determined by and with patriarchy, MacKinnon and Dworkin have risked portraying women as solely derivative of masculine power. In terms of their theory of rape, this has resulted in a necessarily wholesale condemnation of heterosexuality, at least for the present time; and indeed, if the power of compulsory heterosexuality and masculine dominance is as fundamental and pervasive as MacKinnon and Dworkin indicate, it would be a long, hard, and perhaps even impossible road to its undermining. In this way their attempt to define rape as primarily sexual by reducing the violence of rape to its sexual nature serves to call into question the possibility of a female agency that includes sexuality. By pitting women's agency strictly against the social agenda of masculine dominance, and by assuming that the presence of force and coercion necessarily includes the absence of the possibility of choice, they assume dichotomies that are philosophically dubious. Their attempt to reduce the phenomenon of rape to only one of its aspects does not, ultimately, elucidate the full social and political meanings of rape; nor does it serve the interests of women, who, although certainly subject to discourses hostile to their experiences, abilities, and desires, nevertheless are not utterly devoid of agency.

Power and the Body

Both attempts to theorize rape discussed above can be accurately termed reductive. The definition of rape as primarily violent seeks to rid the crime of sexual significance and meaning, and redefine it solely within the existing legal framework of assault. The definition of rape as primarily sexual claims that the violence inherent in the crime is directly due to its particularly sexual nature, and that its wrong is to be found in the context of an overarching system of compulsory heterosexuality and masculine dominance. Neither theory sufficiently accounts for the significance of rape, and the threat of rape, in women's lives.

Lorenne M. G. Clark and Debra J. Lewis, writing in 1977 with regard to Canadian rape law, state even more strongly Brownmiller's thesis concerning the primarily violent nature of rape: "To [the rape victim], the fact that this assault was direct against her sexual organs is—at least at the time—irrelevant. Rape is a physical attack on her person, and she believes she has the right to be protected from such attacks" (Clark and Lewis 1977, 167); not surprisingly, Clark and Lewis strongly urge that rape be redefined as assault. Yet this appeal to female experience does not, it seems to me, hold true. Rape victims are not apt to view this assault, either in the moment or subsequently, as essentially similar to any other type of physical assault. The sexual component of the assault distinguishes it from a beating and endows it with meanings that cannot be achieved through other types of assault (although I agree with MacKinnon that a beating that does not necessarily include or focus on the genitals may also be, properly speaking, sexual; I arrive at this conclusion in importantly different ways, however, later in this work). The reduction of rape to sexuality also speaks against women's experience; for most heterosexual women, the act of noncoerced intercourse does not appear as fundamentally similar to rape. This is not to deny the existence of cases where the victim herself is either loath or uncertain about terming her experience "rape," for the social and legal ramifications of being a rape victim are horrific enough that the victim herself may be eager to deny or ignore the crime that has been committed against her. Such hesitation or uncertainty, however, is due to the social and legal response that a victim can expect, a response that more likely than not will only extend, rather than assuage, her victimization. It has little or nothing to do with the specific phenomenon of the act of rape itself, which cannot be reduced to the "normal" act of heterosexual intercourse.

Indeed, it is the specificity of rape that both theories fail to approach. This failure is essentially due to faulty, or perhaps simply absent, understandings of the intersection of political power and female bodies. It is striking indeed that in both of these theories there is a marked lack of attention paid to the role of the body in agency and social and political being. Although MacKinnon gestures toward the formation of feminine sexual desire in relation to patriarchy's valorization of masculine dominance, the details of this formation are decidedly murky. Likewise, Brownmiller's attempt to distinguish strictly between things sexual (i.e., biologically determined) and things political leaves unaskable the question of the body as politically and socially constructed. Finally, neither theory speaks substantially to the role of rape in the formation of the feminine body, and to the implications of that role in the experience and phenomenon of rape itself.

To begin to locate the place of the body not only in relation to the phenomenon of rape, but also in relation to the dynamics of power, agency, and politics, involves its own potential hazards as well. The body is notoriously difficult to theorize, and the dangers of assuming it to be natural or clearly determined are well documented. Yet the politics of the body and the politics of gender are deeply intertwined, and rape, as a crime against specifically female bodies, takes place at the intersection of the two. Before we can articulate the ethical relevance of rape, its phenomenological significance, or its social and political functions, we need a detailed analysis of the social, political, and phenomenological aspects of the body.

Moreover, given the deep implication of the body and gender politics, this analysis must retain sex and gender as central to its questioning. Insofar as the body and embodiment are significant, sexual difference cannot be far behind, and indeed, any allegedly sex-neutral theories of the body are rightfully suspect. Men's and women's bodies are accorded radically different social significance, subject to radically different discourses, and presented with radically different demands. It is likely, then, that men and women experience their bodies in radically different ways. Class, race, sexual orientation: these axes also distinguish bodies and produce different bodily experiences; therefore, those axes produce differences in the experience of rape and the threat of rape.

By understanding the role of the body in sexual and social politics, we will gain a clearer and more nuanced understanding of rape as that bodily assault that is a disproportionate threat to women. Rather than reducing rape to either sexuality or violence, a coherent and detailed analysis of the body will elucidate the relation of both factors, while also serving to articulate the sex-specific meanings of rape. Most important, it will articulate the relation between the body and agency, thus serving to argue against theories that preclude the possibility of feminine subjectivity, even as, or perhaps precisely because, subjectivity itself becomes redefined.

The theories of Brownmiller and MacKinnon fail on the basis of their inattention to the body. What tools, then, do current feminist theories of the body have to offer to the task of unraveling this knot of violence, embodiment, masculinity, and sexual difference? If those previous theories imply problematic definitions of women, usually to the extent that feminine agency is exposed as a necessary contradiction, what can feminist theories of the body tell us about the subjectivity of those beings subjected to a pervasive threat of rape?

Who are the beings being raped? What is the status and quality of their being? What can their being tell us of the phenomenon of rape?

Subjectivity and the Body

Modern philosophy produces a concept of subjectivity defined by intellectual ability, and more specifically by the ability to reason. Rationality was the distinctive mark of the human, that which set the human being apart from and over the nonhuman, irrational world. Reason marked not only human specificity, but also human superiority, and it was the workings of the mind that justified the mastery of the natural world. In the philosophical journey which is Descartes's "Meditations on First Philosophy" ([1641] 1984), the existence of the mind and its significance to the human being are established well before that of the body; the author concludes that "I am, then, in the strict sense only a thing that thinks" ([1641] 1984, 18). Maturity for Kant consists of the ability to think for oneself, to utilize one's individual capacity for reason, and it depends solely on the "freedom for man to make *public use* of his reason in all matters" (Kant [1784] 1949, 134).

Opposed to these intellectual workings, over which each man had control, were the matters and workings of the material body (the masculine generic, functioning as a universal, was crucial to the overall schema, as the following discussion will demonstrate). Uncontrollable, not directly or consistently subjected to the rational choices of the mind, the body was fundamentally a hindrance to the projects of reason. It interrupted the cool, calm process of rational thought with its frightening demands and incessant urges; such forces should be controlled as much as possible, mastered by the superior (but, it would appear, not always stronger) authority of the mind, which alone guaranteed access to certain truth. Humanity, then, the state of being most fully human, demanded liberation from the wild, ever-changing life of the flesh by means of the domination of the enduring, universal, dispassionate life of the mind.

Reason promised a host of goods that the body could not hope to provide. Bodies lived, grew old, withered; reason worked according to universal laws of logic and produced timeless truths. Bodies distinguished individuals from each other; reason was the common denominator. Bodies were subject to desires, emotions, and drives that were appallingly outside the realm of the subject's control; rational thought was a careful, self-conscious process that the subject could undertake in a context of choice and autonomy. Human agency, then, was defined in terms of the capacity of reason, for only reason made such autonomy possible. Insofar as human beings remained susceptible to bodily dynamics, they were still mired in the realm of the animal, the instinctual, the unfree.

If rationality was the hallmark of humanity, its distinctive mark and its destiny, there were an astounding number of human beings who did not, it would appear, share in the human bounty. Among those excluded, of course, were women. While few of the great modern thinkers, with the exception of John Stuart Mill ([1869] 1911), saw fit to expend much of their philosophical energy criticizing the exclusion of women from the club of reason, it is clear that in the resulting binary categories of body/mind, nature/culture, passivity/activity, and dependence/autonomy (among others), women were consistently defined along with that which should be properly exchanged and dominated. In considering the fitting companion for his Emile, Rousseau notes that

> In the union of the sexes each contributes equally to the common aim but not in the same way. From this diversity arises the first assignable difference in the moral relations of the two sexes. One ought to be active and strong, the other passive and weak. One must necessarily will and be able; it suffices that the other put up little resistance.
>
> Once this principle is established, it follows that woman is made specially to please man. If man ought to please her in turn, it is due to a less direct necessity. His merit is in his power; he pleases by the sole fact of his strength. (Rousseau [1762] 1979, 358)

Kant argues that women's peculiar talents are more oriented toward the beautiful than the sublime:

> Deep meditation and a long-sustained reflection are noble but difficult, and do not well befit a person in whom unconstrained charms should

show nothing else than a beautiful nature. Laborious learning or painful pondering, even if a woman should greatly succeed in it, destroy the merits that are proper to her sex, and because of their rarity they can make of her an object of cold admiration; but at the same time they will weaken the charms with which she exercises her great power over the other sex. A woman who has a head full of Greek . . . or carries on fundamental controversies about mechanics . . . might as well even have a beard. (Kant [1763] 1965, 78)

In the justification for women's inherent inferiority, the role of the body was crucial. Women's more insistent and direct ties to the body, as exemplified by the details of menstruation, childbearing, and child rearing (the role of the mother as primary caretaker being perceived as virtually just as "natural" and necessary as was her role in nine months of gestation), rendered her capacity for reason stunted and just barely above that of animals. If being human was defined as the mastery of the intellect over the body, then it was only right and just—it was only *humane*—to have those more intellectually capable rule over those incapable of transcending their bodily being. According to Rousseau,

Woman and man are made for one another, but their mutual dependence is not equal. Men depend on women because of their desires; women depend on men because of both their desires and their needs. We would survive more easily without them than they would without us. . . . By the very law of nature women are at the mercy of men's judgments, as much for their own sake as for that of their children. ([1762] 1979, 364)

Subjectivity was thus defined as opposed to (perhaps present even in spite of) the body. In a double movement characteristic of the logic of patriarchy, the definition of the generic human was made at the cost of the exclusion of women. Both theoretically and practically, women were pressed upon to absorb, embody, and satisfy material human needs demanded by the fact of embodiment *so that* the (male) intellect might fulfill its project unfettered by such lowly, worldly exigencies. Hegel explicitly turns to the brother-sister relationship because, unlike that between husband and wife or parent and child, it is not marked by the "dissimilarity" of the parties ([1807] 1977, 475). Yet that relationship, which in turn affects the husband-wife relationship, ascribes the private realm to the female and the public realm to the male:

The brother is the member of the family in which its spirit becomes individualized, and enabled thereby to turn towards another sphere, towards what is other than and external to itself, and pass over into consciousness of universality. The brother leaves this immediate, rudimentary, and therefore, strictly speaking, negative ethical life of the family, in order to acquire and produce the concrete ethical order which is conscious of itself. . . . The sister, however, becomes, or the wife remains, director of the home and the preserver of divine law. (Hegel [1807] 1977, 475)

Women were bodies *so that* men could be minds—*so that* men could be human. The male generic which marks the modern subject, the "he" which allegedly stands for the entire species, must be both male and generic in order to accomplish the needs of the patriarchal discourse. If modern thinkers used the male gender specifically, if they self-consciously spoke of men qua men and not qua the gender-neutral figure of the human, then the resulting definition would not have the satisfying ring of the universal. Patriarchal logic needed to understand the exclusion of women as accidental; that women found themselves outside, or at least on the periphery of, the definition of humanness in no way affected the integrity of the totality to which the definition allegedly referred.

Feminist theory has demonstrated that that exclusion, far from being accidental or happenstance, was in fact crucial not only to the political and social domination of men over women, but also to the accepted superiority and authority of reason, and subsequently to the various binaries that have dominated Western philosophical thought. According to Genevieve Lloyd,

It is clear that what we have in the history of philosophical thought is no mere succession of surface misogynist attitudes, which can now be shed, while leaving intact the deeper structures of our ideals of Reason. There is more at stake than the fact that past philosophers believed there to be flaws in female character. . . . Our ideas and ideals of maleness and femaleness have been formed within structures of dominance—of superiority and inferiority, "norms" and "difference," "positive" and "negative," the "essential" and the "complementary." And the male-female distinction itself has operated not as a straightforwardly descriptive principle of classification, but as an expression of values. . . . Within the context of this association of maleness with preferred traits, it is not just incidental to the feminine that female traits have been construed as inferior—or, more subtly, as "complementary"—to male norms of human excellence. Rationality has been conceived as transcendence of the feminine; and the "feminine" itself has been partly constituted by its occurrence within this structure. (1993, 103–4)

Luce Irigaray describes the traditional sexual *in*difference of Western metaphysics—i.e., its relentlessly universal scope, its portrayal of the human species as *one*—as the possibility condition not only for the oppression of women, but also for an entire history of thought. By positioning the masculine as both the norm and the epitome of humanness, and by defining that norm in terms of rationality and intellect, Western philosophical thought cast both the feminine and the body as marginal forces that were to be feared and controlled, even as they were, at times, adored (an adoration that, as de Beauvoir noted [1974], always served to underscore and justify the utter otherness of the adored object). Their only significance was to be found in relation to those forces that dominated them. Women came to be defined (biologically, politically, intellectually) as mere imperfections, whose purpose was to be found in the interests and beings of men, and the body was relegated to the status of the willing or resistant tool of the rational subject. The body and nature existed to be shaped and used as resources for the progress of reason. Women, as beings far more saturated with bodily significance, needed the shaping, guiding hands of a male to achieve full humanity. Apart from men, women literally did not matter, had no meaning, did not exist as full human beings.[1]

The subjectivity of the modern period was not only defined in opposition to the body; it also depended on the exclusion of the body for its constitution. Modern political thought had to exclude the body and bodily specificities in order to construct the rational, surreptitiously gendered, universal, autonomous subject. It is a mistake, therefore, to understand subjectivity in the modern philosophical sense as independent from the body, although that is the promise the modern project makes. This model of subjectivity, defined as the rational, autonomous, intellectual exercise of free choice and free will, needed the body even as, in fact, precisely as, it denigrated and devalued all matters of (and all beings overly associated with) the flesh. Just as men could not assume the mantle of authority—whether in the home or in the public arena—without the presence of properly dominated beings (women and others), so subjectivity could not achieve its intellectual status without the degradation of the body.

Feminist Responses to the Modern Subject

The body justified the exclusion of women from the realm of the subject and thus, in modern political theory, from the realm of the political. The model citizen, such as the one described by Rousseau ([1755] 1984) bore a remarkable similarity to the generic human in his faculties of reason and his jealously protected autonomy; while material needs, and especially the dangers presented to him by other humans, drove him to the necessarily limited freedom of society, within those constraints he strove to maintain as much of his natural independence as possible. His reason, however, properly exercised, allowed him to work with others on common problems, and due to its universal and unchanging nature, it alone was capable of creating a common whole from a set of individuals. For Locke, civil government began when individual beings were "willing to join in society with others, who are already united, or have a mind to unite, for the mutual *preservation* of their lives, liberties and estates, which I call by the general name, *property*" (Locke [1690] 1980, 66). Hobbes too locates the construction of government as the rational response to the vulnerability and fear which marked the natural state, in which the rampant exercise of individual desire rendered security impossible ([1651] 1996, chap. 17).

Women found themselves outside the definitions of both the subject and the citizen by virtue of their relentlessly specific bodies. Marked by the significance of their sex, they could not possibly embody the generic norm, which had been defined against them. They had no access to the "normal," sexually neutral aspects of rational humanity. Women's proclivities concerning their appearance and bodily matters severely limited the exercise of rationality, and their susceptibility to bodily matters beyond their control (not only their own, such as menstruation, but also the satisfaction of the bodily needs of others, especially men and children) as well as to emotional attachments demonstrated their inability to adopt the cool, detached perspective necessary to the self-interested, self-defined citizen. Woman's sexuality, according to Rousseau, tainted the entirety of her being, at least during those years when it was useful: "There is no parity between the two sexes in regard to the consequences of sex. The male is male only at certain moments. The female is female her whole life or at least during her whole youth. Everything constantly recalls her sex to her" ([1762] 1979, 361). Kant writes that "The content of woman's great science . . . is humankind, and among humanity, men. Her philosophy is not to reason, but to sense" (Kant [1763] 1965, 79). Such logic enabled great theorists of equality, such as Locke and Rousseau, to proclaim the equality of all citizens, while simultaneously arguing for the natural inferiority of women with relation to that quality that defined humanness, reason.

Mary Wollstonecraft, in her impassioned response to such exclusionary political theories, especially those of Rousseau, foreshadowed many of the insights of generations of U.S. feminism. Her *Vindication of the Rights of Woman* ([1792] 1983) is a classic immanent critique of the masculinist bias of Enlightenment thought. Despite her at times vitriolic assessment of the modern answers to the "woman question," she remains wholly committed to the values and projects of the Enlightenment. So deep is her commitment that she wholeheartedly agrees with the bulk of the descriptions of women which she finds within the theories of the time:

> The . . . love of pleasure, fostered by the whole tendency of their education, gives a trifling turn to the conduct of women in most circumstances; for instance, they are ever anxious about secondary things; and on the watch for adventures instead of being occupied by duties. . . . In short, women, in general, as well as the rich of both sexes, have acquired all the follies and vices of civilization, and missed the useful fruit. . . . Their senses are inflamed, and their understanding neglected, consequently they become the prey of their senses, delicately termed sensibility, and are blown about by every momentary gust of feeling. ([1792] 1983, 151–52)

Had these sentiments been read outside the context of the larger work, one may well wonder just how free Wollstonecraft was from the misogyny of her time. Her contribution to feminist thought, however, cannot be exaggerated, for she directly (albeit incompletely) attacked the naturalism associated with women's intellectual and social failings. Women, she admitted, may be frivolous, vain creatures, seemingly incapable of mastering rational thought and the "generalizing" of ideas; but if they are so, it is because they have been so created. This concept of "rendering" women weak, rather than assuming their weakness to be an a priori state of nature, called into question the extent of biology and the scope of nature. Wollstonecraft's main insight was as profound as it was simple: women may in fact be irrational and subject to lowly desires and emotions, but *they need not be.*

The immanence of Wollstonecraft's critique, however, proved ultimately to be its theoretical downfall. For while she questioned the scope of nature, nevertheless she accepted the basic dichotomy of nature/culture itself (and hence the concurrent dichotomies of male/female, masculine/feminine, mind/body). The persistence of this dichotomy led her to support women's role as primary child rearers, and indeed much of her argument is devoted to the claim that an increase in the exercise of women's inherently possessed reason would produce better wives and mothers. Her acceptance of the undeniable truth of physical differences between men and women also ensured a grudging acknowledgment of at least one area of male superiority. Although the liberal emphasis on the mind rather than the body allowed Wollstonecraft to downplay this point of hierarchized difference, nevertheless she herself often seemed unsure that women could achieve the same lofty heights as men:

> I will allow that bodily strength seems to give man a natural superiority over woman; and this is the only solid basis on which the superiority of the sex can be built. But I still insist that not only the virtue but the *knowledge* of the two sexes should be the same in nature, if not in degree, and that women, considered not only as moral but rational creatures, ought to endeavour to acquire human virtues (or perfections) by the *same* means as men, instead of being educated like a fanciful kind of *half* being—one of Rousseau's wild chimeras. (124)

Liberalism, Wollstonecraft maintained, could not afford differing standards of virtue, worth, or knowledge on the basis of differing sexes. Either women were fully human and endowed with the same kind of reason as men (although perhaps not in identical quantities), or they were utterly excluded from the species itself, a conclusion that even Rousseau could not accept. Wollstonecraft's point was a stark one: there was either one kind of reason, one kind of knowledge, one kind of truth, or none at all. Sex-specific standards of truth broke liberalism's promise of universality, especially because they contaminated the pristine realm of the mind with meanings based on the changing, sex-specific body.

Wollstonecraft essentially agreed with liberalism's account of the body as a tool of and hindrance to the intellectual (hence unsexed) subject, although she cited the physical education of women as central to their development of rational capacities and their status as fully moral, intellectual beings. Thus she was committed to supporting women's social roles as mothers and wives on the basis of their specific bodily role in reproduction. While she cited women's increased capacity for reason and "generalizing" thought as beneficial for their homemaking tasks, she did not suggest that women's bodily specificity and experience had the potential for changing the scope and nature of knowledge itself. Her doubt that women could achieve the same level of virtue (which depended on the exercise of reason) as men was due to her implicit assumption that in comparison to men, women had a greater degree of bodily being to transcend: "Let it not be concluded that I wish to invert the order of things. I have already granted that, from the constitution of their bodies, men seemed to be designed by Providence to attain a greater degree of virtue" (109).

Because Wollstonecraft questioned only the scope of the naturalism inherent in liberalism's consideration of women, not the dualisms (mind/body, thinking/feeling, masculine/feminine) that underlay that naturalism, she was unable to consider women's *bodies* as a site of the production of knowledge different from that valued by her contemporaries. Insofar as she could not, ultimately, free women from the demands of their reproducing bodies, she continued to name the private realm of children and family as belonging uniquely to women: "the rearing of children, that is, the laying a foundation of sound health both of body and mind in the rising generation, has justly been insisted on as the peculiar destination of women" (313).

The Sex/Gender Distinction

Wollstonecraft's repeated point that various behaviors understood socially as distinctly feminine were not in fact natural, but the products of social conditioning, and were thus distinct from the biologically necessary differences between the sexes (understood, at least ostensibly, as morally neutral), was reiterated in the sex/gender distinction that marked some of the most influential thought of 1970s U.S. feminism. Where the overall goal was political inclusion and equality, feminist activists faced literally the same ideological forces as Wollstonecraft had nearly two hundred years earlier. The winning of the vote some fifty years earlier had not, as some had hoped, ushered in a new era of political equality between the sexes. Women were still vastly underrepresented in leading political bodies and were underpaid (in comparison to their male peers) even in those professions where they were to some extent represented. Like Wollstonecraft, liberal feminists of the 1970s were seeking inclusion into the political institutions that had been formed by and for men. Some opponents maintained that women were simply not sufficiently equipped to function in such worlds. To demonstrate the horrors of a gender-equal world, antifeminists dared society to imagine same-sex bathrooms, women playing football, and (most frightening of all) the prospect of having the responsibility of the existence and protection of the free world in the hands of a rabidly premenstrual woman.

The feminist activists were faced with an impressive conundrum similar to that which fueled the thought of Wollstonecraft. Much of what marked distinctly feminine behavior (submission, sentimentality, unpredictability, coyness, etc.) did in fact seem at odds with the values and structures of the male-based worlds of politics and business. How, then, to argue that women deserved—had a "right"—to inhabit such worlds? The sex/

gender distinction solved the problem. Those behaviors and tendencies marked as feminine, feminist scholarship demonstrated, were not in fact fixed, static, or even "natural," but rather varied widely from culture to culture. The particular traits prevalent in this culture, then, did not necessarily reflect the true being of women, but rather the fact that women were an oppressed class, forced (economically and socially) to submit to the authority of men. These malleable traits, which allegedly could be changed with a conscious effort, constituted the field of *gender*, while those undeniable and biological differences between male and female bodies were relegated to the field of *sex*. What was deemed feminine was thus radically different from—in fact, independent of—that which was female.

The mistake in the patriarchal logic had been to overestimate the relevance of the biological distinction of sex, which was understood as virtually irrelevant when it came to determining capacities for specific jobs. The mere *sex* of women did not, in and of itself, preclude women from working within areas formerly closed to them; if the *gender* of women, as socially constructed, made such positions unlikely, then it was society's moral duty to transform those constructions so that women could achieve what their potential allowed. Likewise, the sex of men in no way necessarily precluded them from work typically deemed feminine, such as child rearing, and if their gender was constructed in such a way as to make such work unlikely, similar changes needed to be made.

A good deal of 1970s liberal feminism centered around an emphasis on the degree to which women are, in all or most relevant political and social matters, similar to men, and that they therefore are entitled to equal participation in all political and social endeavors. This egalitarian feminism was by no means the only feminist position in evidence at the time; the second wave of feminist activism in the United States, coming some fifty years after the suffragists had gained the vote, was far more fractured, far more multiple, than the one preceding it. Radical feminists, for example, wanted to transform or even eradicate mainstream political institutions rather than join them (see Castro 1990). However, liberal feminism, as represented significantly by the National Organization for Women, was in some ways the most visible branch of the widespread feminist movement, and many legal reforms (including those concerning the crime of rape) are squarely based on its insights. I emphasize liberal feminism here because of its political effects on U.S. culture at large, as well as its theoretical debt to the Enlightenment. This is not to say, however, that other feminist positions, many of which directly opposed the underlying theories of liberal feminism, did not have significant influence as well.

The primary political difficulty women faced, according to liberal feminism, was *discrimination*—being distinguished by their sex in a way that justified exclusionary practices. Moreover, it was assumed that the realm of the biological was outside the realm of potential political action; that is, we may be able to change the popular image of women as hopelessly thin and relentlessly sexual through self-conscious social activism; but we cannot change the fact that the bodies of men and women are, prior to any socialization, radically different. That women and men were biologically different was both inevitable and politically insignificant. Moreover, the differences in question did not bear on the specific problem of inclusion, as the possession of a penis or a vagina in no way could be construed as a qualification for the vast majority of occupations.

This is not to say that the body was ignored by 1970s liberal feminism. Certain critics, such as Camille Paglia, have mistaken feminist criticisms of sexual politics for a prudishness concerning all things sexual and bodily (inspiring Paglia's rather memorable, if utterly wrong-headed, warning that "leaving sex to the feminists is like letting your dog vacation at the taxidermist's" [1992, 50]). On the contrary, reproductive rights and a newfound emphasis on control over and knowledge of women's own bodies were central to a distinctly feminist politics. Works such as *Our Bodies, Our Selves* (Boston Women's Health Collective, 1973) insisted that women needed to explore their own bodies, claim their own sexuality and sexual freedom, and question the accepted wisdom of the male-dominated medical institution. However, when it came to gaining entrance to political institutions or professions, the *specificity* of women's bodies was downplayed.

The general tendency of liberal feminism was to transcend difference, whether that difference existed between men and women or among women themselves. The goal was to move beyond it to a more balanced, unified whole. The major feminist legislation was the Equal Rights Amendment, whose terse formula stated only that persons should not be discriminated against on the basis of sex. Since the problem, as formulated by liberal feminism, was that women were unfairly excluded from full and active citizenship, including their role in the business world, on the unjust and illogical basis of assumptions concerning the relevance of sex, the solution was to insist that sex had little or no relevance.

Both Wollstonecraft and the liberal feminists of the 1970s faced the same problem: women were excluded, because of their sex-specific bodies, from realms whose inhabitants were defined by their intellectual capacities (and thus, given the hierarchized mind/body dichotomy, by their ability to transcend their physical being). The sex/gender distinction was essentially the feminist attempt to articulate women's equal capacity for transcending the bodily significance of sex. The realms that had excluded women up to now—not only the political and professional worlds, but also the intellectual worlds responsible for producing and validating knowledge—were, according to this logic, universally achievable. Sexual inequality consisted of men procuring for themselves the best of the human experience, whether those goods were defined economically, intellectually, or socially. Sexual justice consisted of redistributing those goods regardless of sex.

The political goal of liberal feminism could be read, then, as a denial of the relevance of sex. What mattered, in virtually all instances of political leadership, employment, or even matters of desire (a particularly paradoxical claim that seemed incapable of accounting for the possibility of sexual orientation), was what was "inside"; when women (or other groups, most notably racial minorities) were perceived as mere "bodies," they were in effect dehumanized. To perceive women as bodies was to objectify them; specifically, their bodies were wholly sexualized and, when so perceived, constructed as mere objects for the satisfaction of male desires. To become human, women must organize their being not around bodily realities, but intellectual capacities, and must demand that others do the same. Where liberal feminism did address the biological specificities of women with regard to their full political inclusion, the purpose was to ensure that those specificities did not constitute hindrances to that inclusion. Rarely were those specificities perceived as opportunities to question the bases of the institutions in general; certainly they were not perceived as grounds on which to question the model of full citizenship that liberal feminism sought to extend to women.

The problems with the sex/gender distinction have been a prevalent theme in recent feminist theory. Constructing equality on the basis of purely intellectual qualities, that is, claiming that women had the abilities to perform in a "man's world" *despite* their bodies, downplayed the fact that those worlds had been constructed with not only the male intellect but also the male body in mind. The business world, for example, had never had to deal seriously with the specter of the pregnant employee; providing child care was hardly an issue since the generically masculine worker was assumed to have a wife at home, caring not only for those bodily needs but for those of his children as well. When women entered the business world without the material support that a wife represented, their experiences were bound to be qualitatively different from those of their male colleagues. Mere reform could not speak to this qualitative difference. By accepting the basic standards and structures that had assumed the masculine generic, the feminist articulation of equality as in-dependent from (at times, opposed to) bodily realities resulted in women's being measured by a yardstick distinctly not their own. Routinely facing questions that men rarely had (career or family?), judged on the basis of expectations that clashed with the material realities of their lives, women struggled to understand why this hard-won equality wasn't more satisfying.

Regarding the sex/gender distinction, which once held such promise for U.S. women, Moira Gatens (1996) notes that it demands an under-standing of the body as, at the very least, passive in terms of identity. In emphasizing the possibility for conscious, determinate change (that is, the possibility that the feminist subject can locate those structures which are producing the oppressive situation and, given sufficient power, change them in order to produce situations that would be recognizably better), feminist activists and theorists were compelled to locate the problem within the grasp of the conscious subject. Because gender was malleable, constructed, and socially specific, it was possible for the subject to achieve perspective on that specificity and affect it. Gatens points out that both the body (as the biologically necessary) and the psyche (as the unreachable unconscious) are ignored as examples, instruments, and means of politi-cal power. The *differences* between certain types of bodies (most keenly, those between differently sexed bodies) become politically irrelevant. Yet the alleged inevitability of matters bodily provides a kind of insurance for the patriarchal structure: "The point is that the body can and does inter-vene to confirm or to deny various social significances in a way that lends an air of inevitability to patriarchal social relations" (Gatens 1996, 10). The distinction between mind and body which constructs the body as natural and passive—as mere matter—is a crucial part of the overall pa-triarchal ideology, and accepting it necessitates losing the question of women's sexually specific political status. Hence Elizabeth Grosz claims that "the body, or rather, bodies, cannot be adequately understood as ahistorical, precultural, or natural objects in any simple way; they are not only inscribed, marked, engraved, by social pressures external to them but are the products, the direct effects, of the very social constitution of na-ture itself" (1994, x).

Judith Butler notes that the sex/gender distinction results, somewhat paradoxically, in the virtual obliteration of the material, that is, strictly bodily field:

If gender consists of the social meanings that sex assumes, then sex does not *accrue* social meanings as additive properties but, rather, *is replaced by* the social meanings it takes on; sex is relinquished in the course of that assumption, and gender emerges, not as a term in a continued relationship of opposition to sex, but as the term which absorbs and displaces "sex," the mark of its full substantiation into gender or what, from a materialist point of view, might constitute a full *de*substantiation. (1993, 5)

The emphasis on gender rather than sex (that is, on social constructivism), Butler continues, results in a hopelessly vicious circle whereby sex, by virtue of its opposition to gender, is necessarily, but contradictorily, *constructed* as *natural*. If sex, however, is understood as constructed, a "contrived premise," in Butler's words, then the distinction fails to hold, and the result is "linguistic monism" (6). The problem, as Butler sees it, is the very understanding of matter, that is, materiality, itself. Insofar as feminist theory has assumed that "matter" is a self-evident concept, it inevitably lands itself between a rock (essentialism) and a hard place (social constructionism).

Lest we think that the sex/gender distinction presented nothing but problems for feminists of the second wave, Rosi Braidotti, despite her criticism of the antimaterialism inherent in the dichotomy, notes that it had real and positive political ramifications for politically active women. While it problematized the inclusion of women in worlds previously inhabited solely by men, it also allowed for the creation of distinctly feminine public endeavors and the politicizing of areas formerly understood as nonpolitical.

> I just want to stress that what made the second wave significant in the history of feminist struggles, is that it posited a common link among women, insofar as they are constructed as the second sex, subjected to the authority first of fathers, and later of husbands—linked by a bond of oppression, of servitude. The positive side of this analysis is that women become valid and trustworthy interlocutors for other women. The novelty of the sixties was that women started talking to other women, to compare notes on their respective conditions. (Braidotti 1994, 264)

Braidotti is correct, of course, to remind us that despite the philosophical inadequacy of the sex/gender distinction as well as the political problems it engendered, it also allowed women to think of themselves as a distinct class with a clearly delineated political objective. However, that "common link among women" was no sooner posited than it was threatened. The National Organization for Women nearly splintered under the weight of the question of whether lesbians should be included (whether, that is, lesbians were to be recognized as included in the class of "women" for whose rights that organization would struggle). Women of color repeatedly, and for good reason, disputed the ability of the overwhelmingly white women's movement to serve as "valid and trustworthy interlocutors" on their behalf. These problems were exacerbated by the implicit devaluing of difference that was inherent in the definition of justice and equality as the transcendence of that which distinguishes persons from each other, especially factors (such as race and class) that had served primarily to ensure the dominance of one group over another.

These criticisms of the sex/gender distinction indicate that the strategy of mere inclusion was faulty in that it too quickly accepted the desirability (and, importantly, the sexually neutral quality) of male-oriented institutions and standards. It also failed to question the assumptions on which those institutions and standards were founded, assumptions that included the unpolitical, unconstructed quality of nature and the necessarily devalued perception of difference. Unlike radical feminism, liberal feminism concentrated its efforts not primarily on the transformation of political institutions, but on the increasing degree of representation of women in them, a goal that by and large left unquestioned the degree to which those institutions were distinctly marked as masculinist. One clue to the failure of the sex/gender distinction for women is that it could lead to a peculiar kind of self-disparagement. By radically separating the realm of masculine/feminine (gender) from that of male/female (sex), while simultaneously considering the unsexed intellect more politically relevant than the sexed body, feminism risked accepting the pejorative associations of those cultural activities deemed "feminine." Even the demand that men share in those activities usually associated with women (especially child care) did not necessarily raise the social status of such work, as it could be perceived as a redistribution of lower-paid, tedious work, just as women's inclusion in various professional realms was a redistribution of higher-paid, respected work. How and why, then, was a society—or even groups of women within that society—to celebrate the cultural contributions of women qua women? Under such a rubric, such typically feminine endeavors as child rearing and cooking could remain socially undervalued work.[2]

Given the model of the modern subject, then, it was precisely the body, and bodily differences, that hampered women's full political participation. Subjectivity came at a heavy price: the denial of the (political) relevance of sexual difference, which found itself distinctly on the "sex" side of the sex/gender dichotomy. Subjectivity was in women's grasp only insofar as they were willing to become sexually neutral; and as Luce Irigaray and others have argued, the myth of sex neutrality has always included a hidden masculinist bent. To free themselves from the burden of sex that they had disproportionately carried, women would have to become what men in the public world had always been—unmarked by sexual specificity: for all relevant political purposes, disembodied.

The Postmodern Subject

Just as feminism thought it had enough on its plate trying to solve the Gordian knot of subjectivity, agency, equality, and difference, postmodern theory radically (and, of course, controversially) changed the playing field. Theorists such as Jacques Derrida, Michel Foucault, Gilles Deleuze, and Jean-François Lyotard began challenging the fundamentals of the modern conception of the subject. Psychoanalytic theory undermined the belief in the possibility of fully conscious action by describing the hidden workings of the unconscious, whose drives revealed that the rational forces of the human being were not always, and perhaps never, in full control of the organism. Where modernism emphasized the unity of the subject, predicated on the autonomy and superiority of the mind, postmodern theories drew a portrait of a being who was radically divided from itself, whose identity, rather than being a static *thing*, was an ongoing process, affected by historical and cultural forces and undergoing constant change.

Postmodernism and feminism have coexisted uneasily for some years now, and their history has been marked with both alliances and serious oppositions. On the one hand, the postmodern emphasis on difference, rather than the unifying principles and standards adopted by modern theorists, provided a way out of the modern maze that inevitably ended up trapping women in a corner rather than liberating them. On the other hand, the most basic claims of postmodernism left women wondering if there was anything left worth struggling for. At least modernism promised the possibility of agency, autonomy, self-determination; all these were dismissed in the postmodern framework as mere illusions, the chimeras of arrogant minds. As Christine Di Stefano observes,

In applying and extending the modernist insistence on the essentially conventional nature of sociopolitical arrangements and their (increasingly important) representations, postmodernism renders the conventional into the arbitrary and promotes a politics and theory of disbelief toward the language of rights, rationality, interests, and autonomy as presumed characteristics of a humanistic self that was thought to provide the legitimizing foundation for modern social life. (1990, 63–64)

The situation could be termed cruel. Just as women and other so-called minorities were seeking to achieve rights, to be perceived as autonomous rather than dependent, to claim the equality of their rational faculties and thus their deserved status as fully equal beings, the goals they were pursuing disappeared. One could hardly blame feminists if they wondered whether the claims of postmodernism amounted to a philosophical iteration of some all too familiar masculinist behavior, with only some slight adaptations: if I can't own you, then I will destroy the notion of ownership itself, so that no one else (including yourself) can.

And what of the body in postmodernism? One of the great points of agreement between feminist scholarship and postmodern theory was their common criticisms not only of the political use of the concept of "nature" but also of the epistemologically foundational character of nature itself. As feminism was demonstrating that many allegedly politically innocent biological claims were in fact the result of a distinctly male bias in the sciences, postmodern theory was claiming that scientific knowledge was as located and situated as any other discipline, and that it had no privileged access to truth or reality. Biology, as the science that purported to discover the truth of the human body, was recast as a particular *type* of knowledge, limited by its own specificity and underlying assumptions, and not as the authoritative source of bodily knowledge.

For postmodern theory, the body as lived by the human being could not be confused with the body as approached by the scientific disciplines, that is, the mechanistic, knowable object subjected to the medical gaze. That medical body was *constructed* by the particular gaze which beheld it, and could not be understood as independent of the particular discourse which purported to study it. The objective spectator of modern theory, who was able to perceive a reality whose existence and truth preceded and exceeded its status as perception, gave way to a subjective, situated spectator who, by the act of perceiving, caused the object of that perception to be organized in particular ways.

While postmodern theory was virtually unanimous in its dethroning of scientific knowledge as the arbiter of objective truth, there was hardly the same degree of agreement when it came to producing various accounts of the significance and quality of the human body. Many postmodern theorists, most notably Foucault, noted that the body, far from being a "natural" and therefore politically innocent entity, is marked indelibly by the political discourses that surround it. Through this marking, this inscription, certain *types* of beings, particular kinds of subjects, are produced. This description of the body as a privileged site of the forces of power emphasized the complex workings of socialization and threatened the modern model of both power and resistance by locating power not in an easily identifiable, single source, which could be resisted by means of a self-conscious and willful subject. If the body itself, its behaviors and comportments, is constructed in accordance with a given (although constantly shifting) set of power relations, then no one body, no one person, can be understood as outside of or free from the tenacious influence of those relations.

In other instances, most notably the phenomenology of Maurice Merleau-Ponty, the body was taken not primarily as a product of socialization, but rather as the condition of possibility for any human agency at all. The "lived body" was posited as the object of philosophical inquiry, whose mandate was to articulate the structures and implications of embodiment for the human subject. Psychoanalysis represented yet another strand of postmodern thought, a strand that constituted the body as a reflection and expression of interior dynamics and struggles. The body is, again, no mere matter, no "natural" substance, but rather a particular incarnation of a complex and intersecting group of desires. According to Elizabeth Grosz, "What psychoanalytic theory makes clear is that the body is literally written on, inscribed, by desire and signification, at the anatomical, physiological and neurological levels. The body is in no sense naturally or innately psychical, sexual, or sexed. It is indeterminate and indeterminable outside its social constitution as a body of a particular type" (1994, 60).

Few of these particularly postmodern theories of the body were primarily interested in the sexual differentiation of bodies, in the sense that they were seeking, for the most part, to produce a general theory of the body. While feminist theory found in phenomenology, psychoanalysis, and Foucauldian genealogy useful methodological tools, most of these theories were found lacking in relation to the question of feminine or female bodies, usually by virtue of their failure to account for bodily experiences or dynamics that were specific to women. The mistake committed by modern political theories of (implicitly or explicitly) accepting the masculine/male body as the norm, thereby positing the feminine/female body as exception or aberration, seemed to have been doomed to repetition. Because the feminine/female body is not taken as the generically human body—or, to put it another way, because the allegedly generic human form is always implicitly masculine—such embodied experiences as pregnancy or menstruation are not perceived as relevant to questions of subjectivity or being. These experiences may speak of women's subjectivity (mostly to limit or deny it), but not of human subjectivity itself. The exclusion of such distinctively female experiences, of course, means that the resulting theory itself is not universal, but speaks only of the particularly male body. Feminist analyses such as Iris Marion Young's discussion of pregnant embodiment (1990, 160–74) seek to demonstrate that the exclusion of the feminine/female body serves to maintain certain distinctions and dichotomies (self/other) which in turn participate in the exclusion of women from social and political activities.

Another major problem with postmodern theories of the body for feminist purposes is that they construct the body as purely pliable, the blank slate on which political discourses or psychosexual drives wrote their narratives. This emphasis on the function of the body in service to either interior or exterior impulses seemed to deny, or at least dismiss, the significance of the materiality of the body. The body *as matter* was again posited as passive and inert: a familiar residue of the modern body/mind split. Yet feminist theory maintained a healthy suspicion of the dualism of such thinking and of the persistent definition of materiality (perhaps taking the place of dethroned nature?), notoriously associated with the feminine, as the inactive, limitlessly malleable stuff of human existence. To construct materiality in this way was to render embodied sexual difference purely fictional, purely constructed, making an articulation of specifically feminine or female ways of being logically impossible. According to Carol Bigwood,

> While we should applaud poststructuralism's criticism of metaphysical foundationalism, as well as its attempt to free gender from our modern conceptions of a biological fixed body, the postmodern disembodied body, which privileges culture over nature and the body, reinforces the same phallocentric metaphysical structures that have contributed to the domination of women and nature. (1991, 60)

Here again we see that the move away from sexual difference—that is, the rendering of sexual difference as wholly malleable, artificial—effectively undermines the grounds for feminist inquiry by positing the class of "women" (formerly defined, much to women's disadvantage, in strictly biological terms) as illusory. The body, it would seem, even when distinctively disembodied, continues to thwart feminist attempts to develop women's agency.

Sexual Difference, Subjectivity, and the Body

Both modern and postmodern theories of the body and subjectivity fail to account for the bodily structures and experiences that are specific to women. Moreover, it appears that the body itself is central to women's struggle to achieve an agency equal to that of men. At least one of two situations seems to hold. Either the particularly female body does not fit into standards shaped for the particularly masculine body, thus rendering feminine specificity hopelessly detrimental to the goals of feminist theory and activism; or the body itself, and both sex and gender along with it, is defined out of existence, perceived as solely derivative of non-bodily forces, incapable (as, indeed, is anything else) of constituting the integrity of the class of "women" that feminism implicitly assumes.

The above questions deal directly with the issue of sexual difference, that is, the relevance and ramifications of the ways men and women are different. However, subjectivity is also closely linked to a person's sexuality—not only how she or he is sexed, but the various ways he or she engages in sexual behavior, achieves sexual pleasure, and so forth. Traditionally, of course, the ontological sexual difference was utilized to construct, enforce, and perpetuate certain standards of sexual behavior. Because one was sexed female, one was expected to have a certain kind of sexuality and to behave according to certain sexual norms. Moreover, as Rousseau reminds us in the quotation above, woman's sexuality was all-encompassing in terms of her being; she was her sexuality, and little more (or once her sexuality was of no use, she was also of little worth). In contemporary theory, of course, the relationship between one's sexedness and one's sexuality is not nearly so clear or distinct. Nor do we wish to construct a theory of subjectivity that defines women solely in terms of their sexuality. Nevertheless, it must be recognized that whatever the relation to one's sex, one's sexuality is a crucial element of selfhood and being, even for those persons who choose to abstain from sexual behavior. Theories that understand subjectivity in terms of embodiment must also therefore be capable of exploring the role of sexuality in the construction of the self.

The challenges to feminist theories of subjectivity and the body, then, are as follows: How does one account for sexually differentiated bodies without reducing women to their bodies (essentialism) or rendering impossible a commonality among women (relativism)? How does one account for subjectivity in such a way as to avoid the dualistic, hierarchical thinking that has traditionally excluded women from agency, and that concomitantly degrades the bodily in favor of the intellectual or the cultural? If traditional definitions and expressions of subjectivity deny both the possibility of women's agency and the significance of sexed bodies, how will a theory of subjectivity that includes women's experiences and specificities differ? How can subjectivity be understood in terms that honor the role of sexuality without reducing women in particular to solely sexual beings? How will the material and corporeal differences of women's existence affect the subjectivity that women seek? In short, how are we to understand the embodied, sexed, sexual subject?

Feminist Theories of the Body
The Material Subject

Given the large and ever-growing field of feminist theories of the body, it would be nothing short of impractical to attempt a comprehensive survey of the theorists who touch on this topic. Moreover, such a survey is not necessary for the needs of the current discussion of the phenomenon of rape. This chapter will not seek to compare and contrast the diverse feminist theories of the body that are so central to current feminist thought, however instructive such a project could be. Rather, in this chapter I am searching for conceptual tools that will help to unravel the problem of rape in such a way as to avoid the problems encountered in previous feminist theories, and to shed light on the specificity of the phenomenon of rape and its relevance to women's bodily experience.

Growing up, I often heard disparaging comments directed toward those people recognized as "cafeteria Catholics," who chose and adopted attractive elements of the Catholic faith while rejecting those that were more discomfiting or problematic. The pejorative term assigned to such allegedly quasi-believers reflected an all-or-nothing moral imperative regarding the tenets of this particular faith. In this chapter I adopt a distinctly cafeteria-like style in my discussion of such thinkers as Judith Butler, Moira Gatens, Rosi Braidotti, Elizabeth Grosz, and others. This is not to say that I will avoid that which is unsettling or difficult. Rarely is feminist theory, or feminism in general, accurate, telling, or significant without a concurrent and at times predominant moment of discomfort. It is, rather, to say that instead of accentuating the differences and disagreements among these various thinkers, my main purpose is to discover concepts, ideas, and perspectives that will elucidate the problem at hand.

Rosi Braidotti's Nomadic Subject

Where previous theories of subjectivity, agency, and the body seem incapable of accounting for, or even including, the feminine/female body, the source of that failure often derives from an insistence on both the unity and the universality of the human subject. The subject so understood is marked by an inalienable wholeness as well as an essential similarity with other subjects. The feminine/female body presents itself as relentlessly, irreducibly *different* from that model, and given the primacy of that unifying category, those differences need to be either denied outright or perceived as merely derivative. In this way, women's bodily differences from men are explained away as aberrations of a more perfect form.

In *Nomadic Subjects,* Rosi Braidotti (1994) attempts to articulate a materialist theory of feminist subjectivity. She locates patriarchy's insistence on sameness and persistence of identity as a major obstacle in the search for agency undertaken by women and other excluded groups. Therefore, she accepts and appreciates the postmodern disruption of the unified subject: "the postmodern dissolution of identity and alleged decentering of hegemonic formations displays an amazing capacity to reabsorb and recycle the peripheral others into a newly undifferentiated economy" (1994, 52). However, she maintains that the fragmentation that postmodernism articulates and celebrates, particularly as applied to the body, paradoxically invokes a notion of sameness, of undifferentiation, rather than a recognition of differences. She notes that the increasing traffic in bodily organs supposes a disquieting sense of bodily sameness, where any part of any one body can stand in for a part of another.[1] This assumption of bodily sameness carries with it a denial of sexual difference that, Braidotti claims, bodes ill for a feminist politics that rests on the recognition of that difference: "Blurring sexual difference, desexualizing masculinity precisely at the historical moment when the feminism of sexual difference is calling for the sexualization of practices seems to me an extraordinarily dangerous move for women" (54). Postmodern theories offer an emphasis on openness and indeterminacy that was of enormous theoretical significance to the purposes of a feminist politics; however, when pushed to its ultimate conclusion (in her words, the "ever-receding fragmentation" [53]), such an emphasis serves to undermine the possibility of a feminist politics of sexual difference per se. Braidotti's self-assigned challenge is to articulate a theory of subjectivity that maintains that openness but also secures a place for the articulation of sexual difference, and thus a place for the significance of the body.

Braidotti's answer to this puzzle is to be found in the figure of the nomad. Her wandering yet embodied subject, whose specific characteristics are derived from the particular environment in which it is developing (the nomad is never complete, but always in process) is "a figuration for the kind of subject who has relinquished all idea, desire, or nostalgia for fixity" (1994, 22). The nomad moves among languages, situations, and roles, and is constituted not by attachments to particular groups, but by the possibility of movement. It is crucial for Braidotti that the nomadic subject is, to a certain degree, nomadic by choice; she dismisses alternative models of the exile or the migrant due to their inherently acted-upon status. The movement of the nomadic subject is not a reactionary one, nor is it a flight from commitment or engagement. Rather, it is a positive denial of the standard of sameness. The nomadic subject refuses to submit its inherently indeterminate state of being to a unified identity that necessarily denies certain possibilities. "Nomadic consciousness is a form of political resistance to hegemonic and exclusionary views of subjectivity" (23).

While Braidotti insists on the ability of the nomadic subject to act and to change its surroundings in meaningful ways, she is not describing a self-moving, autonomous subject capable of self-constitution. Such a modern conception of the subject betrays the deeply intersubjective aspects of human being and action, and in so doing denies the deep implication of the self in the other. One of the many dualisms that Braidotti (implicitly and explicitly) attacks in her work is the self/other distinction, which assumes that the human self is isolatable from its relationships to others, and hence is in some crucial way self-producing. On the contrary, alterity, the fact of otherness that is constitutive of the self, is fundamental to the nomadic subject. Rather than grounding her model of the subject on the capacity for rational thought, Braidotti locates its constitution through the intersection of desire and will:

> The vision of the subject as an interface of will with desire is therefore the first step in the process of rethinking the foundations of subjectivity. It amounts to saying that what sustains the entire process of becoming-subject, is the will to know, the desire to say, the desire to speak, to think, and to represent. In the beginning there is only the *desire to,* which is also the manifestation of a latent knowledge-about desire. Desire is that which, being the a priori condition for thinking, is in excess of the thinking process itself. (120)

If the subject is a desiring subject, it is oriented at its most basic level toward what it is not, its other, that which it itself does not incorporate. Moreover, the specifically desired actions, especially those involving language (and perhaps they all involve language), are themselves intersubjective. The compelling force behind the development of the actions and behavior of the nomadic subject is the yearning for the other, for communication, for an experience of alterity. Through alterity, through the experience of and desire for the other, and not the development of a static, self-produced identity, the subject comes to be in its intersubjectivity. The peculiar unity of the nomadic subject is not self-defined: "And yet this living sexed organism has a unity of its own, which hangs on a thread: the thread of desire in its inextricable relation to language and therefore to others" (56).

Desire is not the only constituent of the nomadic subject, but is part of a complex interplay that also includes the factor of will. If the nomadic subject is compelled by the desire for the articulation and experience of alterity, it is also marked by the capacity to act on that desire, to willfully achieve its goals, *to act*. Without this concomitant and irreducible factor of will, the nomadic subject would be wholly other-defined, which is to say, wholly unmarked by its own specificity and particularity. In order for meaningful action to be possible—and thus in order for feminist action to be possible—the nomadic subject must be, in some way, not independent but unique, that is to say, particular. Braidotti accounts for this particularity by stressing the significance of embodiment.

The nomadic subject, in contrast to the intellectually defined subject of modern political theory, is insistently embodied. This description is not a reiteration of the biology-is-destiny implications of scientific discourse, for the body that constitutes the basis of the possibility for subjectivity is not the body as the object of the medical gaze, but the body as lived and experienced by the situated subject:

> The subject is not an abstract entity, but rather a material embodied one. The body is not a natural thing; on the contrary, it is a culturally coded socialized entity. Far from being an essentialistic notion, it is the site of intersection between the biological, the social, and the linguistic, that is, of language as the fundamental symbolic system of a culture. (238)

Embodiment, for Braidotti, accounts for both alterity (as it is the means by which intersubjective activity is possible; it is the location of the desire for language, that is, the desire for the other) and particularity (as each subject is embodied individually; that is, each particular body is its own unique incarnation of the intersection of various forces and dynamics).

To say that all subjects are embodied is not an essentialist claim, for it is at the level of embodiment that difference is produced. Nomadic subjects share a common status of being embodied. Yet, precisely because they are embodied, all subjects are distinct from each other.

If embodiment is a defining characteristic of the nomadic subject, then the question of sexual difference becomes crucial. The tangle that women faced in seeking to integrate—that is, to infiltrate—the realm of subjectivity was due to the ostensibly sex-neutral basis of the subject, the capacity for rational thought. Sexual difference was deemed by definition irrelevant with regard to subjectivity per se, *even if,* as in fact it turned out, that model of subjectivity resulted in the virtually complete exclusion of women. To ground the concept of the subject in the fact of embodiment, as Braidotti does, forces an acknowledgment of the relevance of bodily differences among subjects. We can no longer imagine the generic "human," marked by allegedly sex-neutral traits; if we are faced with an embodied subject, we are necessarily faced with a sexed subject.

In grounding her model of the nomadic subject in embodiment, and thereby securing a central role for sexual difference, Braidotti is quite consciously walking a fine and controversial line in feminist theory. On the one hand, an invocation of sexual difference risks a slippage into essentialism, by which women become defined wholly by their bodily specificities and by which differences among women (especially those along the axes of class and race) become at best problematic and at worst silenced. On the other hand, without the notion of a fundamental difference between the sexes, the dangers of relativism become quite real, and with them a threat to the possibility of feminist thought and feminist action. The challenge, in other words, is to articulate a difference that is not necessarily determinate, but that can nevertheless challenge the hegemonic character of patriarchal thought:

> The central question here is the extent to which sexual difference meant as the difference that women can make to society—that is, not as a naturally or historically given difference, but as an open-ended project to be constructed—also allows women to think of all their other differences. Foremost among these differences are race, class, age, and sexual lifestyles. The female subject of feminism is constructed across a multiplicity of discourses, positions, and meanings, which are often in conflict with one another; therefore the signifier *woman* is no longer sufficient as the foundational stone of the feminist project. (Braidotti 1994, 105)

That the signifier *woman* is no longer sufficient—that it no longer refers to a determinate, easily definable class of people—does not render feminism impossible *as long as sexual difference remains central to the feminist project*. What feminism must struggle against is the modern desire for universality, sameness, oneness; the bodily fact of sexual difference serves as an effective challenge to that universalism. It undermines the desire for oneness at the most basic level, opening up the possibility for the articulation of other pertinent differences among women (and among subjects in general). The fact that basic bodily differences exist between men and women—and that those differences influence significantly their experience of subjectivity—does not necessarily imply that all women have identical bodily experiences or are in fact identical in some discernible ways. Rather, the lack of symmetry between the sexes is the source of the acknowledgment and realization of the primary role of difference itself, not as a negative, exclusionary principle, but rather as a positivity that makes action, change, and subjectivity itself possible. Patriarchy degraded women in its attempt to make sameness out of difference by placing differences in a unified hierarchy, whereby one aspect of being was always dominated by another, thus relegating the dominated aspect to a merely derivative status while the superior aspect enjoyed the status of the norm. The embodied subject, always already marked by sexual difference, denies the possibility of a unified norm itself and thus presents difference without the concomitant structure of a hierarchy.

If Braidotti is correct—if sexual difference is a project that has been thwarted by the modern project, whose universal claims were in fact specifically masculine and thus importantly incomplete—then the female embodied subject, once allowed to speak outside of the demands of a sexual hierarchy, will have quite different things to say.

> The assertion of the positivity of sexual difference challenges the century-old identification of the thinking subject with the universal and of both of them with the masculine. It posits as radically other a female, sexed, thinking subject, who stands in a dissymmetrical relationship to the masculine. Given that there is no symmetry between the sexes, women must speak the feminine—they must think it, write it, and represent it in their own terms. The apparent repetition or reassertion of feminine positions is a discursive strategy that engenders difference. (118)

Sexual difference, that which marks women as different from men (and, importantly, men as different from women, for the recognition of difference must result in the sexualization of masculinity, which has enjoyed the alleged innocence of sex neutrality), constitutes the power and the possibility of feminist action. The challenges women have faced in their attempts to integrate existing fields of knowledge and activity without questioning their most basic assumptions are due to the mistaken belief that women are, in all relevant aspects, identical to men. With this denial of difference, women were left without the conceptual tools necessary to grapple with the nagging feeling that somehow these new opportunities were not an easy fit.

The nomadic, embodied, material subject which Braidotti describes is one that is intimately intertwined with the other, capable of significant and meaningful action, always in process, and never wholly reducible to its membership in one class (be it sexual, racial, or other) of beings. Change, including feminist change, is possible not because of the autonomy of the subject, but because of its necessarily indeterminate and shifting nature. The movement of the subject, its never-ending development, opens up the possibility of critique and makes nonsense of the hierarchization of differences:

> [W]hat emerges from these new developments in feminist theory is the need to recode or rename the female feminist subject not as yet another sovereign, hierarchical, and exclusionary subject but rather as a multiple, open-ended, interconnected entity. To think constructively about change and changing conditions in feminist thought today one needs to emphasize a vision of the thinking, knowing subject as not-one but rather as being split over and over again in a rainbow of yet uncoded and ever so beautiful possibilities. (158)

Echoing Irigaray, Braidotti notes that without recognition of differences, with only the celebration of sameness, there can be no wonder, no newness. It is only in the recognition of both the proliferation of differences and the embodied, material, sexually marked experience of subjectivity that significant change—political, social, metaphysical, philosophical—can occur.

Elizabeth Grosz and the Volatility of Embodiment

In her work *Volatile Bodies: Toward a Corporeal Feminism,* Elizabeth Grosz (1994), like Braidotti, attempts a refiguring of subjectivity that posits the body as a central location of identity and agency. To place the body at the heart of subjectivity is to change our conceptions not only of subjectivity and agency, but also of the body itself, which Grosz wants to approach "as the very 'stuff' of subjectivity" (1994, ix). In remarkable agreement with Braidotti, Grosz locates the body as the crux in feminist struggles:

> [W]hat is at stake [in definitions of the female body in struggles between patriarchs and feminists] is the activity and agency, the mobility and social space, accorded to women. Far from being an inert, passive, noncultural and ahistorical term, the body may be seen as the crucial term, the site of contestation, in a series of economic, political, sexual and intellectual struggles. . . . If women are to develop autonomous modes of self-understanding and positions from which to challenge male knowledges and paradigms, the specific nature and integration (or perhaps lack of it) of the female body and female subjectivity and its similarities to and differences from men's bodes and identities need to be articulated. (19)

Grosz considers a series of contemporary philosophical views of the body, which she separates into two distinct threads: those that take the body as an exterior expression of interior dynamics (psychoanalysis, neurophysiology, phenomenology); and those that address the body as an inscribable surface, on which exterior forces etch the values and truths of the dominant paradigm (Nietzsche, Lingis, Foucault).

In the work of the first group of theories, the body is generally perceived as the unconscious work of the individual subject. It takes its form and its meanings from the subject's internal psychical play of desires. However self-motivated, this process does not indicate an all-knowing self that determines, freely and consciously, the form of the body that it inhabits. Rather, the body becomes an expression of those desires and drives that are buried in the subconscious or that are structurally present but not consciously perceived. The movement of the process, however, is distinctly from "the inside out" (in Grosz's terms); the origins of the specificities of the external body are to be found in the specificities of the internal dynamics.

The other group of theorists perceive the body as an expression not of individual, internal dynamics but of the dominant social discourses that surround the subject, as well as a network of complex and interlocking relationships and dynamics. Here, especially in the theories of Foucault, the specificities of individual bodies are determined by the play of power, which creates subjects and bodies of particular and identifiable types. Rather than the interior determining the exterior, it is the bodily inscription of power that in turn creates psychical realities. The body becomes the medium and the object of a vast set of interactions, a site of intersubjective intersection, and the possibility not only of the repressive mode of power but also of agency and action. Because it is not perceived as the culmination and expression of interior forces, the body loses a certain unity and appears as the fragmented locus of a host of differing (and often contradictory) ways of knowledge and experience:

> The notion of corporeal inscription of the body-as-surface rejects the phenomenological framework of intentionality and the psychoanalytic postulate of psychical depth; the body is not a mode of expression of a psychical interior or a mode of communication or mediation of what is essentially private and incommunicable. Rather, it can be understood as a series of surfaces, energies, and forces, a mode of linkage, a discontinuous series of processes, organs, flows, and matter. . . . The body is thus not an organic totality which is capable of the wholesale expression of subjectivity, a welling up of the subject's emotions, attitudes, beliefs, or experiences, but is itself an assemblage of organs, processes, pleasures, passions, activities, behaviors linked by fine lines and unpredictable networks to other elements, segments, and assemblages. (Grosz 1994, 120)

The body, rather than being that which is most private, emerges as the public surface of the subject. Through it, the subject is both subjected (formed in the likeness of the dominant discourses, shaped by the play of power, literally—although again not consciously—created for certain purposes) and subjectivated (rendered capable of action, movement, in the particular environment and discourse within which it was created). The movement here is from "the outside in"; the body is acted on by forces that, although themselves disparate and fluid, are nevertheless positioned over and against the subject itself.

These two general approaches to the body appear significantly contradictory, producing an either/or situation that seems to demand loyalty to one camp or the other. Grosz, however, refuses this dichotomy. In fact, she notes that it is precisely on the basis of dichotomies per se (interior/ exterior, mind/body, etc.) that the allegedly singular concept of "the" body comes into being. What is needed, she asserts, is a complication of the very dualisms that consistently relegate women to the role of the submissive, inert, inactive factor. As those dualisms become complicated, "the" body will be revealed as an illusory unity. Thus, for Grosz, "there is no body as such: there are only *bodies*" (1994, 19). Rather than being forced to choose either the interior or the exterior as the creative force behind the body, Grosz complicates the distinction between the two realms. She relates the need for such a complication to a familiar feminist problem: the tension between the need to honor women's experiences as the basis for feminist thought and action, and the recognition that much of women's experience is predicated on (often internalized) patriarchal assumptions. The recognition of the degree to which women themselves are determined by a discourse that demands their inferiority (and, more sadly, the acceptance and perpetuation on the part of women themselves of structures that uphold such demands) prohibits the acceptance of experience as an innocent resource.

> If, as feminists have claimed, "our politics starts with our feelings" and if the very category of experience or feeling is itself problematized through a recognition of its ideological production—if, that is, experience is not a raw mode of access to some truth—then the body provides a point of mediation between what is perceived as purely internal and accessible only to the subject and what is external and publicly observable, a point from which to rethink the opposition between the inside and the outside, the private and the public, the self and other, and all the other binary pairs associated with the mind/body opposition. (20–21)

Perceiving women's experience as solely internal, free from any external determination or influence, would be dangerous, given that women are certainly capable of harboring misogynist ideas, values, and beliefs. The innocence of experience would demand that the clearly masculine-identified positions of persons such as Phyllis Schlafly would be equally as "feminist" as those of women who are directly challenging the fixedness and social evaluation of gendered roles. Yet to claim that the totality of women's experience, as well as their interior, psychic lives, is determined by patriarchal social structures risks positioning women as only pliable, only inert, incapable of any autonomous action whatsoever. Note that this problem regarding the experience of women is exactly parallel to problems concerning the status of the body. Just as various theories of the body seem forced to perceive the body either as wholly determining (biology is destiny) or wholly determined (the extremes of social constructionism), women's experience tends to be understood as either completely innocent of patriarchal discourses, and thus capable of undermining such discourses, or wholly constituted by them. The fates of women and the body are apparently (if somewhat mysteriously) inextricably linked.

For Grosz, bodies are neither primarily interior nor exterior in origin, but are rather the edge of the intersection between the two. She uses the model of the Möbius strip, a winding, three-dimensional looping figure eight, to demonstrate the way bodily exteriors ultimately, and without an identifiable, single moment of transition, lead to bodily interiors, and vice versa. It is impossible to define bodily interiors as ultimately distinct from the exteriors; the two are inextricably linked and mutually defined:

> The Möbius strip model has the advantage of showing that there can be a relation between two "things"—mind and body—which presumes neither their identity nor their radical disjunction, a model which shows that while there are disparate "things" being related, they have the capacity to twist one into the other. This enables the mind/body relation to avoid the impasses of reductionism, of a narrow causal relation or the retention of the binary divide. It enables subjectivity to be understood not as the combination of a psychical depth and a corporeal superficiality but as a surface whose inscriptions and rotations in three-dimensional space produce all the effects of depth. It enables subjectivity to be understood as fully material and for materiality to be extended and to include and explain the operations of language, desire, and significance. (209–10)

Note that the model of the Möbius strip resists the temptation to reduce either interiority or exteriority to its counterpart; Grosz is not attempting to replace the dualisms of traditional theory with a unitary, unifying model. What is compelling about the Möbius strip is not its contained integrity (although it is a closed system, an aspect of the model that Grosz does not explore) but rather its twistedness, its blurring of distinctions, and its inherent movement. Following what appears to be the exterior surface of the strip inevitably leads to the interior surface, and it is impossible to indicate precisely where the change occurred. Likewise, Grosz claims, the interior aspects of the subject lead inextricably to the exterior surfaces of the body. Each is constituted by the other, which is not to say that there is no distinction between the interior and exterior aspects of subjectivity, but rather that they are mutually constructed, developed in a kind of interlocking tandem that renders any radical separation between them impossible. The body is not, then, limited to the outside or the inside, but is precisely the interplay between them, that place where they interact simultaneously. In this way the body, especially the surface of the body, can be both acting on itself and acted upon by itself *simultaneously,* an experience that serves to break down the familiar opposition of subject/object.

> The information provided by the surface of the skin is both endogenous and exogenous, active and passive, receptive and expressive, the only sense able to provide the "double sensation." Double sensations are those in which the subject utilizes one part of the body to touch another, thus

exhibiting the interchangeability of active and passive sensations, of those positions of subject and object, mind and body. . . . This is the twisting of the Möbius strip, the torsion or pivot around which the subject is generated. The double sensation creates a kind of *interface* of the inside and the outside, the pivotal point at which inside will become separated from outside and active will be converted into passive. (35–36)

Bodies are volatile for Grosz precisely because they refuse the determinations imposed by the traditional dichotomies of active/passive, mind/body, form/matter. They are the site of the construction of the subject precisely insofar as they provide a locus for the interplay of such factors. Constantly in movement, relentlessly material yet psychically compelled, individual bodies are specific expressions and incarnations of these interactions.

To define bodies as processes, intersections, movements, and reversibilities is to render impossible any one, unifying theory of the body or the experience of embodiment. As noted earlier, there is no body, there are only bodies. However, if subjectivity is created along the axes of these movements and interactions and if the generated subject in turn serves to constitute the particularity of the subjectivated body, then it is possible to claim that a given, always developing subject may have vastly different, even contradictory, experiences of his or her body. On an experiential level, it may appear, or rather, it may literally be that the body of one year is significantly different from that of the year before. Experiences that can radically shift a subject's perception of his or her body can range from the allegedly "natural" (pregnancy, the onset of menopause or puberty), to the traumatic (being the object of physical violence), to the medical (undergoing major or, for some, even minor surgery). All such experiences can cause the subject to experience his or her body in radically different (and differing) ways, sometimes to the extent that the body appears to the subject as an utterly unfamiliar, alien object. If the subject survives these experiences, these new understandings and experiences of the body can become integrated into the person's subjectivity. To have been pregnant, to have been the object of the medical gaze, or to have been physically brutalized, precisely because these are bodily experiences, is to experience shifts in one's subjectivity. It is, perhaps, to become a different person; however, it must be remembered that it is precisely insofar as subjects are embodied that they are constantly becoming different persons. We cannot reduce such shifting experiences of the body to mere revelations of hidden selves. It is not the case that there was an impregnable self buried somewhere in my subjectivity that I become aware of only through a certain experience. These shifts in subjectivity do not represent unveilings of existing but concealed (or repressed) selves, but rather constitute qualitative changes in the subjectivity of the person who underwent them.

Not only, then, is there not one, generically human body that can be explored and theorized; apparently subjects themselves can experience, quite literally, different bodies. This is not to say that the subject can choose freely, from among a clearly proffered smorgasbord of possibilities, specific bodily characteristics or experiences. By emphasizing the materiality of subjectivity, Grosz is at once articulating the indeterminateness of bodies—their infinite array of differences, their resistance to any unifying theory—as well as their individual determinateness. To understand subjectivity as grounded in the material is to emphasize a certain degree of limitation. Because subjects are embodied, they are limited, finite, to a certain extent, given. Bodies are the sites of infinite possibilities, but their materiality (the fact that they grow, change, die, break, fail) limits the possibilities that may be experienced at any one time. The embodied subject is not the free, autonomous, rational subject of the modern period, but rather a situated, located, specific subject with specific, individualized abilities and characteristics.

Grosz's emphasis on the materiality of bodies, and thus the materiality of subjectivity, includes an acknowledgment of the material fact of sexual difference. She is "reluctant to claim that sexual difference is purely a matter of the inscription and codification of somehow uncoded, absolutely raw material, as if these materials exert no resistance or recalcitrance to the processes of cultural inscription. This is to deny a materiality or a material specificity and determinateness to bodies" (1994, 190). One of the many differences among bodies is sexual difference, which Grosz takes to be material and therefore irreducible to merely social and political forces. This is not to say that that difference is not taken up and expressed in specific historical and cultural ways, but rather to say that that difference itself exists in such a way that individual cultures are forced to codify it. *How* individual cultures take up sexual difference, how they hierarchize it, arrange it, symbolize it, varies widely; but it seems inevitable that any given culture must integrate the fact that women's bodies differ from men's into its structure.

The fact that there is no one human body, but that human bodies are always male or female (or, rarely, both, as in the case of the hermaphrodite, which Grosz does not address) demonstrates the limitations that embodiment involves. Any individual, embodied subject, sheerly by virtue of his or her embodiedness, is confronted with the human otherly-sexed, who represents a wondrous and at times threatening image of the unknowable. If sexual difference is recognized *as a difference*, if male and female are not placed in a hierarchy that results in the latter being reduced to the former, then the totality of human experience and being is always outside any one individual's comprehension and in a significant way does not exist for subjects in general. The embodied subject is always other, always different, because it is always sexed. It is never a complete, closed system, but is always in relation to that which it is not.

> [Bodies] are no longer either independent units each with their own internal cohesion; nor are they unbounded relations with no specificity or location. Bodies themselves, in their materialities, are never self-present, given things, immediate, certain self-evidences because embodiment, corporeality, insist on alterity, both that alterity they carry within themselves (the heart of the psyche lies in the body; the body's principles of functioning are psychological and cultural) and that alterity that gives them their own concreteness and specificity (the alterities constituting race, sex, sexualities, ethnic and cultural specificities). Alterity is the very possibility and process of embodiment: it conditions but is also a product of the pliability or plasticity of bodies which makes them other than themselves, other than their "nature," their functions and identities. (209)

The various alterities within and among bodies allow and account for the movement that marks bodies as processes, as ongoing projects, and challenge the understanding of bodies as self-contained, static, unified entities. Sexual difference constitutes a basic alterity that makes possible the formation of individual, specific, embodied subjects. The denial of difference with regard to subjectivity inaccurately relegates to one particular sex (male) the boon and the burden of the universal, while denying full subjectivity to that sex which is different from it (female). Where women alone bear the onus of difference—where they and their bodies are perceived and constructed as different, but men and their bodies are perceived and constructed as the norm—they alone also bear the onus of sexuality, that is, of sexual difference.

The alterity that Grosz articulates is distinctly mutual, and so the ethics we may read in the model of the embodied, situated, sexually specific subject is one of mutual asymmetry. Bodies are both other to themselves (in the sense that they are not reducible to any one aspect of themselves, and that they are as constituted by exterior forces as interior ones, and that they are constantly developing and shifting) and other to other bodies (insofar as they are irreducibly specific, in terms of sexual and other differences). The lack of identity among bodies and the lack of self-sameness within individual bodies do not speak the impossibility of equality, but the impossibility of equality as sameness. The challenge presented by the figure of the volatile body is the challenge of insistent difference. Embodied subjectivity becomes possible because of and in relation to difference. Thus we must address the embodied other not with the assumption of similarity (although clearly some similarities are possible) but always with an eye to the play of difference.

Judith Butler and the Material Performance of Sex

Judith Butler's description of gender as performative, developed in her work *Gender Trouble: Feminism and the Subversion of Identity* (1990), was a new blow against the various forces that would define sex as an innately held, naturally determined force, or even those feminist theories that invoked a particularly feminine identity or set of values. Gender in Butler's analysis lost its meaning as a knowable, determined trait, and appeared as an action (performance) that constituted itself. Simply put (although simplifications are dangerous when applied to Butler's thought), subjects became gendered in their *acting* as gendered. The performance of given gendered roles created the sexed subject: "There is no gender identity behind the expressions of gender; that identity is performatively constituted by the very 'expressions' that are said to be its results" (1990, 25).

At first consideration, Butler's theory seems susceptible to two possible threads of criticism. One thread would question the idea of performativity on the basis of its seemingly volunteeristic implications. If (gendered) identity was the product of the performing of gender norms, it would appear that individual subjects were, in a sense, free to choose which gender roles they would in fact perform. Subjects who had been performing as men could, apparently, suddenly choose to perform activities and behavior distinctly female, and in so doing become equally "female" as those subjects who had been performing the feminine for their entire lives. Pushed to its logical conclusion, such an understanding of performativity threatened the privileged position of lifelong women with regard to feminist activity and thought.

The second thread of criticism would be almost directly opposite to the first. It notes that if subjects became gendered by performing—aping, mimicking, miming—existing gendered roles, and if it was assumed that those gendered roles consistently constructed women as inferior, then the totality of the identities of real-life women was reducible to the values and meanings inherent in a patriarchal structure. This understanding of performativity threatened the possibility of resistance, that is, of feminist thought or action, by portraying real-life women and their bodies as nothing more than mere reflections of a system of values that demanded their submission. Performativity taken in this way implied that there was no corner of any particular woman's identity or being which did not directly originate from an outwardly hostile source, and if that was the case, then individual women had virtually no weapons against the massive monolith that was patriarchy (in fact, it was worse than this: the women themselves were constructed as weapons against themselves).

Butler returned to these and other problems in her subsequent work, *Bodies That Matter: On the Discursive Limits of "Sex"* (1993). There, she abandons the concept of construction that has pervaded feminist theory in favor of a questioning of materiality itself:

> The discourse of "construction" that has for the most part circulated in feminist theory is perhaps not quite adequate to the task at hand. It is not enough to argue that there is no prediscursive "sex" that acts as the stable point of reference on which, or in relation to which, the cultural construction of gender proceeds. To claim that sex is already gendered, already constructed, is not yet to explain in which way the "materiality" of sex is forcibly produced. What are the constraints by which bodies are materialized as "sexed," and how are we to understand the "matter" of sex, and of bodies more generally, as the repeated and violent circumscription of cultural intelligibility? Which bodies come to matter—and why? (1993, xi–xii)

This move from construction to materialization precludes both the notion of a constructing agent (the choosing self who may perform different sexes and sexualities at will) and the problem of determinism. It does so by understanding the body not as a natural, hence inactive, surface, but as a dynamic (but in no way autonomous, a priori, or pre–socially given) participant in the formation of the self. Given that constructivism seems unable to account for, on the one hand, any form of human agency, and on the other hand, any limit to human agency, Butler suggests a strategy that emphasizes that which has been constructed as the most unconstructed: matter.

> What I would propose in place of these conceptions of construction is a return to the notion of matter, not as site or surface, but as *a process of materialization that stabilizes over time to produce the effects of boundary, fixity, and surface we call matter.* . . . Thus, the question is no longer, How is

gender constituted as and through a certain interpretation of sex? (a question that leaves the "matter" of sex untheorized), but rather, Through what regulatory norms is sex itself materialized? And how is it that treating the materiality of sex as a given presupposes and consolidates the normative conditions of its own emergence? (1993, 9–10, emphasis in the original)

This articulation of performativity as materialization not only questions the integrity of the sex/gender distinction, but also implies that the way matter itself is theorized is directly (albeit complexly) linked to the construction of gender identities. By reversing the assumption that matter, including the material aspects of sex, precedes the regulatory norms of gender, so that matter itself is unveiled as always already gendered, Butler places the body again at the center of the performativity of gender while refusing to endow it with even the slightest degree of naturalness. The matter that is body, in other words, is not cast as the blank slate on which the regulatory norms of gender are inscribed, but rather as the possibility and product of those norms themselves.

Butler notes that traditional theory not only has linked matter with the feminine, to the extent that each concept takes on the characteristics of the other, but also has ultimately excluded the feminine from the form/matter distinction. It is only insofar as the feminine remained untheorizable that that distinction becomes possible: "The problem is not that the feminine is made to stand for matter or for universality; rather, the feminine is cast outside the form/matter and universal/particular binarisms. She will be neither the one nor the other, but the permanent and unchangeable condition of both—what can be construed as a nonthematizable materiality" (1993, 42). The feminine becomes constructed as that exception that literally makes the rule possible, in the same way that the masculinist definition of the generic human is possible only if women are constructed as somehow other than human. The feminine has been constructed as more material than the masculine, providing only the stuff of life, or, more precisely, the empty space within which the stuff of life is formed, and relying on the masculine capacity for that possibility of form. Butler contends that the feminine so constructed is actually a mere reflection of the masculine; she cites Derrida's and Irigaray's shared point that "what is excluded from this binary is also *produced* by it in the mode of exclusion and has no separable or fully independent existence as an absolute outside" (1993, 39). What is necessary to the possibility of those hosts of dichotomies is the refusal of the feminine itself. The *refusal* of the feminine is to be distinguished from the *absence* of the feminine; phallocentric thinking needs the constant denial of the feminine, the relegation of the feminine to the unknowable and untheorizable, in order to theorize along the lines of those binarisms. Yet this constant denial already assumes, prior to those dichotomies, the functioning of sex, which implies that the theorizing of matter as opposed to form is predicated upon the regulatory norm of sex. "The very formation of matter takes place in the service of an organization and denial of sexual difference, so that we are confronted with an economy of sexual difference as that which defines, instrumentalizes, and allocates matter in its own service" (52).

If matter itself is dependent on the at once necessary and denied sexual difference, then the materiality of the body cannot be opposed to the workings of the regulatory norms of sex and gender, as is usually the case. The materiality of the body affords the possibility of those regulatory norms; the specific nature of power is thus itself constituted by materiality. This is so in two distinct senses. First, the functioning of the regulatory norms of sex and gender depends directly on the construction of materiality as that which is outside construction. In order for the production of sex and gender roles to appear not as productions but as natural occurrences, they must be linked to an obviously neutral realm that is allegedly free from the influence of society or power. The body as matter, that is, as natural, provides the necessarily stable ground on which to build the fixed sexed identities and roles; without this stable ground, those identities and roles would surely collapse. Second, given a Foucauldian analysis of power (which Butler in general accepts), material bodies provide those regulatory norms the necessary locus at which to work. Those norms, in order to work effectively, must not only be stated, enforced, or repeated, they must be incarnated, made flesh: "[T]he regulatory norms of 'sex' work in a performative fashion to constitute the materiality of bodies and, more specifically, to materialize the body's sex, to materialize sexual difference in the service of the consolidation of the heterosexual imperative" (1993, 2).

For Butler, the sexed body is the literal materialization of the norms that demand and enforce static and stable genders. This is not, however, to place the body in a strictly submissive relation to those norms, nor is it to portray materiality as a merely exploited factor in the production of the gendered self. Rather, Butler is defending a co-constituting effect, whereby the materiality of the body (not the specific characteristics of bodies) is itself produced along the lines of assumed sexual difference while, simultaneously, the same materiality is a necessary condition for the play of sexualized norms. Any invocation of the necessity of sexual difference and the fixedness of gendered identities (especially those that take the material characteristics of the body as their basis), fails to appreciate sufficiently the forcible imposition of gendered norms, an imposition that reaches far beyond the conscious realm and extends as far as the flesh of the constructed self. Precisely because gendered identities are not necessary in the strict, metaphysical sense, they demand rearticulation, enforcement, and incarnation. To appeal to fixed identities is to forget these demands and their radical implications, among which is the irrefutable fragility of those identities: "Identifications are never fully and finally made; they are incessantly reconstituted and, as such, are subject to the volatile logic of iterability" (1993, 105). That gender has to be performed, that the regulatory norms of sexual difference must be constantly incarnated, is precisely why the ostensibly certain realm of sexual difference is, in fact, so radically delicate—delicate because it is so insistently, so continually in need of reinforcement and repetition.

Materiality can no longer be depended upon to ground the stability of gender identities, for to appeal to the innocence of materiality would be to repeat the mistake of the assumption of the "natural" realm as opposed to the cultural/political one, and Butler's concern is the political construction of nature itself. Yet resistance to the regulatory norms of sex is possible. The need for repetition necessarily carries with it the possibility of disloyalty, the failure to materialize those norms in obedient accordance. Every repetition, precisely insofar as it is a repetition, is not identical to the norms themselves, but is always different, displaced, warped, imperfect. "It is this constitutive failure of the performative, this slippage between discursive command and its appropriated effect, which provides the linguistic occasion and index for a consequential disobedience" (1993, 122). If, as Butler insists, that repetition of norms literally brings subjects into being, then the failure to repeat them faithfully will produce subjects who are, to varying degrees, opposed to the dominating discourses.

This is not to say that beings are in some sense free to contradict those norms at will, or consciously, or predictably. Performativity of gendered norms can take place only in the context of constraint, of limit, of the unthinkable:

The "performative" dimension of construction is precisely the forced reiteration of norms. In this sense, then, it is not only that there are constraints to performativity; rather, constraint calls to be rethought as the very condition of performativity. Performativity is neither free play nor theatrical self-presentation; nor can it be simply equated with performance. Moreover, constraint is not necessarily that which sets a limit to

performativity; constraint is, rather, that which impels and sustains performativity. (1993, 94–95)

One performs gendered roles because there is nothing else to perform,
because to be subjectivated, to exist in any meaningful way, is already to
exist in relation to regulatory norms. To come to be a subject demands
performativity, which means that the subject is always already subjected.
The subject, because it is a subject, must perform; it is always already functioning under constraint. Resistance is possible only upon the recognition
of performativity *as performativity*, that is, upon the denial of the ground of
nature. Authority, the production of that which is to be obeyed, is predicated by its construction as unconstructed: "[I]t is precisely through the
infinite deferral of authority to an irrecoverable past that authority itself is
constituted. That deferral is the repeated act by which legitimation occurs.
The pointing to a ground which is never recovered becomes authority's
groundless ground" (1993, 108). Butler's analysis of the construction of
nature and of materiality threatens this groundless ground by giving it a
political history, thus eradicating the innocence that bolsters the authoritative norms. Nature and materiality are thus uncovered as those
realms that are constructed as unconstructed so that authority and the play
of power are made possible, and in that uncovering, the illusion of authority
is revealed.

Because regulatory norms are inherently troubled (by virtue of their
dependence on iterability, which contradicts the very stability which they
attempt to produce and celebrate), identity is similarly fractured. It is only on
the basis of the mythically irreducible bases of nature and materiality that the
concept of fixed identities comes into existence, and it is those bases that
Butler ultimately finds to be profoundly constructed. The body is a major
medium of iteration, and as such, it is both the effect of and the condition of
possibility for the imposition of regulatory norms. It is also, however, the site
where that iteration inevitably falls short of the demands of such norms, and
as such, it is central to the project of resistance. Butler warns, however, that if
such a project is to be truly effective, it must not avail itself of the concept of
identity as that which exists beyond matrices of power. Where other feminist
theories, including those discussed above, describe sexual difference as irreducible and inevitable, Butler refuses to locate any groundless ground, especially that of a gendered or sexed difference. Sexual difference exists only in
the context of a particular discursive regime that demands, produces, and
depends on the integrity of that difference. Materialization itself, as well as
the material aspects of sexual difference, is as implicated in this regime as
any other facet of sex and gender.

Moira Gatens and the Imaginary Body

In her work *Imaginary Bodies: Ethics, Power and Corporeality,* Moira Gatens (1996) distances herself from the materiality that Butler so insistently emphasizes. Rather than confronting the material body, Gatens seeks to approach those representations of and associations with the body that affect (and at times constitute) the concept of subjectivity:

> I am not concerned with physiological, anatomical, or biological understandings of the human body but rather with what will be called *imaginary* bodies. . . . The term "imaginary" will be used in a loose but nevertheless technical sense to refer to those images, symbols, metaphors and representations which help construct various forms of subjectivity. In this sense, I am concerned with the (often unconscious) imaginaries of a specific culture: those ready-made images and symbols through which we make sense of social bodies and which determine, in part, their value, their status and what will be deemed their appropriate treatment. (1996, viii)

The imaginary bodies that are central to the constitution of subjectivity are historically and socially specific. Moreover, they are not utterly separate from the real, live, living bodies of subjects, but serve to shape, organize, and evaluate them. While Gatens does not directly approach the problem of materiality (at times, the concept of the "imaginary" seems to necessitate a raw material that is shaped by its representations and demands), it is clear that the characteristics of lived bodies, especially sexual characteristics, are directly, if not necessarily, linked to the elements of the imaginary body. Gatens relates her notion of the imaginary body to the phenomenon of the phantom limb:

> Schilder maintains that both "phantom limb" and hysteria can be understood only if we take into account the fact that all healthy people are, or have, in addition to a material body, a body-phantom or an imaginary body. This psychical image of the body is necessary in order for us to have motility in the world, without which we could not be intentional subjects. The imaginary body is developed, learnt, connected to the body image of others, and is not static. (1996, 12)

The imaginary body is both intimately linked with the physical, material body and distinct from it. In the event of great trauma or amputation, the psychic force of the imaginary body is so strong that it can take on a kind of disembodied fleshiness. Thus, even in the absence of the material arm, the imaginary arm can literally be felt.

With regard to sexual difference, Gatens notes that the imaginary body is the site of the production of the historically specific elements of masculinity and femininity (1996, 12). The ways the material body is organized and privileged give rise to assumptions of gendered characteristics and traits; however, Gatens refuses a thoroughly relativistic notion of gender by noting the "contingent, though not arbitrary" (13) connection of masculinity and femininity with sexed bodies. The imaginary body is not independent of the material conditions of the physical body (to the extent that masculinity is utterly autonomous from the male body, or femininity from the female body) but is rather a particular interpretation of a material reality. "Masculinity and femininity as forms of sex-appropriate behaviours are manifestations of a historically based, culturally shared phantasy about male and female biologies, and as such sex and gender are not arbitrarily connected" (13).

In her description of the imaginary body, Gatens assumes a certain, given, sexual difference. That this sexual difference is, ultimately, located in the material rather than the imaginary body, and that it is the imaginary body rather than the material body that accounts for and produces subjectivity, implies that the formation of any historically specific subjectivity is predicated on the ways that sexual difference is taken up in the imaginary body. If the imaginary body is not utterly independent from the material body, neither is the material body utterly independent from the imaginary. Only the representations and organizations of the imaginary body allow the material body to function as a subject. Given that women have traditionally been excluded from full subjectivity and all its requisite rewards and responsibilities, Gatens's project is to articulate the specific complicity between the imaginary body and subjectivity, a complicity that has served to define women and their bodies as inferior, less worthy, and, in general, troublesome.

In describing the conditions of the "twin birth" (50) of the modern subject and the body politic, Gatens notes an exclusion of the feminine with regard to both progeny. The feminine is placed outside the relevant category and thus makes that category (or norm) possible. "Woman in fact never makes the transition from the mythical 'state of nature' to the body politic. She *becomes* nature. She is necessary to the functioning of cultural life, she is the very ground which makes cultural life possible, yet she is not part of it" (51). The construction of the sexed subject is thus linked intimately with the explicitly political goals of modern theory. Gatens insists that any feminist theory of the body must account for this linkage and must remain suspicious of the concepts derived from it. What must compel feminist theories of the body is that which remains unthinkable in the modern schema, that which does not rest, as those schema do, on the simultaneous erasure and domination of the feminine. "The distinction between the sexes is taken to be a fundamental feature of nature that could only be represented in culture in this dichotomous way. The notion that culture constructs nature or that cultural practices construct bodies as dichotomously sexed is theoretically *inadmissible* in the modern account" (*ibid.*, 51).

What troubles Gatens is not the claim of sexual difference, but rather that difference can be organized only in comparative terms of inferiority and superiority. Such organization is the role of the imaginary and of imaginary bodies, which arrange essentially different types of bodies into evaluative systems such that some are endowed with greater social and political value than others. In this sense, although the modern project depends utterly on the sexual distinction, it nevertheless seems ultimately incapable of sufficiently theorizing it *as difference;* rather, the difference melts into sameness by virtue of women's exclusion from the public world and their construction as derivations of the masculine. The body politic— that abstract "artificial man" of Hobbes's construction— feeds off the feminine body, and in order to render that dependence invisible, it must banish the feminine body to the realms of the unpolitical, the private, the untheorizable, those realms where (conveniently enough) the standards of freedom, autonomy, and self-determination are no longer relevant. "The modern body has 'lived off' its consumption of women's bodies. Women have serviced the internal organs and needs of this artificial body, preserving its viability, its unity and integrity, replacing its bodyparts, without ever being seen to do so" (23).

Not only does the body politic refuse the presence of feminine bodies, but it allows masculine bodies to function as generically unsexed. The refusal of female bodies results in the denial of bodily specificity and the relevance of the body itself. The birth of the body politic, the organism of public reason and civic participation, must be accompanied by the birth of the disembodied modern subject, whose bodily specificity is erased in its construction as generic. In order for the body politic to function effectively, its subjects must be understood as basically the same ("human," that is, rational). To understand them as profoundly different from each other in some basic and unhierarchized sense seems to undermine the possibility of public discourse as well as the values of equality and autonomy on which the body politic rested.

The exclusion of women from the public realm, then, is not (as the modern theorists so often claimed) justified on the basis of women's inferior mental capacities, but is rather predicated more profoundly on the modern need to disallow the relevance of bodily differences. That dependence results in a structurally necessary inability to recognize and account for bodily differences, including sexual difference, without reducing those differences to a single standard (by which standard certain bodies have "more" or "less" of a socially valued characteristic, thus justifying either their superiority or inferiority). Hence the inclusion that many feminist movements sought and continue to seek is problematic at its core, for it is an inclusion into a realm that necessarily demands the disavowal of bodily specificities that are a large part of many women's experience and lives. To speak of those bodily specificities in the context of the body politic is to speak nonsense: "If what one is fascinated by is the image of one body, one voice, one reason, any deviation takes the form of gibberish" (26). The futility of the goal of inclusion is manifested in its price: in order to enter the body politic as it is traditionally known, women must subject themselves to the norms of unity and oneness. They must deny their sexual specificity and implicitly accept the valorization of the masculine as the generic. They must accept the masculine imaginary as their own in order to become the subjects that have always inhabited the body politic. They must become generically human; they must become men.

A feminist activism that seeks equal political participation must consider at the outset the problem of the representation and autonomy of the female body. At an even more basic level, the challenge facing a feminist politics is the problem of difference. Gatens's analysis, like those of Braidotti and Grosz, claims that the problem is not one of difference, but of hierarchy. Insofar as subjectivity is defined as unmarked by difference, that is, as a unified whole, any difference must appear as an inferiority or aberration. The challenge as Gatens sees it is to allow the play of difference without the context of hierarchization. "Difference, as it has been presented here, is not concerned with privileging an essentially biological difference between the sexes. Rather, it is concerned with the mechanisms by which bodies are recognized as different only in so far as they are constructed as possessing or lacking some socially privileged quality or qualities" (73).

If feminism does not find a feasible or desirable goal in inclusion, a redefining of the category of subjectivity remains its best hope. Gatens claims that the existing political structures, given their inherently masculine bias, are incapable of representing women's diverse realities in a nonderivative way, that is, as autonomous in relation to men's realities. What is needed is change at the level of the organization and valuation of realities and bodies themselves, a change in the dominant imaginaries that ascribe to different types of bodies inferior status than those of white men. Moreover, Gatens indicates that women, as beings with differing social statuses than men, have access to different imaginaries, different ways of understanding and organizing bodies and subjectivity, and that those imaginaries need to be endowed with social and political power:

> The problem, as I see it, is that dominant masculine sexual imaginaries are politically, legally, economically and socially legitimated through existing networks of power, whereas women's imaginings about men are not. Such legitimation entrenches sexual imaginaries that tell us only about the affective relation in which men stand to women. They tell us nothing about the various powers and capacities which women possess independently of their power to affect, or be affected by, men. (147)

In order for women's imaginings to find a place in the construction of subjectivity, a necessary step in the process of achieving full and equal political participation between the sexes, subjectivity itself must not be centered around a unifying, allegedly universal standard, but must rather begin with the assumption of difference. As long as women (and their bodies) are constructed as mere reflections of men, as the satisfiers of male desire or the pale imitation of a greater, more real, masculine being—that is, as long as the dominant male imaginary retains virtually all meaningful power, so that it is virtually the only standard with any social force—full female subjectivity will remain beyond their reach, indeed, beyond the pale. To begin with differing imaginaries (and it may be assumed that, due to the neglect with which feminine imaginaries have been treated, it is they who deserve a greater degree of attention at the moment) is necessarily to leave hierarchies behind and to approach the multiplicity of bodies and subjectivity.

The first step in this rethinking of subjectivity as difference involves a stress on the significance of embodiment. Through an emphasis on the embodied, situated subject, the urge to articulate a generic, "normal" subject, the standard by which other beings are judged (and by which, inevitably, large groups of persons fall short), is stifled. Those situated bodies, not only material but also imaginary, are always already marked as different from each other in a myriad of significant ways, not the least of which is the mark of sexual difference. To struggle against the imaginary structure that insists that these differences be prioritized, hierarchized, organized as "superior" and "inferior" will result in a qualitative change in the definition of "masculine" and "feminine" (or at least in the evaluation of traits and characteristics defined as such). Rejecting the alleged sex neutrality of the subject, with its lurking masculinist character, opens the possibility for defining the subject in such a way as to render significant sex-specific bodily experiences. Viewing women's experiences and imaginaries as independent, or at least not derivative, from those of men is necessary if we are to avoid the demand of sex neutrality which the goal of simple inclusion inherently contained.

To be embodied, for Gatens, is not only to be mere flesh or materiality, but is importantly to participate in (as well as be produced by) a culturally and historically specific imaginary that both constrains and produces subjectivity. It is the imaginary body, as the site at which subjectification occurs, that needs to be at the center of both a liberating feminism and a rethinking of the subject. Drawing interestingly on Spinoza, Gatens develops an understanding of both subjectivity and the body that values at once a degree of bodily autonomy and a necessarily nonhierarchical view of difference. By understanding reason as embodied and the process of creating a communal civilization as not innate, but a rational choice on the part of embodied beings, Gatens emphasizes the degree to which members of a society can view themselves as communally responsible for its structure.

This different view of responsibility provides a challenge to individualistic morality (which, implicitly or explicitly, considers the political structure or surrounding environment of any given action or behavior to be morally irrelevant): "A community of rational beings would look to the structural, as well as to the immediate, causes of violent behaviour and assume responsibility for such causes where appropriate—for example, attitudes to women that are embedded in the customs and laws of the civil body" (1996, 121). In other words, members of the community would acknowledge a shared responsibility for the imaginaries that structure and organize beings in such a way as to make certain actions possible and even likely (imaginaries that, in order to be just, must acknowledge the differences among embodied subjects in ways that refuse hierarchization). In this way, each member's actions would be considered not as those of an autonomous moral agent, but as actions of an embodied citizen who both participates in the formation and perpetuation of the pertinent imaginaries and is formed by them. In the complex interplay between the imaginary body and the material body, Gatens locates the possibility of a political agency that recognizes differences among subjects while acknowledging the influence of overarching systems of thought and organization.

Thinking from the Feminine Body: Luce Irigaray

All the theorists discussed so far have been developing new understandings of the body and its connection to subjectivity. Luce Irigaray, by contrast, presents a way of theorizing from the feminine body that differs significantly from other theorists, and as such, her theories will offer significantly different conceptual tools. Her thought will prove crucial to my analysis of the ethical wrongs of rape in a subsequent chapter, as she connects the very possibility of ethics to the recognition of sexual difference, a difference she establishes by privileging the significance of the feminine body.

Rather than attempting to establish what the body or the feminine body is, Irigaray constructs the feminine body as the ground on which her thought is built. Irigaray utilizes the specificity of the feminine body to construct an alternative metaphysics, one that challenges and undermines the historically Western valorization of unity and identity. Her philosophical project involves the dismantling of the masculine generic, the universalism that at once refuses to recognize sexual difference and assumes the normativity of the male. According to Irigaray, it has been the philosophical and historical *denial* of sexual difference that is at the root of the oppression of women. It is not the distinction between the sexes that has justified the domination of women, but rather the refusal to confront the fact that the human species is irrevocably split, (at least) doubled, and that therefore there exists no universality to human being. The logic of patriarchy has attempted to create a stultifying unity out of this doubleness by positing women, and the feminine, as a mere derivative of the masculine, thus forbidding the possibility of a distinct and discrete femaleness. Science and philosophy have adopted the male generic as the model of the human, and by claiming that the female consists of nothing more than a pale shadow of the male (or the projection of masculine needs and desires), have justified the exclusion of the female from the universal. Because the female is understood as merely the subset of the male, as that which only lacks some of the traits and abilities of the male and has nothing uniquely its own, any exploration of the human being itself need address only the most complete type of human, that is, the male. The allegedly neuter, generic human, therefore, is relentlessly masculine by nature:

> Given that *science* is one of the last figures, if not the last figure, used to represent absolute knowledge, it is—ethically—essential that we ask science to reconsider the nonneutrality of the supposedly universal subject that constitutes its scientific theory and practice.

> In actual fact, the self-proclaimed universal is the equivalent of an idio-
> lect of men, a masculine imaginary, a sexed world. With no neuter.
> (1993a, 121)

The body plays a crucial and productive role in Irigaray's theorizing of difference. Western metaphysics, she claims, rests upon a particular reading of the particularly masculine body. The feminine body, by contrast, has not been thought from: it remains a model unexplored in its own specificity. When Irigaray approaches the feminine body, she does so not in an attempt to describe that which is either common among all women or alien to the male experience. Rather, Irigaray explores the feminine body to see what it can tell us of the human condition (which, as it turns out, does not exist in the unity which the phrase implies). In the details of the feminine genitalia, she finds a challenge to the singularity of the phallus.

Irigaray presents the distinctly female body as a model of difference that resists the reduction into unity: "Now, the/a woman who doesn't have *one* sex organ, or a unified sexuality (and this has usually been interpreted to mean that she has no sex) cannot subsume it/herself under *one* generic or specific term" (1985a, 233). The plurality of feminine sexuality, the fact that there is not one sex organ but many, as well as the indeterminate openness of the female genitalia, provides an image of an indeterminate, fluid way of being that cannot be contained within definitive limits. "The/a woman cannot be collected into *one* volume, for in that way she risks surrendering her own jouissance, which demands that she remain open to nothing utterable but which assures that her edges not close, her lips not be sewn shut" (1985a, 240). In addition, the/a woman's genital lips are examples of an irreducible twoness: "Woman 'touches herself' all the time, and moreover no one can forbid her to do so, for her genitals are formed of two lips in continuous contact. Thus, within herself, she is already two—but not divisible into one(s)—that caress each other" (1985b, 24).[2]

The centrality of the specifically feminine body in Irigaray's thought constitutes a philosophical attempt to think subjectivity not from the generic (and persistently male) human body, but from one kind of sexed body. Irigaray is not arguing that the details of the feminine sex organs give rise to a fluid, doubled subjectivity that applies only to women, but that their doubleness and irreducibility reflect the doubleness and irreducibility of the human species. Given the historic exclusion of the feminine body from models of personhood, experience, and subjectivity, Irigaray is attempting to correct a loss that, she claims, has resulted in the

universalism of traditional philosophical thought. To think from the female body is to recognize difference, not only methodologically, but sub-
stantively, as the female body itself resists the models of unity and sameness that dominate discourses of science and philosophy. Irigaray's
thought is then (at least) double: both the choice of the subject of her
analysis and the content of that analysis reflect the fundamental significance of difference. Women's sexuality is always already differentiated;
" 'She' is indefinitely other in herself" (1985b, 28), and it is this primacy
of differentiation that has been forgotten, lost, in the historically traditional pursuit of the universal.

It is not surprising, then, that the sexual indifference that has marred
traditional philosophical, political, and scientific thought has been accompanied by a distinct somatophobia. Those projects that such a culture
has deemed the most valid, valuable, and productive have traditionally
demanded a separation from, or denial of, the material body. "It is also
significant that in our cultures man thinks or prays by estranging himself
from his body, and that thinking or praying do not assist him in becoming
incarnate, becoming flesh" (1996, 40). Both intellectual and spiritual
pursuits have failed to recognize that matters of the body and matters of
the spirit, *precisely because they are differentiated from each other,* are the conditions of possibility for both thought and prayer. In valuing one over
another or reducing one to the other, such pursuits have been incapable
of recognizing the primary nature of movement which depends directly
on difference.

> We must reexamine our own history thoroughly to understand why this
> sexual difference has not had its chance to develop, either empirically or
> transcendentally. . . . It is surely a question of the dissociation of body and
> soul, of sexuality and spirituality, of the lack of a passage for the spirit, for
> the god, between the inside and the outside, the outside and the inside,
> and of their distribution between the sexes in the sex act. (1993a, 14–15)

The dissociation to which Irigaray refers is not a recognition of difference,
but a hierarchical organization that reduces difference to a coherent,
closed unity (a unity that gains its nature primarily from the dominant
and domineering element). Hierarchies that at first appear to be creating
injustice out of sexual difference, by treating women and other groups as
inferior and endowing them with fewer rights and privileges, are actually
means of reducing the differences embodied by those different groups to
quantitative variations of a single, unified standard. The difference that is
modeled in the distinctly feminine body cannot be reduced to such a

unity ("she is already two—but not divisible into one[s]") but persists in its (at least) doubleness.

At least two ethical aspects of the recognition of sexual difference are related directly to the body. First, and perhaps primary in Irigaray's thought, is the demand to constitute and understand individual beings in relation to their sexuation, that is, to place their bodily specificity at the center of their social and political identities. The fact of sexual difference indicates that the reduction of an individual to a mere example of a generic, unsexed model of personhood is a violent act that inevitably recasts that individual not in his or her own specificity but in the terms of an implicitly hierarchized system. In order to approach any individual in an ethical, just manner, we must approach them as they are: men and women, differentiated from each other, specific, incarnate, embodied beings.[3]

Second, there exists the demand to explore the philosophical significance of those bodies that have, until now, been deemed unworthy of intellectual attention. Since sexual difference is a primary difference among bodies, especially insofar as it is necessary to the existence of the species as we know it, and because it has been so relentlessly ignored and denied, those bodies marked as female are particularly in need of intellectual attention. Or perhaps that is putting it backwards: if we are to correct the sexual indifference that has dominated Western thought and metaphysics, it is that history, the validity of that thought, that finds itself in need of the feminine.

An ethics of sexual difference is thus marked by a recognition of the ways every embodied individual is differentiated, limited, yet indeterminate. Not all women represent or experience an identical femininity, but—and this is Irigaray's point—all men and all women, insofar as they are sexed and therefore not universal, represent and experience only a limited portion of the possibilities of human being. An ethics of sexual difference thus demands a humility that a belief in universalism or unity cannot include, a humility that is expressed in that first passion of wonder:

> To arrive at the constitution of an ethics of sexual difference, we must at least return to what is for Descartes the first passion: *wonder*. This passion has no opposite or contradiction and exists always as though for the first time. Thus man and woman, woman and man are always meeting as though for the first time because they cannot be substituted one for the other. I will never be in a man's place, never will a man be in mine. Whatever identifications are possible, one will never exactly occupy the place of the other—they are irreducible one to the other. (1993a, 12–13)

Conclusion

Obviously, this chapter has not provided a complete survey of all feminist theorists who are currently working on problems of the body, nor has it exhausted the theoretical richness of any one of the theorists discussed. Nonetheless, it has served to locate the problem of the body as central to feminism's struggle with the problems of subjectivity and inclusion. While these theorists differ from each other in important and obvious ways—Butler would wince at Grosz's invocation of the "irreducible" factor of sexual difference, and Gatens's emphasis on the imaginary conflicts with the materiality which Braidotti highlights—they also, as a whole, represent a set of theoretical tools that will prove useful in the articulation of the phenomenon of rape. While not underplaying the significances of the differences among these theorists, I seek to cull from all of them a more or less common understanding of some basic characteristics of what may be called the feminist material subject. The discussion of rape as an embodied experience that will follow in the ensuing chapter will depend heavily on this constellation of characteristics, and so will draw not only on specific theorists, but on the (admittedly fractured and contradictory) field of contemporary feminist theories of the body.

Given the trenchant critiques of modern concepts of subjectivity and the body that these contemporary feminist theories represent, it is clear that traditional, and perhaps even some feminist, concepts of the raped and rapable subject will prove insufficient. Moreover, insofar as rape is defined in terms that surround and constitute the modern subject, it is likely that that definition would serve to repeat the masculinist bias inherent in that conceptualization of the subject. To rethink rape in such a way as to avoid that mistake of repetition necessitates an understanding of subjectivity that differs radically from that of modernity. The subject that arises out of this burgeoning, still expanding field of feminist scholarship on the body has a number of traits that are literally unspeakable in the context of modern theory. These traits will ground our discussion of rape as an embodied experience. Principal among them are the following:

1. Embodiment

Perhaps most importantly, the feminist subject is taken to be a material, embodied being. Rather than being marked as an essentially intellectual being, defined by the abstract and distinctly nonbodily capability of reason, who merely "inhabits" a fleshy vessel, the embodied subject is not separate from its specific bodily form. Subjectivity, the ability to act, speak, and move, is defined in terms of, rather than against, the material aspects of the body. This definition does not preclude reason or rationality from the definition of subject or subjectivity, but rather denies the strict dichotomy between the mind and the body, as well as the hierarchy that privileged the former over the latter. Reason itself is perceived as an embodied activity, or, more generally, the body is understood as an active participant in the project of reason.

The embodied subject is necessarily specific, situated, and particular, precisely because it is a literally incarnated being. While embodiment is a trait that all known subjects share, it is by no means shared identically by all subjects. To be embodied is already to be radically different from others in a variety of ways. These ways of differing are neither strictly biological (as if they were necessarily determined by an apolitical nature) nor strictly social (as if they were imposed on a passive, blank slate); ways of embodiment in their dynamic workings confound such distinctions. Because political and social power works directly on bodies, literally shaping them in often pernicious ways and for particular purposes, the political specificity of a given culture can give rise to certain kinds of subjects. The emphasis on the significance of embodiment in the formation of subjectivity can highlight the significance of bodily customs in the perpetuation of oppressive regimes (whereas if the mental existence of the subject is perceived as more important than and radically separate from the material conditions that surround that subject, then bodily customs can be dismissed as merely superficial).

That the embodied subject is understood, to some extent, as constructed by her or his social, historical, and political situation does not necessarily imply that such a subject is wholly and relentlessly determined by that situation. The fact that forces of power act on bodies and affect their literal shape and habits does not indicate that those forces act identically or with equal force on every single body. Any theory of constructivism needs to account for the fact that individual subjects—even those who are developed in strikingly similar environments—respond to the play of forces in radically different ways, and in doing so, develop radically different bodily habits and behaviors. In order to account for these differences, we must be understood the body on which political and social forces act not as an inert surface, which soaks up and then reflects the dominant claims and values of the discursive regimes without permutation, but rather as an active and at times resistant factor in the process of subjection. We may claim with some certainty, then, that the play of power is consistently directly against and upon the bodies of subjects, but we must understand those bodies as essentially moving targets, which adopt some practices and eschew or refuse others.

Moreover, the body itself cannot be placed in strict opposition to the play of power, as the process of subjectification also produces the enforcers of the dominant discourse. Power is not a disembodied force, strictly exterior to any given subject, which forms and shapes that subject to its dominant model. Power is embedded both in its source and its object; and while it is not located in any one body or even one group of bodies, it nevertheless claims the subjectivated body as its medium and the subjected body as its object. In the end, all bodies are subjectivated to the extent that they are subjected to the play of power (although not all bodies are equally or similarly subjected). The same embodied subject that resists one aspect of bodily discipline may well in turn enforce another.

The embodied subject is thus a particular incarnation of a particular constellation of political, social, historical, and material forces. Insofar as it is incarnated, it is limited by its specificity; yet it is this limitation of specificity that endows that particular embodied self with specific abilities and behavior. Embodied subjects, in order to become subjects recognizable in their own milieu, must develop in relation to the specific discursive regimes that surround their formation. For example, those bodies marked as feminine in contemporary Western culture must, in some fashion, engage with and respond to ideals of feminine beauty. However, that engagement is a continual and indeterminate process. There will exist feminine subjects who reproduce those ideals to the letter and at any cost, those who resist any and all trappings deemed womanly, and those (the vast majority) who fall somewhere in between. All these subjects, however, as well as their bodily experiences and their sense of embodiment, are (dissimilarly) marked by the same discursive regime. Because the body is neither utterly free from the play of power, as the "natural" body was understood to be, nor wholly determined by it, the subject is similarly constrained and capable of resistance.

2. Intersubjectivity

The feminist subject is not defined primarily as autonomous or self-created. The specific characteristics of various subjects arise always in the context of a particular environment and a particular community, and the development of any subjectivity is directly dependent on the existence and care of other subjects. Here, feminist theorists are arguing against the modern conception of individualism, where subjectivity becomes understood primarily as a private project and the goal of maturation is understood as a freedom from the claims and demands of other beings. Such a model of subjectivity assumes a strict distinction between self and other, whereby the integrity of the former is dependent on the limitation of the influence of the latter. Feminist theorists note that the radical individualism and freedom celebrated by modernism, and most explicitly by Rousseau's "savage man," are strictly illusory, and can be constituted only if the work of women (traditionally, the child rearers who provide for the material needs of growing subjects) is rendered invisible and invalid. In contrast, feminist theorists understand subjectivity as a project undertaken among subjects in the course of a variety of relationships, and any given trait (including many bodily characteristics) of a subject as a result of the complex interplay between the subject and his or her society. The self cannot be understood as opposed to the other or to society, because it is only in the context of others and a particular society that that self comes to be.

While the intersubjectivity that marks the embodied subject is grounded in a variety of types of relationships, its significance should also remind us of the importance of the subject's sexuality. Sexuality itself, however coded or organized, is oriented around desire, which, as Braidotti reminds us, is fundamental to the constitution of the intersubjective subject. Sexual preferences and acts, with the possible exception of autoerotic acts, involve another subject in a vital way, and in their intersubjectivity speak to the inherent openness (and, as we shall see, the vulnerability) of the embodied subject. An understanding of the subject as embodied and therefore intersubjective presents a challenge to a model of sexuality whereby one person is "acting" and the other person is "acted upon." Rather, sexual desires, actions, and experiences are taken up as a means by which an individual's subjectivity is shaped by the play of alterity.

3. Sexual Difference

The material subject of many of the theories explored above is always already sexed; that is, it always carries with it the mark of sexual difference. This is not to say that individual subjects can be wholly determined by their sex, nor that subjects who share the same sex can be assumed to share a defined set of characteristics or behavior. Rather, the emphasis on sexual difference, including the bodily manifestations of that difference, constitutes a criticism of the sex-neutral, generic subject that dominates modern theory. To approach the subject as always already sexed is to preclude a sole, universal, unifying definition of subjectivity and to place difference rather than sameness at the basis of an understanding of human agency. This privileging of difference (although certainly controversial, even and perhaps especially within the realm of feminist scholarship) disallows the possibility of one dominant model that, by exclusion, defines other types of beings as inferior or less worthy. Theorists of sexual difference note that the standards of subjectivity, worth, and value are predicated on the assumption of the male generic. To emphasize difference at a fundamental level is to call into question the applicability of those norms (which women, by definition, cannot hope to fulfill to the same extent that men have been able to) rather than to adopt them in a wholesale fashion. To view all subjects as sexed is to view them in their particularity, rather than as representations of either the norm or the failure of the norm.

Moreover, theories of sexual difference note that the development of subjectivity as currently undertaken necessitates a process of sexing or gendering. Despite the modern promise of and insistence upon the gender-neutral model of the subject, in fact, in contemporary Western society, a subject comes into being only insofar as it is subjected to gender roles, that is, insofar as it is sexed. It is not the case, then, that the subject (or the body of the subject) is a blank, neutral slate upon which the cultural characteristics of gender are imprinted. Rather, the subject becomes a subject only to the extent to which it is gendered. This, in short, is Butler's point: gender roles, indeed, male and female sexualities themselves, rather than being determinate, static, and naturally derived, are both artificial (in the sense of being culturally and historically specific, as well as being forcibly imposed) and constitutive (in terms of their necessity for subjectivity itself). While Butler argues against the idea of fixed, certain sex identities, she nevertheless places the act and process of sexing at the most basic level of the development of the subject.

As a theoretical concept, sexual difference must be differentiated from the sex/gender distinction prevalent in earlier feminist theories. The sex/gender distinction functioned to dismiss the biological fact of sex as already given, known, and relegated to a specifically nonpolitical (and nonmalleable) area of discourse. Its purpose was to free women from the culturally specific mandates of gender roles by separating them from that which was biologically necessary, namely, sex. Moreover, the distinction benefited the feminist political goal of inclusion by arguing that what was biologically given was often and perhaps almost always irrelevant in terms of political subjectivity ("biology is not destiny"). The biological distinction of sex, then, was often portrayed as irrelevant, or at least nondeterminative, with regard to subjectivity. The job of a patriarchal society was to get over its obsession with the sex difference and to recognize that with regard to personhood, it was a false means of demarcation.

Obviously, the sexual difference that is theorized by these contemporary feminists is not the sex difference that emanates from the sex/gender distinction. The sexual difference that theorists such as Grosz and Braidotti articulate is not, strictly speaking, reducible to biological differences between the sexes, although its material manifestations are certain relevant. Given that embodiment is fundamental to subjectivity, the radical difference between male bodies and female bodies is understood to affect the kinds of subjectivity and indeed the kinds of experiences that are available to these differing subjects. Sexual difference thus understood emphasizes the lack of symmetry between the sexes, which should result in a call to integrate those embodied experiences particular to women into a new model of subjectivity (whereas they had previously served to justify women's exclusion from full subjectivity). As Braidotti insistently points out, it will not serve feminist purposes well to construct women as essentially identical to men. The denial of sexual difference, especially at this historical juncture, is in effect the erasure of that which is particular to female experience. By contrast, the emphasis on sexual difference requires that men share the burden of sexualization, which, until now, women have disproportionately carried.

Whereas the sex/gender distinction delivered the biological factor of sex to the realm of science, understood as at least allegedly neutral and nonpolitical, the concept of sexual difference encourages a philosophical reevaluation of subjectivity and its relation to politics, law, and ethics. The sex of the sex/gender distinction was constituted as known, fixed, and in many ways politically uninteresting. Theorizing sexual difference, by contrast, is constituted by these thinkers as the primary goal of feminist theory. Yet it is important to realize that these theorists resist the urge to define sexual difference in a static or fixed way. Irigaray, for one, insistently refuses to characterize the category of women, as crucial as that category is to her theory. Recognizing sexual difference is not necessarily, or perhaps at all, to arrive at any conclusions about some characteristics, traits, or tendencies that all women, as members of a delineated category, hold. Rather, such recognition involves the presumption that differences between and among the sexes are relevant, and that that relevance, given a history of sex-indifference and false inclusivity, is often buried, denied, or ignored. To approach the material subject as marked by sexual difference is to bring to bear a mode of inquiry that would otherwise be deemed—sometimes by the very use of the sex/gender distinction—irrelevant, and that is in fact vital to the understanding of that subject.

4. Discontinuity

If subjectivity is directly related to the fact and particular experience of embodiment, then it stands to reason that significant bodily changes may produce significant and qualitative changes in the subject who undergoes them. Feminist theorists note that the body, and therefore the subject, is not a static, stable entity, but is constantly in the process of change, development, and deterioration. In its search for a fixed and universal subject, modern theory celebrated reason as that which was most permanent, and the self, the being capable of rational thought, as a unified, constant entity. The embodied subject of feminist theory, however, is radically discontinuous in that there is no one abstract core of being that persists through necessary bodily changes. Any individual embodied subject is thus properly understood not as a distinct and stable entity, but rather as a constantly shifting conglomeration of physical, psychical, emotional, and intellectual characteristics.

Many feminist theorists turn to the particularities of the female body to demonstrate this discontinuity. The cyclical occurrence of menstruation, the upheaval of pregnancy, the onset of menopause—all these distinctly female bodily experiences (although not experienced by every woman, and certainly not experienced in identical ways) emphasize the shifting abilities and characteristics of a body that is never completed, never finished, but always in movement. Iris Marion Young discovers in the phenomenon of pregnancy a challenge to the possibility of a determinate, self-identified body, and thus to the possibility of a purely self-contained subject:

> The pregnant subject . . . is decentered, split, or doubled in several ways. She experiences her body as herself and not herself. Its inner movements belong to another being, yet they are not other, because her body boundaries shift and because her bodily self-location is focused on her trunk in addition to her head. . . . Pregnant existence entails, finally, a unique temporality of process and growth in which the woman can experience herself as split between past and future. . . . Pregnancy . . . reveals a paradigm of bodily experience in which the transparent unity of self dissolves and the body attends positively to itself at the same time that it enacts its projects. (1990, 160–61)

The concepts of the autonomous self and the self-contained body fail in the light of the phenomenon of pregnancy, an experience that cannot sufficiently be described in the terms allowed by the definition of the rational subject. By placing bodily experiences that are particular to women at the center of the process that is subjectivity, feminist theorists effectively demonstrate that the "transparent unity of self" is an illusion directly predicated on the exclusion of feminine experience.

The discontinuous, ever-changing characteristics of the body—and therefore of the subject—allow for the possibility of a new kind of ethics that emphasizes the significance of material and bodily changes and transformations. Bodily experiences no longer happen to a persistent, immutable self; instead, they are part of the ongoing construction of the self and are in fact central to the development of particular modes of subjectivity.

All these characteristics of the subject of feminist theories of the body serve to challenge the dualisms inherent in modern theory. The ostensible dichotomies of self/other, mind/body, interior/surface, nature/culture are complicated and in many cases revealed as mutually defining and co-constitutive dynamics whose factors cannot be separated from each other. The dichotomous thinking of the modern period demanded that differences be resolved in the unity, the oneness, of a hierarchy, and hierarchies, in order to be effective, necessitate a radical opposition between that which dominates and that which is dominated. By demonstrating that these roles are always already mutually dependent, feminist theorists of the body refuse the possibility of an innocent, neutral standard.

The subject is thus defined not as the autonomous, rational, and virtually disembodied creature of modern philosophy, but rather as an embodied, fluid, intersubjective being whose materiality is the basic condition of possibility for existence. To begin with corporeality is necessarily to begin with difference, not only sexual difference, but the differences of class, race, sexual orientation, and material resources. Legal, political, and social attempts to approach individual beings and behavior in such a way that demands the denial of difference inevitably replicate the sexed, raced, and classed standards of a patriarchal, white-dominated society. The standards that depend on the disembodied, rational subject as its model will always fail to explicate and account for the experiences of those beings automatically excluded from the category of the normal.

Rape as Embodied Experience

Grounded by the various models of embodied subjectivity that contemporary feminist theories of the body provide, our discussion now turns to the embodied experience of being raped. Immediately the problem of definition arises. Any definition of rape seems doomed to be either too broad or too narrow, and the mutual dangers of misidentifying an experience as rape and of failing to recognize a case of rape seem paralyzing indeed.[1] This chapter will not, ultimately, solve this conundrum. Its purpose is to elucidate the meanings of the phenomenon of rape as an embodied experience, not to produce some generally applicable definition of the crime itself. Indeed, I will argue that such general definitions, precisely because of their ostensibly universal nature, inevitably fail to describe any particular instance of rape sufficiently.

My approach to the phenomenon of rape as an embodied experience is not without its own assumptions. It is, for example, grounded in the specificity of female bodies and feminine experiences, an assumption that will attempt to correct for the masculine bias inherent in previous definitions and analyses. Specifically, then, I am interested in rape as an embodied experience *of women.*

This is not an uncontroversial move, especially insofar as it explicitly assumes that the victim of rape is a woman. While not all rape victims are women, rape is a crime disproportionately committed against women; in general this assumption is fairly safe, although not foolproof.[2] It is, of course, limiting, insofar as it will cause some aspects of some rapes to remain unexplored. However, a gender-neutral approach to rape, as will be discussed below, despite its seemingly broader scope, has similar limiting effects, ones that cause the sexually specific aspects of rape to be studiously ignored.

Another controversial element of this approach is its privileging of the experience of the victim. J. H. Bogart's analysis of the nature of rape explicitly refuses a victim-centered approach, claiming that relying on the experiences of women necessarily demands the articulation of a unifying element of the experience, an impossible goal:

> Requiring an experiential element leads to serious problems. It requires that there in fact be *an* experience common to all cases of rape. It is clear that there is no common experience temporally extensional with rape. A looser temporal connection will not remedy the lack. The experiences of rape victim [*sic*] vary significantly. Some victims are in states which preclude relevant experiences (the unconscious, for example). We should also have to exclude those cases where the victim does not have disfavored experiences. Further, the experiential requirement raises serious barriers to a proper understanding of sexual oppression on a multicultural and historical basis.
>
> A focus on experience also leads to legal snares. If rape has an experiential core, then it is natural for evidentiary inquiries to permit, indeed encourage, investigation of a putative victim's experiences. The place in an inquiry of "how it felt" is then assured. (1991, 122)

Note that for Bogart, an emphasis on experience with regard to the definition of rape leads to an inherent paradox, since experience is fraught with a specificity that cannot sustain a generally applicable definition. It is only by casting the definition of rape in abstract terms—that is, as a violation of abstractly held and defined "rights"—that one can avoid the paralyzing relevance of the specificity of each victim's experience. Moreover, by setting aside the particular experience of the rape (to such an extent that the victim's own recognition, or lack of same, of the harm visited upon her is deemed irrelevant; whether her rights were denied or trampled upon is the only meaningful question), one can spare victims the unpleasant and often horrifying prospect of describing the emotional and bodily effects of the assault.

Bogart's position is problematic in several ways. The desire to block the possibility of the "inquiry into 'how it felt' " constitutes a repetition of the feminist attempt to remove sexuality from the definition of rape so that women would not be further damaged by questions of complicity. While explicitly insisting that any definition of rape must include its sexual aspect, Bogart retains a desire to protect women from being forced to describe a sexual act in the public forum of a courtroom. Yet why such an inquiry should be avoided in not explained directly; one can only assume that the results of the inquiry would either embarrass the victim or perhaps call into question the plausibility of the victim, both of which constitute revictimization. Laura Hengehold has noted that the demands of the courtroom on the rape victim inevitably construct her as a hysterical, hence untrustworthy, voice:

> This "second rape" is often formalized in court proceedings, when a witness who enters cross-examination with complete faith in her own self-understanding nevertheless finds herself unable to explain why she did certain things or why she chose to explain them in a certain way. As the victim's increasingly prolific explanation diverges farther and farther from the ideal of self-contained subjectivity, she appears "beside herself," "hysterical," even to herself. (1994, 100)

Bogart's assessment of the danger of an articulation of women's experience is therefore not incorrect. In the masculinist setting of the courtroom, the depth of the psychic and emotional response to an experience of rape appears nonsensical and is easily dismissed. However, the suggested solution—to remove the possibility of the victim's articulation of her experience, including her bodily experience, which is even more removed from that discourse that recognizes and privileges abstractly held rights—only serves to reinforce a discourse where the full spectrum of the ramifications of rape is denied. That a victim's description of an experience of rape within the context of a courtroom can constitute a "second rape" is not the fault of the quality or content of that description. The fault lies in a systematic discourse that refuses the significance of anything not rational, not abstract, not universal, that is, anything bodily or sexually specific. The solution to such a difficulty is to render women's articulation of experiences of victimization such as rape audible and respected. Hengehold concludes:

> [A] woman's attempt to publicly reassert herself as a rational and powerful speaker in the aftermath of rape may demand the creation of another speaking community (such as the women's movement) besides that which is mediated by law, and that only an alternative (feminist) discourse capable of analyzing the asymmetrical speech situation within the courtroom can confirm the sanity and communicative agency of the supposed hysteric. (1994, 104)

This alternative discourse, which Hengehold locates strictly outside legal discourse, would demand the decentering of the rational such that the non-rational, specific, and situated effects and significances of the crime of rape would be recognized as central to the phenomenon itself.

Bogart's concern about the specificity of the experiences of victims of rape is similarly linked to the bodily meanings of rape. Again, to a certain degree, Bogart (whose gender is unknown to the reader) is correct. To attempt a definition of rape that is centered on victims' experiences is necessarily to invoke a host of contradictory narratives that are not necessarily bound together by any one "essence" or meaning. For Bogart, the threat of multiplicity is sufficient to discourage a strategy that privileges the role of experience. However, given the discussion in chapter 3, it is unclear that multiplicity itself, as opposed to the unity and universalism afforded by a generic abstract, is unattractive or even inaccurate. In fact, a strategy which explicitly seeks a universal and all-encompassing definition of rape—especially one that, like Bogart's, is distinctly unmarked by sexual difference—should inspire suspicion as to its ability to describe a phenomenon that is so profoundly gendered as well as raced.

In the virtual abandonment of the significance of experience, Bogart is forced to abandon the significance of the body itself. Although Bogart recognizes the sexual element of the act of rape, he or she subsumes that element under a discourse of rights that eradicates the differential factor of sex. Interestingly, Bogart notes that rape is "an attack on a person through their sexuality" (121) yet fails to recognize that sexuality itself is experienced differently by persons of different sexes. The sexual significances of rape, in Bogart's view, precisely because they are bodily, must be abandoned or denied because of their lack of universality; rape becomes defined in terms of that which is unmarked by bodily meanings, namely, abstract rights. The meanings of the body are traded for the illusion of universality.

Contrary to Bogart, an analysis of rape as embodied experience will remain centered on the significance of the experience of victims, especially female victims. More specifically, it will approach female victims of rape not as subjects as defined by traditional modern theories, but rather as instances of the kinds of subjectivity developed by contemporary feminist theorists, as articulated in chapter 3. In short, I will approach rape as experienced by an embodied, situated, moving, sexed subject.

The Multiplicity of Rape

The problem of multiplicity, as noted above, is solved—that is, it disappears—with the introduction of the universal standard of rights. When the subject is approached and defined as the holder (or perhaps owner) of abstract rights, who is harmed primarily through the denial or theft of those rights, the bodily specificity of the subject (his or her sex, race, economic status, or physical condition, to mention a few) is considered irrelevant. The rights remain the same regardless of the specificity of their holder or owner, and thus the harm of any specific action is also identical across any spectrum of individuals.

However, when we approach rape as an experience of the embodied subject, the universality of the experience of the act of rape is undermined. Although every subject is embodied, there are few if any aspects or qualities of embodiment that are shared identically by all subjects. Embodiment is precisely the site of the possibility and necessity of difference; as such, it constitutes both that which is most shared by subjects qua subjects and that which differentiates subjects from each other. Precisely because all subjects are embodied, all subjects are embodied *differently*.

Embodiment gives rise to an enormous scope of differences. The quality and nature of an individual's embodiment is significantly affected by such factors as historical location, cultural environment, economic status, gender, race, sex, sexual orientation, physical limitations, psychical limitations, emotional experiences, and others. To claim that these factors are relevant with regard to embodiment is not to claim that their effects are necessarily determinative or even identical among individuals. It is rather to claim that the development not only of a subject's body, but also of a subject's conceptualization and experience of his or her body, takes place in a particular, situated context and thus is linked in important ways to the various specific discourses that constitute that context. It is also to claim that that bodily development is central, not peripheral, to the subject's subjectivity or being. That a person has developed in the context of a particular discourse concerning race or gender, for example, does not allow for determinative predictions concerning that person's particular subjectivity and embodiment. However, it does provide a possible explanation for certain aspects of that subjectivity. Subjects are not utterly determined by their bodies and the forces that produce and shape those bodies, but the development of an embodied subjectivity must take place within and in reaction to a particular, localized situation. The responses to a given situation, the ways discourses are taken up, repeated, and resisted, are by necessity diverse, and so any given subject cannot be exhaustively reduced to the discourses that surrounded its development.

To approach the embodied subject, then, is necessarily to approach a particular, not an example of the generic. Any given experience is taken up differently by different subjects. Moreover, any given experience *only* occurs to individual (and individually embodied) subjects. This is not to deny the possibility of commonality among experiences. There are some particular subjects who share my delight in a good cup of tea, or who, like me, find the music of Kate Bush stirring and beautiful. Subjects who attended the same college as I did will quite likely remember with similar revulsion the quality of the cafeteria food, and those who share a common family history with me may experience a similar sense of nostalgia when viewing a particular piece of furniture. However, someone who did not sit at my family's oval kitchen table regularly for decades will necessarily perceive it in a radically different way than I do. More to the point, there is no *one* experience of that table, even among members of my immediate family.

Are we not committed, then, to a radical relativism? Not necessarily, and it is here that embodiment comes into play. Rather than claiming that each individual subject is just as likely to have a certain experience as any other subject, the emphasis on embodiment necessitates a consideration of the embodied effects of the discourses and environments that have surrounded the always-becoming subject. Although those discourses will have effects that are to a degree indeterminate, it is certain that they will leave their mark; they will become embodied, but in different ways among different subjects. An individual's particular experience of that oval kitchen table, for example, will reflect not only the various family dynamics that were played out around it, but the distinct role that person played within those dynamics. The particular material conditions of that person's development are thus partly shared, allowing for communal experiences and significant similarities, and partly unique, because no two subjects, regardless of similarities in their environments, are identically embodied.[3] Moreover, there seems to be, in some instances, some limit to the differences that embodiment allows. Pain is almost always unpleasant, and some tastes seem universally repulsive. The particular individual is not relentlessly autonomous, without relation to other beings. The individualism demanded by embodiment is not a radical one, but one that, while necessitating the play of difference, also requires the formative and productive interaction of the embodied subjects with other embodied subjects.

How does this play of difference affect the experience of rape? Most importantly, it serves to contradict the possibility of any one, unified, determinate and determining experience of the phenomenon of rape. Rapes that occur in different situations and to different (and differently embodied) subjects can have radically different meanings to the victim, and indeed can constitute radically different harms. However, in all the differences that are possible in a given example of the crime of rape, the fact of embodiment persists in its relevance. Because all victims of rape are embodied, rape always has bodily significance; because embodiment is always marked by difference, that significance varies widely among victims.

To say that every victim of rape has a significantly different experience of the crime and suffers a significantly different harm does not appear to further our understanding of the phenomenon. For if every rape is different, if every victim is radically different from every other, what can we claim of the crime in general? Isn't it necessary to articulate some universal aspect of rape in order to fix its meaning (and hence its appropriate punishment) in the legal system, as well as to provide a generally acceptable and coherent understanding of the crime in society at large? Are we not compelled to determine an ostensibly comprehensive definition of rape, despite the obvious futility of such an attempt? The difficulty here (encountered with remarkable persistence in this discussion) is the difficulty of difference. While experiences of rape are significantly differentiated by such factors as race, age, political climate, and many others, the differences among them do not, by their sheer multiple nature, imply that rape itself has no specificity. As a particularly sexual, bodily attack on an embodied subject, rape constitutes a fundamental and sexually specific undermining of that person's subjective integrity. This specificity of the act of rape can produce a variety of experiences, because that undermining can be expressed and experienced to differing degrees and in differing ways. However, that variety is not limitless, and the nature of those experiences can be (although not, perhaps, exhaustively) understood through the lens of the significance of embodiment.

For example, because bodies and bodily experiences are marked by race, rapes that occur between differently raced people can have a host of meanings that are not necessarily present in rapes that occur between people of the same race.[4] This is a problem that has long plagued feminist political movements of the United States. With regard to race, rape has been constructed not only as an expression of power (the white slave owner claiming his ownership of the body of the black female slave, a claim directed not so much to the woman as to the black male slave) but also as an expression of resistance to power, as in Eldridge Cleaver's description of his commission of rape:

> Rape was an insurrectionary act. It delighted me that I was defying and trampling upon the white man's law, upon his system of values, and that I was defiling his women—and this point, I believe, was the most satisfying to me because I was very resentful over the historical fact of how the white man has used the black woman. I felt I was getting revenge. (Cleaver 1968, 14)[5]

Moreover, there is a long-standing history of African American men being falsely accused of raping white women, part of the construction of the black man as sexually predatory and as a constant threat to the sanctity of white womanhood. This distorted image too often provided the justification for lynching.

The ways rape has been implicated in the discourse of race in general and the oppression of African Americans in particular has made for some perplexing difficulties in feminist politics. These difficulties often get cast in the model of competing loyalties: when faced with the prospect of a European American woman accusing an African American man of rape, whose "side" does a person committed to ending both racism and sexism take? To believe the story of the accusing woman seems to be dictated by a feminist politics, which include a commitment to honoring women's voices and to challenging their presumed unreliability. To defend the accused man seems necessitated by a racially aware politics, which includes a commitment to refusing the construction of the black male as sexually dangerous. One must choose to champion women's rights, it appears, or those of people of color.

Of course this must be a false set of options, one that originates in the demand to choose between one set of wrongs (those of sexism) and another (those of racism). The assumption is that only one wrong must be accentuated, to the detriment (or, more precisely, the exclusion) of the other. The wrong, then, is either sexism, in which case the races of those involved are irrelevant, or racism, in which case the alleged sexual crime is assumed to be nonexistent.If we understand rape as differentiated by such factors as race as well as by sex, it is possible to avoid this dichotomy. The racial politics of rape is an example of the co-constitution of race and gender, in that the production of a particular type of femininity (white) depended heavily on the racist stereotype of black masculinity. This complex co-constitution allows for no easy solution to any particular case of disputed interracial rape; it is impossible to argue for the position of either the accused or the accuser on its basis alone. However, such a theoretical understanding of the ways the constructions of race and gender are intertwined and mutually dependent urges us to consider the racial aspects of such an instance of rape, not to the exclusion of its gendered aspects, but rather each in relation to the other. In her consideration of interracial rape, Valerie Smith states:

> [T]o the extent that the discourses of race and rape are so deeply connected, cases of interracial rape are constituted simultaneously as crimes of race and of gender. The inescapability of cultural narratives means that instances of this sort participate in the ongoing cultural activity around ide-

ologies of gender, race, and class. Rather than attempting to determine the primacy of race or class or gender, we ought to search for ways of articulating how these various categories of experience inflect and interrogate each other and how we as social subjects are constituted. (1994, 168)

The historical construction of race included a particular construction of the phenomenon of rape to the extent that it is impossible to understand one without the other. Because race was always also gendered and gender was always also raced, the phenomenon of rape, especially in cases of interracial rape, is subject to both discourses simultaneously. Therefore, any experience of rape will be profoundly influenced by the race of the particular victim and assailant. The rape of a black woman by a white man, for example, may contain an element of an insistence of racial superiority, a reinvocation of the right of the master race over the slave race. The harm incurred by such a rape would be significantly different from that incurred by a rape that involved only white persons (this is not to say that the harm would necessarily be less, or less acute, but rather that race is a differential axis that affects significantly the particular quality of a particular incidence of rape). Similarly, a rape such as the ones committed by Cleaver, though similar to the one described just above in terms of its racial asymmetry, would also be distinct in its explicitly (but different) racial motivation.[6] The woman who is attacked at least in part because of her race has a distinctly different experience from that of the woman whose race is, at least in terms of the attack itself, ostensibly irrelevant; differently raced women will have different experiences of interracial rape precisely because of the differential construction of race itself. The impulse to define rape exclusively of race, to erase this differentiating factor, is another example of the desire to eradicate difference in favor of simplifying unity.

Race is not the only differentiating factor in the spectrum of the experience of rape. Rapes experienced at different ages, for example, may have widely different meanings to the victim. Being attacked by an acquaintance, lover, or relative is strikingly different from being attacked by a stranger. Again, the point of exploring these different experiences of rape is not to create a hierarchy whereby certain rapes are acknowledged as more harmful, more "serious," than others. It is rather to begin to comprehend the vastly varying meanings that acts similarly termed "rape" can hold. To be attacked by a stranger while exercising in a neighborhood park, for example, may result in an intense and reasonable fear of open and public spaces. One of the many harms of this crime, then, would be a limitation of the public mobility of the victim. In contrast, one harm incurred by a rape committed by a relative, especially if the assaults were frequent and/or constant over a period of time, may be a systematic destruction of a sense of personhood for the victim, or perhaps the emotional inability to enter and maintain intimate relationships. This constant erosion of an individual's sense of self would constitute a specific harm not present in all rapes, but central to the experience of that particular victim.

A universal, generic theory of rape is incapable of recognizing these salient differences among experiences of rape. At best, such theories produce a single standard by which all rapes are judged, such that some are considered "worse" or more "real" than others. Susan Estrich (1987) took it upon herself to argue that so-called simple rape (that is, one that does not include a physical beating or the presence of a weapon) is, to quote the title of her book, "real rape." That such an argument was necessary reflects the use of a standard, one that dictates which rapes are "real" and which are not, that is not based upon women's experiences. Analyzing rape as an embodied experience, by *assuming* difference rather than trying to eradicate it, allows us to consider the particular conditions of a case of rape without subjecting that particular experience to a universal standard of harm. *All* rapes, whether they involve weapons or not, whether they are committed by a stranger or an acquaintance, whether they are a singular occurrence or part of an ongoing abusive relationship, are real. The differences that surround different instances of rape contribute qualitatively and fundamentally to the victim's experience. To claim that one person's experience of rape is more or less "real," more or less "harmful," than another's is to fail to engage directly, accurately, or honestly with either.

Rape itself, as a phenomenon, is profoundly multiple, deeply differentiated by a host of diverse and at times conflicting discourses. Yet its possible meanings, while diverse, are always directly related to that complex interplay between the body and subjectivity. That is, it is precisely *as* an embodied experience that rape gives rise to a wide-ranging spectrum of significances. Rather than insisting on a universal, hence necessarily nonbodily, understanding or definition of rape, as Bogart does, we need to approach the phenomenon with an eye to relevant, bodily differences that contribute to the particularity of individual experiences.

Rape, Sexual Difference, and Sexuality

In various considerations of rape, two elements in particular have often been ignored, denied, or suppressed: the sexuality of rape and the relevance of sexual difference. In considering both of these elements, I argue that both the sex and the sexualities of the victim and the assailant are crucial factors to consider in approaching both individual rapes and rape as a social phenomenon.

In many feminist approaches to rape, the fact that sexuality was used as a means of violence was invoked as evidence that the phenomenon was reducible to violence. In other words, these approaches claimed that the sexualized locus and means of the assault were irrelevant, and that the effects of sexualized assault were by and large identical to the effects of any kinds of assault, and should in fact be approached as such. Rape was not sex, as a sexist society often claimed: it was violence. As I argue in chapter 1, I find this dichotomy to be faulty. However, the distinction between sex and violence was invoked for honorable purposes, namely, to ensure that women who had been the victims of rape were not blamed for their own victimization. Nancy Venable Raine embodies the frustration of the rape victim whose experience is interpreted as "sexual" and therefore private, shameful, and personal:

> I was irritated with this woman because I resented the fact that talking about rape (as a personal experience rather than a social phenomenon) produces a cringe in the people around me. This cringe feels silencing, although that is not always its intent. It confuses me when I feel it. I'm attempting to define my experience in terms of a violent assault and the residual trauma. But other people seem to be defining me in terms of a shameful sexual encounter. Words, no matter how precise, seem only to get me deeper into the briar patch. Where are the words? I need to find them so I don't have to feel that I am talking about something "embarrassing" when I talk about rape. (Raine 1998, 207)

> The difference between sex and rape is consent. What "worried and upset" the grand jury [in a case where a victim tried to talk the rapist into wearing a condom to prevent STD's] is what has worried, upset, and, more important, silenced rape victims for centuries. Rape is so very personal because if you live to speak of it, there's always the possibility you consented to a sexual act. (Raine 1998, 210–11)

Raine here seeks to de-emphasize the sexual aspects of rape because invoking them risks positioning herself as blameworthy. If rape is understood as a violent act, the question of victim culpability does not arise. If it is understood as a sexual act, suddenly the specter of shame arises. It is rape's *sexuality* that is socially interpreted as embarrassing, shameful, and inappropriate as a topic of civil conversation. As a society, we laud war heroes, listen intently to their sufferings (and the sufferings they imposed on others). We do not wish to hear the sufferings of rape victims. Such stories embarrass us and bring shame on those who tell them, and it seems that the main reason they do so is that we are never quite certain that the victims are innocent.

The difficulty with the feminist desire to eradicate the shameful factor of sexuality from rape is that it is impossible to understand rape without addressing its sexual nature. The way out of this conceptual difficulty is to separate sexuality from its overtones of privacy, shame, and (distinctly feminine) culpability. There is no reason to assume that sexuality per se is always marked by desire, autonomy, and lack of freedom, such that if an experience is sexual it must be, by definition, mutually agreed to by the parties involved. There is no paradox in the phrase "sexual assault." While rape is clearly violent and clearly constitutes an assault committed on the victim's body, it is relevant that the assailant has chosen to assault the victim in a particularly sexual way. Patriarchal society, when it makes the kinds of mistakes Raine refers to above, limits that relevance to the question of the victim's consent. That interpretation is obviously false and obviously harmful to the victim and her healing process. However, an understanding of rape as an embodied experience needs to recognize the sexuality of rape, not with relation to the victim's culpability, but rather with relation to the particularity of the experience and the harms it visits on the victim. Rape is sexual because it uses sexualized body parts and the very sexualities of the victim and the assailant as a means to commit physical, psychic, and emotional violence. To say that it is sexual is only to recognize the experiential relevance of the means of the violence committed, and not to undermine in any way the recognition of the crime as a horrifically violent one.

Like sexuality, the role of sexual difference has often been ignored in interpretations of rape. However, many feminist theorists of the body assert that sexual difference can never be ignored in the interpretation of any given experience. Braidotti (1994), Grosz (1994), and others insist that subjectivity be understood not in terms of an abstract quality of rationality or reasonableness, but rather as grounded in an experience of embodiment and the necessary differences accompanying that experience. Sexual difference is one of the primary differences if not the primary difference among embodied beings. The embodied subject, as it exists in a particular social, political and historical context, is always sexed, or, perhaps more precisely, is always being sexed: the process of becoming sexed is necessary to the continuing development of any given subject.

To approach rape as an experience that is imposed on a sexed subject is to recognize that there will be major differences among various experiences related to the sexes of the subjects involved. Hence, any theory that attempts to describe rape independently of the sexes of the attacker and the victim will necessarily fail to articulate meanings that are central to any particular victim. The experience of rape is always substantially informed by the sexed quality of the bodies involved in the assault.

Women's bodily experiences, as will be discussed in the following chapter, tend to incorporate at a basic level an assumption of the threat of rape, to the extent that it forms a kind of backdrop for daily, even seemingly trivial, decisions. The fact that women are constantly subjected to the threat and possibility of rape is itself an integral part of any one experience of rape. To be the victim of an assault whose danger has been persistently reiterated virtually guarantees an emotional reaction of guilt and responsibility. Given the daily measures women are encouraged to take for their own safety, it can seem hardly believable that any woman is surprised to find herself being sexually assaulted (and yet, even amid the shame, there is surprise, perhaps due to the strength of the belief in those daily protective practices). The common response of "Didn't she know any better?" is still common, though it is challenged by feminist analyses of the tendency to blame the victim.[7] More to the point, however, that response is likely to have been already internalized by the rape victim, who is as apt to blame herself as anyone else. The masculine experience of rape does not have the same, or even vaguely similar, set of meanings attached to it, since men are not subject to such a reiterated threat, and are therefore not exhorted to protect themselves against sexual attacks as a matter of daily life.[8]

Rape is not only sexed on the level of individual experience, a level to which I will return shortly. It is also sexed on a larger, social level, in that it is a crime overwhelmingly committed by men against women. The exhortations to which women are subjected with regard to their own safety are not completely off the mark (although they serve to veil the fact that women are more likely to be sexually assaulted by men they are acquainted with than by a stranger).[9] In contemporary U.S. culture, women are, by virtue of their sex, at serious risk of sexual assault. The risk to women with regard to sexual assault is so much greater than that facing men that it constitutes a qualitative and sexually differentiated distinction between the social lives of women and those of men. The degree to which the phenomenon of rape and the threat of rape affect a subject's perception of their own safety and mobility is directly related to the sex of that subject; thus rape itself is a means of social sexual differentiation. A study undertaken by Margaret T. Gordon and Stephanie Riger indicated that "fear of rape is central to the day-to-day concerns of about a third of women, a sporadic concern for another third, and of little concern to another third even though these women take precautions to prevent it" (1989, 21). What is interesting about this conclusion is not only that a large amount of women fear rape on a daily basis, but that even those who profess not to be concerned take precautions, perhaps reflecting a belief that the possibility of rape can be significantly reduced, or even eradicated, by correct behavior on the part of the woman. Regardless of the ways this threat is taken up by individual women, it remains that the threat of rape is one that is imposed on a particular segment of the population, a segment defined by its sex.

That rape constitutes a sexual differentiation in contemporary Western society does not establish its status as an unethical and unjust act. *Distinguishing* between the sexes is not, in and of itself, problematic. Many of the theorists discussed in the previous chapter indicate that justice for women depends precisely on some kind of recognition of the differences that do exist between the sexes. The ethical difficulty with the kind of differentiation enacted by the social phenomenon of rape is that it marks one group not merely as different, but as *inferior* to another. As Keith Burgess-Jackson (1994) asserts, it saddles one group with a danger to which the other is not subject, thus decreasing the safety, mobility, and freedom of the threatened group. Burgess-Jackson thus interprets sexual violence as an example of the unjust distribution of fear and insecurity. In the context of this chapter, however, my concerns with the sexually differentiating function of rape are less ethical than phenomenological. I am concerned with the way the social function of rape both produces and accounts for qualitatively differing experiences of rape among men and women. Because women are subject to a pervasive threat of rape, a threat to which the vast majority of men remain virtually immune, women will experience individual acts of rape in a qualitatively different way than men will. The phenomenon of rape is thus insistently and fundamentally sexed.

To consider rape as a sex-neutral phenomenon—as something that happens similarly to both men and women—precludes the possibility of recognizing the sexually differentiating social function of rape. Indeed, it is striking that, despite the obviously disproportionate degree to which rape affects women's lives, many theoretical considerations of rape insist on an approach that attempts to set aside any and all sexually specific elements of the phenomenon. Such an approach implicitly claims that the fact that rape happens disproportionately to women is incidental and does not affect the true nature of the crime or the experience itself. Yet the social functioning of rape does not exist separate from sexual differentiation; the "true nature" of rape (which is not, as discussed above, universal or constant among different experiences) cannot be elucidated without reference to its sexually differentiating social function.

The denial of difference inherent in a sex-neutral theory of rape can be motivated by both feminist and patriarchal interests. Feminist theories of rape that define the crime as primarily violent and urge legal reforms such that the sex of the victim will be rendered virtually irrelevant in the context of the courtroom seek to mitigate the possibility of the further victimization of women. And indeed, in a context where sexual difference is persistently hierarchized, the sexually specific status of women can be a detrimental position, by which women's voices and perspectives are constructed as unreliable, nonsensical, and not worthy of social import. The sex neutrality suggested by these feminist perspectives was a means of endowing women's voices and experiences with an import equivalent to those of men. Yet, as the previous chapter has indicated, there is no reason to believe that sex neutrality, or the denial of sexual difference, is any more likely to be a liberating force for women than the recognition of sexual difference. Because of both the particular, historical construction of the sexes and the bodily differences among differently sexed subjects, women are not identical to men. Demanding that they be treated as just humans (that is, as not sexed) is not, therefore, necessarily a step away from sexual hierarchization. Rather, because such a demand invokes an illusory generic that is implicitly sexed male, the result is that the meanings that are specific to women's lives are rendered invisible.

Specifically with regard to rape, the feminist flight from sexual difference sought to protect women from sexist assumptions concerning the victim's own culpability for the assault. However, that strategy also precluded the consideration of the sexually specific significances of rape, at least in the courtroom, a limitation that prohibits the articulation of some basic elements of a victim's experience within the discourse that, at least ostensibly, represents the societal response to a horrendously violent victimization. Being raped is different in significant ways from other types of assault, and one major difference in the experience is the centrality of its sexual meanings. For example, a woman who is raped may well find herself unable or unwilling to engage in sexual intercourse with her partner following the rape; because her victimization was particularly sexual, it has affected the associations she has with sexual behavior. This destruction of the positive connotations of sex is part of the crime that was committed against her, and it cannot be articulated without reference to the sexuality inherent in that crime. More generally, because of the disproportionate degree to which women are the victims of rape, many rape victims may experience the assault as part of an overall domination of women by men, that is, as part of a sexual hierarchy, a point that cannot be elucidated in a sex-neutral legal category, which does not recognize the relevance of the sex of the parties involved. Despite their good intentions, feminist theories of rape that are distinctly sex-neutral in their analysis cannot elucidate some of the most dominant and pertinent meanings of the experience of being raped.

Patriarchy too has a stake, albeit a strikingly different one, in representing rape as sex-neutral. In my discussions about the problem of rape in a variety of contexts, from the professional to the personal, my analysis of rape as a formational aspect of the daily lives of women has frequently been met with an insistence that men too are raped, and that therefore an emphasis on women as the sole victims of rape provides an inaccurate portrayal of the problem at large. The fervor with which my partners in conversation insisted on the equal victimization of men in relation to rape surprised me in at least two ways. First, to claim that men were as victimized by rape as women are reveals a disturbing lack of understanding concerning the prevalence of sexual violence inflicted on women, not to mention the surrounding implications of that violence. In just such a discussion, a close male relative of mine reacted to various statistics concerning the numbers of women raped while in college by defiantly claiming that none of his women friends had ever mentioned being sexually assaulted. Given his unwillingness to accept the fact that women were regularly abused in the context of relationships, it seems hardly surprising that his women friends would be reluctant to inform him of such an experience. His assumption that women who were attacked would feel free to speak of the crime committed against them demonstrated an incomprehension of the shame attached to being a rape victim, as well as the well-documented trauma of bringing charges against one's attacker. Because there are few, if any, crimes that would inspire a similar kind of shame in a male victim, my relative was assuming a specifically masculine perspective of the victim. If a man wouldn't be ashamed to disclose an act of violence that had been committed against him, why should a woman?[10] The question, of course, implies one of two possibilities: either there is simply nothing to tell, that is, women have little or no direct experience of rape; or there is a feminine deficiency that is itself the cause of victims' silence. The former possibility, it would seem, is simply empirically false. The latter fails to recognize a sexual hierarchization that would reward such disclosure with more shame, more guilt, and little chance of justice.

The second surprising element of such conversations is the eagerness to claim for men an equal status of rape victim. My relative, for example, was arguing that just as many men as women are raped, or at least in similar numbers such that the distinction is merely quantitative rather than qualitative. The empirical claim, of course, is squarely ridiculous; the facts that 99.6 percent of rape offenders are male and 94.5 percent of rape victims are female demonstrate that the sexual differentiation practiced by rape is rarely challenged (Greenfeld 1997, 21, 24).[11] However, more interestingly, the claim hardly seems appealing. Given the preponderance of sexual violence aimed at women, few would wish an extension of the scope of this violence such that it included men in equal numbers. What, then, is to be gained by this argument? Why was this person committed to asserting that men are raped in similar, if not equal, numbers to women?

Clearly, this distinctly masculinist position only makes sense in conjunction with the assumption that, in fact, few women are subject to sexual violence. Assuming that few men in general society have been victims of rape, and that men *as a group* do not confront the possibility of such victimization regularly, an equalization of the phenomenon itself implies that the victimization of women is similarly rare and similarly free from the classificatory significance of sex. According to this logic, it is a mistake to emphasize the sex of the rape victim; we need to understand rape as a crime that is visited on persons in general, and not define it as a threat specifically imposed on the sexually specified class of women. This, generally speaking, is the perspective of Christina Hoff Sommers, who, it will be remembered from chapter 1, noted that "to view rape as a crime of gender bias . . . is perversely to miss its true nature. Rape is perpetuated by criminals, which is to say, it is perpetuated by people who are wont to gratify themselves in criminal ways and who care very little about the suffering they inflict on others" (1994, 225). For Sommers, women aren't raped because they are women. If this were the case, men would never be raped. Because men are in fact raped—to a greater degree, my opponent was asserting, than I was admitting, and in fact to a similar degree as that of women—the sex of the victim is irrelevant. This position serves patriarchal aims by rendering invisible the gendered nature of rape itself (not such that men are never raped, but such that women are far more likely to be raped than men), thus disallowing any sexually specific analysis of rape that would result in an emphasis on justice *for women specifically*. Keeping the question generic, that is, sex-neutral, retains the masculinist privilege that underlies not only legal discourse, but also other fundamental aspects of the general social structure.

The phenomenon of rape is sexed in at least two ways. First, it is a means of sexual differentiation and hierarchization among the subjects of contemporary Western society. Rape as a social phenomenon affects men and women in distinctly different ways, ways that not only depend on sexual difference but actually produce experiences and subjects that are differentiated by sex. Rape here can be understood—as indeed it has been understood in traditional feminist theory—as a society-wide means of producing and perpetuating a system of oppression that privileges men and dominates women. As I will argue in the next chapter, the prevalence of rape and the threat of rape literally forms aspects of feminine bodily comportment. Rape not only happens to women; it is a fundamental moment in the production of women qua women.

Simultaneously, the quality of any given, particular experience of rape is directly related to the sexed nature of the bodies of both the victim and the assailant. On this more individual level, sex becomes one of the major axes that account for differences among diverse experiences of rape. Each instance of rape, then, precisely because it is primarily an embodied experience (not, at the most fundamental or meaningful level, an abstract experience of a loss of rights, for example), and most intensely because it directly involves the sexualities of the parties involved, contains a set of sexual meanings for both the assailant and the victim. A given act—for example, vaginal penetration by a nonbodily tool—will have radically different meanings for a victim depending on the sex of the assailant. If committed by a man, the act invokes an ongoing history of sexual violence against women by men; as such it emphasizes and reinforces an oppression that exists throughout the social structure. If committed by another woman, it has no such history to invoke, and thus cannot carry similarly loaded cultural meanings. This is not at all to say that the harm which a male-on-female rape inflicts is necessarily any less than that of a rape with a different sexual structure. Again, the point is not to automatically endow certain types of rape with greater "reality" or seriousness. Nor does an emphasis on sexual difference imply that every male-on-female rape has an identical set of harms (precisely because rape is also differentiated by such factors as class, age, relationship of the assailant to the victim, etc.). The category of sex cannot exhaust the possible differences among experiences of rape any more than it can exhaust the possible differences among subjects. It can, however, account for many relevant differences among experiences; more to the point, it is a necessary element of every act of rape. Every experience of rape is, in some form and to some degree, differentiated by sex.

The social function of rape deeply affects individual experiences of rape, and individual experiences in turn shore up that social function. The two levels are intricately related, for just as contemporary feminist theorists of the body insist that the individual subject and his or her sur-

rounding political, social, and historical context are ultimately insep-
arable—and that therefore it is both futile and undesirable to attempt to
approach the subject in isolation from his or her context—so too any individual experience of rape is deeply embedded in the surrounding social
and political environment, which is itself affected by the ways the victim,
the assailant, their families, and various public institutions react to and
represent the incident. The shame and guilt that many rape victims experience are a direct reflection of society's tendency to blame them for their
own assault. The silence surrounding many women's experiences of sexual
assault leads to a societal failure to recognize the pervasive effects that
rape and the threat of rape have on women's lives.

I can think of no better example of this dual functioning of rape and
sexual assault than a conversation I had with four women while research-
ing a book about their college experience. They were two sets of best
friends, all graduates of a small, Jesuit liberal arts college in Massachusetts.
When I first asked them about their experiences of security on campus,
each declared that she had felt very safe within its iron gates; that she was
always able to tell who "didn't belong"; and that she had felt secure in the
distinctly familial environment of the college. As the conversation pro-
gressed, one woman mentioned that she had been assaulted by a male
dormmate. Forty-five minutes later, two women had related experiences
of attempted rape, while another told of being held against her will in a
male student's room. None had, previous to this evening, told these stories. Best friends looked at each other in amazement and claimed that
they would never have felt safe had they known how many of their friends
had been attacked. When I asked them why they didn't report their attackers, they replied that they knew they wouldn't have been able to prove
their allegations and that nothing would come of any such efforts. Moreover, they feared that no one, even their women friends, would believe
them, since their attackers were well-liked, upstanding members of the
community. Some responded to their attacks with anger, some with
shame, but none felt confident that the familial community of the college
would take their experiences seriously.

In this case, the women's (quite accurate) knowledge about the likely
response of the community served to render their individual experiences
invisible. Their individual experiences of being attacked were directly related to a social refusal to recognize the violence done to women on campus. Moreover, their communal silence directly contributed to what
amounted to a false sense of security on the part of the women of the college. Individual women privatized their experiences of assault, some out
of shame and embarrassment, and as a result the phenomenon of vio-

lence against women continued unseen and unabated. Because sexual violence is committed disproportionately against women, and because
women's representations of that sexual violence are met with social disbelief and suspicion, women remain at risk from a threat that is as pervasive as it is invisible.

Rape and Intersubjectivity

The subject of contemporary feminist theory, as described in
chapter 3, is decidedly intersubjective. She or he develops in the context
of intersubjective relationships and therefore cannot be perceived as utterly distinct from those other subjects that made up his or her social and
emotional environment. The intersubjective subject of contemporary theory is to be contrasted with the autonomous subject of modern philosophy, one of whose primary goals, with regard to social responsibility, was to
safeguard as much personal freedom as possible. This subject was understood as standing apart from other subjects, and the mutual dependence
that society presented was not only artificial (for the natural state of "man"
was freedom, independence), but also a necessary evil that was to be
borne in exchange for the protection that only a group of individuals
could provide. The intersubjective subject, however, is understood as necessarily interdependent, marked and constructed by a series of different
relationships (some of which demand the subject's dependence, such as
the maternal relationship). The particularities of any one subject—his or
her desires, preferences, abilities, fears—are inextricably intertwined with
those of the beings encountered throughout the subject's ongoing development. Were one to attempt to remove or eradicate all traces of the
influence of these relationships, there would be no subject left; the intersubjective subject is *indelibly* (although not predictably and not determinately) constituted by intersubjective relationships. There is no true "self"
that precedes one's social being or underlies the various influences of a
specific society.

Intersubjectivity is rooted in the primacy of embodiment in at least two
ways. First, the tenuousness and fragility of the body necessitate the most
fundamentally dependent relationship, that of a child on his or her caretaker (usually his or her mother). Because human children are born well
before they are capable of self-sufficiency, because infant bodies are not
equipped to satisfy their most basic needs, the development of a mature
human being demands the care of another subject. There are precious
few statements that can apply to literally every human being, and yet this

is one: each embodied subject has by definition existed in a distinctly dependent relationship. That relationship may have been characterized by love, neglect, or institutional efficiency, but regardless of these variations, it was always an irrevocably unequal dynamic, by which the infant child depended utterly and completely on those responsible for his or her care. Given this necessity of dependence, it seems questionable to claim independence as a primary or defining state of human being. Modern theory succeeded in doing so only by defining the human subject essentially in terms of the abstract capacity for rational thought, thus denying the significance of bodily existence. Because human subjects are bodies (and not primarily intellects trapped in a fleshy prison), they are profoundly interdependent.

The significance of bodily intersubjectivity extends well beyond the bounds of infancy, however. The shape and habits of individual bodies are directly related to their surrounding political and social environments. That which can appear or be sensed as the most "natural," in the sense of the most physically intuitive—my particular gait, or the way I cross my legs while sitting—is in fact the most socially specific. In the details of the bodily comportment of an individual subject are indications of the particular environment in which that body developed and took shape, as well as of the particular subjects that inhabited that environment. The way a person moves his or her mouth and tongue to pronounce the word "mall," for example, can fairly accurately indicate whether that person grew up in the privileged streets of Cambridge, Massachusetts, or the surrounding suburbs of Revere. Because the embodied subject is always in process, always changing and developing, bodily habits and comportments are constantly being reshaped or, in some cases, reinforced. To improve one's social status, one may concentrate on dropping the Revere accent in favor of the Cambridge one, or, if one merely attends Harvard for four years, the change can happen far less intentionally. As the embodied subject continues to encounter new and different subjects and new and different discourses of power, new bodily experiences and new ways of understanding those experiences become possible. The bodily intersubjectivity of the subject means that relationships with other subjects can produce real bodily changes. Nor are such changes merely superficial; changes in bodily habits inevitably involve a degree of change in the personhood of the affected subject. To return to a Revere household with a Harvard accent is no small matter.

How does the intersubjectivity of the subject described by contemporary feminist theory shed light on the phenomenon of rape? Primarily, it encourages us to explore the extent of the significance of the bodily violation of rape. Because the subject is not defined by reference to intellectual ability or abstractly held rights, a physical assault such as rape should be perceived as an assault on the whole body-self of the victim. Precisely because the assault is visited upon the victim's body, it will have profound effects on the victim's personhood and being.

In her article "Outliving Oneself: Trauma, Memory, and Personal Identity," Susan J. Brison (1997) explores the apparently peculiar claims of survivors of traumatic experiences that they are literally not the same persons they were prior to their experience. Brison, herself the survivor of rape (see Brison 1993), experienced the sense of being other than what she once was, and relates this shift in being directly to her experience of her body:

> I was no longer the same person I had been before the assault, and one of the ways in which I seemed changed was that I had a different relationship with my body. My body was now perceived as an enemy . . . and as a site of increased vulnerability. But rejecting the body and returning to the life of the mind was not an option, since body and mind had become nearly indistinguishable. My mental state (typically, depression) felt physiological, like lead in my veins, whereas my physical state (frequently, one of incapacitation by fear and anxiety) was the incarnation of a cognitive and emotional paralysis resulting from shattered assumptions about my safety in the world. The symptoms of post-traumatic stress disorder gave the lie to a latent dualism that still informs society's most prevalent attitude toward trauma—namely, that victims should "buck up," put the past behind them, and get on with their lives. (1997, 16–17)

The exhortation to "buck up," to pack the experience away neatly and forever, fails so spectacularly because it assumes that there is a self that exists independently of the traumatic experience, a self that can voluntarily choose to interpret and take up that experience in a variety of ways, the best of which is simply to ignore it. It also assumes that this true self is significantly separate from the self's body, so separate as to be relatively untouched by the physical experience of assault. The recognition of the bodily self disallows the notion of such an abstract or intellectual self buried beneath the layers of skin and bone.

Brison describes the reconstruction of the self which constitutes the healing process following a traumatic experience. The purpose of this reconstruction, however, is not to re-create the person who existed prior to the trauma—victims experience that person as irretrievably, and regrettably, lost—but rather to create a new person. This person can be radically other than the person who experienced the trauma, or one for whom the significance of the trauma is integrated within, although not permitted to dominate, the new self. The failure or inability to remake oneself after a traumatic experience can often indicate the impossibility of survival, to the extent that the person may commit suicide (Brison 1997, 32). The process of remaking oneself, as Brison describes it, is not a matter of applying one's own sheer will, but rather necessarily includes intersubjectivity, including the telling of one's story and the experience of caring for, and being cared for by, others.[12]

The intersubjectivity of the body, and therefore of the subject, encourages us to perceive such physically traumatic experiences as rape as potentially radically transformative occurrences. To be raped—to have one's body violated by another person's body in a particularly sexual way—can mean the destruction of the person one has become up to that point. Brison agrees with Cathy Winkler (1991) in terming rape a kind of "social murder," or death: "Indeed, the victim's inability to be—and assert—her self in the context of a rape constitutes at least a temporary social death, one from which a self can be resurrected only with great difficulty and with the help of others" (Brison 1997, 18). This resurrection is not a rebirth of the same self who existed prior to the attack, but rather a replacement of that self with a new being.

Because the body of the embodied subject is both the physical separation between himself or herself and other subjects (my skin tells me, usually, and in a limited way, where I end and you begin) and the condition of possibility for intersubjective interactivity, and because the body and embodiment are central, not peripheral, to the development and construction of the self, we as human beings are doubly vulnerable. Not only do our bodies present the opportunity for physical pain and abuse, as well as the opportunity to inflict such abuse, but they necessitate that the implications of that abuse extend well beyond the purely physical. More precisely, they call into question the existence of a strictly physical realm. The continual development of the embodied subject is profoundly affected by the actions of other subjects; therefore, the violence inflicted by another subject threatens not just the victim's bodily integrity, but their subjective integrity as well. Or, rather, *because* such violence threatens the victim's bodily integrity, the integrity of the body-self is *necessarily* threatened.

The interdependence of embodied subjects indicates that their individual wholeness relies in some part on the actions of others. Brison asserts that one of the many meanings of traumatic experiences is the collapse of a necessary trust in other subjects. "When the trauma is of human

origin and is intentionally inflicted ... it not only shatters one's fundamental assumptions about the world and one's safety in it but also severs
the sustaining connection between the self and the rest of humanity"
(1997, 14). Without this sustaining connection, a self cannot exist as a
recognizable self; and so the victim of the traumatic experience, until
such a time as he or she can rebuild that connection in the context of a
new self, can experience a kind of walking social death. Rape, in its total
denial of the victim's agency, will, and personhood, can be understood as
a denial of intersubjectivity itself. Here in a radical way, only one person
(the assailant) is acting, and one person (the victim) is wholly acted on.
This imbalance, in its total nature, renders the victim incapable of being
truly engaged intersubjectively. The self is at once denied and, by the totality of this denial, stilled, silenced, overcome.

The intersubjectivity of rape is a complex matter, in that the intersubjective effects of the experience (that the self is significantly, qualitatively
undermined by the attack) are results of the denial and subsequent impossibility of intersubjectivity itself. Another way to understand this complicated turn of events is to perceive the intersubjectivity of rape, insofar
as it is profoundly imbalanced, as necessarily destructive. Rape itself does
not produce a transformed self; only the healing process that follows the
traumatic experience can properly be termed productive. Rather, the intersubjective effects of rape, strictly speaking, include necessarily the violent destabilizing of the existing self. Rape is an example of the exploita-
tion of the vulnerabilities that an embodied intersubjectivity necessarily
entails.

When one person rapes another, the assailant utilizes his power to affect, destructively, another person's being and experience—a power that
is a necessary aspect of embodied intersubjectivity. At the same time, the
assailant severely limits (and, assuming he is successful, effectively albeit
temporarily nullifies) the power of the victim to practice her intersubjective agency. A fundamental part of the violence of rape is that intersubjectivity becomes a one-way street, rather than the dynamic engagement that
embodiment calls for. Because that intersubjective agency is essential to
embodied personhood, an act of rape is more than a temporary hindrance of one's bodily movement, more than a merely unpleasant sexual
encounter. The actions of the rapist eclipse the victim's agency in a particularly sexual manner. Because it renders impossible for that moment
the victim's intersubjective agency, rape is a bodily, sexual assault on a
woman's underlying conditions of being.

And what does the act of rape tell us about masculine embodied subjectivity? If the intersubjectivity of rape accounts for the scope of severe

harms it imposes on victims, it must also account in large part for the experience of the rapist. Although rape is an act by which the intersubjective being of the victim is denied, and in which only the will of the rapist is both active and effective, still the fact that the rapist needs the victim to fulfill this particular desire is notable. There is a paradoxical dependency at work here. The rapist, who seeks to establish his sexual, physical power over his victim through this particular means (a means that connects him to a history of patriarchal, sexually specific authority), cannot accomplish that goal independently of his victim. Obviously, this dependency does not demand that the victim actively aid the rapist in the achievement of those ends. Rather, what is necessary is the victim's mere bodily presence, as unwilling or defiant as that presence is. This paradoxical dependency in no way establishes any kind of equality or symmetry between the rapist and the victim. It does, however, demonstrate that the phenomenon of rape from the perspective of the assailant is also intersubjective, in that the meaning of rape for the assailant cannot be produced without the presence of the victim. In other words, the rapist *needs* the destruction of the victim's being in order to construct his being as rapist—a need that ties the fate of his being to his victim's at the very moment where he seeks to express his utter dominance.

As a traumatic, violent, embodied experience, rape thus does not merely attack the victim's sexuality, or her sense of safety, or her physical being. It does all of this, and more. It destabilizes the personhood of the victim and the victim's intersubjectivity at the most fundamental level. It cannot be assumed that there is one aspect of that person's being that is untouched by the experience of rape. There is no pristine, untouched corner to which to retreat. To demand that the victim revert to her previous being—that she simply rise above the experience—implicitly denies the overwhelming implications of such an attack. This is not to say that it is impossible to recover from an experience of rape or that one's reconstructed self is utterly determined by that experience. The extent of the rapist's influence is broad, but not infinite. It is, however, to say that the reconstructed self will irrevocably be marked by this experience. Its intensity may wane, or it may not; the victim's relationships with her family and friends will almost certainly be strained, may erode entirely, or may ultimately be strengthened; the paranoia, depression, and physical scars of the attack may fade, or they may linger. But the self that emerges from the process of healing will always be qualitatively and profoundly different from the self that existed prior to the assault. To know oneself as not only rapable, but as raped, is to become a different self.

Rape and Victimhood

While chapter 6 will delve more specifically into an exploration of the ethical wrongs of rape, it seems appropriate here to consider some thoughts concerning the quality of the victimhood that rape imposes. This topic is of particular concern given some recent, allegedly "antifeminist feminist" perspectives that insist that feminism's continual emphasis on sexual violence risks defining women solely as victims. In her criticism of the sexual policies inspired by contemporary feminism, Katie Roiphe writes:

> The image that emerges from feminist preoccupations with rape and sexual harassment is that of women as victims, offended by a professor's dirty joke, verbally pressured into sex by peers. This image of a delicate woman bears a striking resemblance to that fifties ideal my mother and the other women of her generation fought so hard to get away from. They didn't like her passivity, her wide-eyed innocence. They didn't like the fact that she was perpetually offended by sexual innuendo. They didn't like her excessive need for protection. She represented personal, social, and psychological possibilities collapsed, and they worked and marched, shouted and wrote, to make her irrelevant for their daughters. But here she is again, with her pure intentions and her wide eyes. Only this time it is the feminists themselves who are breathing new life into her. (Roiphe 1994, 6)

Roiphe here is, of course, missing a crucial point: the feminists of the second wave in the United States were not marching against a particular type of woman. They marched against the dominance of the image and the social structures that produced women in its likeness. The "excessive need for protection" did not originate in the quality of women themselves, but in a world organized in such a way so that women were (through no fault of their own) constantly in danger. To claim that women are strong and capable of tasks hitherto denied them, as the feminism of the 1960s and 1970s did, is not to say that women are invincible or that they face no great danger. Agency and passivity are not quite so dichotomously defined.

However, Roiphe's point is not without its insight. As chapter 1 demonstrated, certain feminist theories concerning rape seemed predicated on women's necessary lack of agency. Rather than complicating the allegedly distinct fields of agency and passivity, these theories emphasized the degree to which women were actually produced, determinately, in the likeness of the image to which Roiphe refers so indignantly above. Such theories repeated the mistake of the dichotomy of self/society; because they portrayed women solely as the product of a social structure, they could not conceive of any degree of women's agency in relation to society. The self that was imposed on women, they claimed, was imposed in a wholesale fashion. It was begat *of* society and thus was incapable of achieving a critical perspective on (and thereby actively changing) society itself.

As contemporary feminist theories of subjectivity and the body have demonstrated, this distinction between the self and society fails to hold. It is not the case that individual subjects are replicated in utter obedience to existing power structures; the iterations Judith Butler describes always include the possibility of disloyalty, that is to say, resistance. Moreover, it is not the case that women, despite their inferior social status, have had no effect on social structures themselves. The fact that women have been oppressed by a patriarchal social structure does not imply that they themselves have not been participants in it. To assert women's victimhood is not, therefore, to imply necessarily their utter and definitive passivity. Linda Gordon and Ellen DuBois, in an early criticism of feminist analyses of sexual danger, note that "the feminist understanding of sexual danger, expressed so poignantly in the fear of prostitution, must be seen as part of a sexual system in which they were participants, sometimes willingly and sometimes unwillingly, sometimes conscious and sometimes unaware" (1983, 12). In other words, women were not only, or not purely, the passive victims of a system that placed them in a socially submissive role with regard to men. They were also, in a complicated and unequal fashion, implicated in it.

Roiphe's perspective, as represented by the quote above, actually ends up repeating the mistake of liberal feminism rather than rectifying it. She implicitly demands that feminism choose between viewing women as strong, capable, self-sufficient, and decisive and viewing them as passive, determined, helpless victims. Women are either utterly other than their socially acceptable construction or hopelessly mired within it. One can choose to adopt the role of victim or, alternatively, distance oneself utterly from the possibility of victimhood. What's more, Roiphe places the responsibility for the victimhood of which women have become aware strictly on the shoulders of feminism itself:

At the most uncharted moments in our lives we reach instinctively for the stock plots available to our generation, as trashy and clichéd as they may be. In the fifties it was love and marriage, or existentialism and Beat poetry in smoky bars. Now, if you're a woman, there's another role readily available: that of the sensitive female, pinched, leered at, assaulted daily by sexual advances, encroached upon, kept down, bruised by harsh real-

ity. Among other things, feminism has given us this. A new stock plot, a
new identity spinning not around love, not marriage, not communes, not
materialism this time, but passivity and victimhood. This is not what I
want, not even as a fantasy. (Roiphe 1994, 172)

The sexual dangers that feminism articulates are not, Roiphe claims, "the
facts of life . . . but a way of interpreting them," (162), and it is the feminist interpretation, not the pervasive targeting of women specifically as
objects of sexual violence, that creates the victimhood of women. According to Roiphe, women are conscious of the sexual dangers that face them
not because those dangers are real, socially integrated, and in fact fairly
likely to be imposed on individual women; rather, women have been
brainwashed by feminism into understanding themselves as helpless. The
"other things" feminism has "given us"—the increased political power,
improved working conditions, and ways of honoring women's voices and
social contributions, for example—remain virtually unmentioned. More
important, however, the distinction between victimhood and agency is
presented as a matter of choice. One can either fulfill the social stereotype
or defy it; the options are as clear as that.

Except, of course, that they aren't. As intersubjective, embodied beings,
we are simultaneously subject to and implicated in the social structures
that surround us. Developed in relation to these structures, yet capable of
a limited degree of resistance and productive agency, we are neither determined utterly by them nor capable of complete freedom from them.
Agency and passivity are not competing choices. Individual women
cannot, by sheer will alone, eradicate the possibility of their own victimhood (a victimhood that, given the masculinist bias of social and political
discourses, is qualitatively different, as well as quantitatively more likely,
than that which faces men). Roiphe is correct: women are not primarily or
essentially victims, and feminist theories concerning sexual violence that
assume they are err in significant ways. However, she fails to consider the
real, albeit not determinative, ways women are, by virtue of their social
definition, victims of a patriarchal structure. Roiphe struggles against this
fact because she is eager to define herself as self-determining and free.
Her mistake is to assume that radical freedom is possible, and that
women's disproportionate experience of victimhood is directly opposed to
any possibility of agency.

With regard to the experience of rape specifically, it is impossible to
deny the virtually total passivity of the rape victim. Or, more exactly (for a
rape victim can actively struggle against her assailant), the commission of

the rape itself at the very least constitutes a conquering of (and therefore an implicit denial of the efficacy of) the victim's agency. The woman who is raped is a victim of another person's actions and choices, actions and choices that she, as victim, was incapable of thwarting. She cannot, by her own individual will and rational choice, limit determinately the effects of this experience. It has been imposed on her, without her consent, without her participation.

That women, as embodied subjects, are vulnerable to such victimhood does not eradicate the possibility of agency itself. Instead, it is precisely as embodied and intersubjective beings that women are capable of action and decisive change. Moreover, while the rape victim individually is not capable of delimiting the effects of the assault (that is, she cannot herself will that certain aspects of her life and her relationships remain untouched by this experience; she cannot simply "buck up" and put it behind her), her intersubjective being allows for the possibility of the reconstruction of a healthy, albeit indelibly marked, self. The very vulnerabilities that render rape and its appalling scope of influence possible—that our bodies and therefore our selves are deeply and fundamentally influenced and shaped by the actions of other subjects—also provide for the possibility of healing. As Susan Brison asserts, our agency (in her words, our autonomy) is decidedly dependent on other subjects:

> Not only is autonomy compatible with socialization and with caring for and being cared for by others, but the right sort of interactions with others can be seen as essential to autonomy. . . . [T]he main reason all of us, especially women, have to fear violent intrusions by others is that they severely impair our ability to be connected to humanity in ways we value. It is this loss of connection that trauma survivors mourn, a loss that in turn imperils autonomous selfhood. . . . The autonomous self and the relational self are thus shown to be interdependent, even constitutive of one another. (1997, 28–29)

Our dependence on others for the formation of our agency (our intersubjectivity) is therefore not opposed to our vulnerability (the possibility for victimhood). Rather, the two are mutually necessary aspects of a being that is not wholly self-determining and not wholly abstract. This means that the victimhood that rape (and the threat of rape) represents is fundamental to, that is, constitutive of, the being of those who are subject to it, without being determinative or exhaustive.

Conclusion

Theories of rape that failed to account for the role of the body either overestimated or underestimated the effects of rape and the pervasiveness of the threat of rape. They portrayed women as wholly defined by an oppression whose most trenchant threat was rape, or they described rape as essentially similar to other, nonsexual physical attacks, thus neglecting the sexually specific aspects of the experience. By understanding rape as an embodied experience, as an attack on an embodied subject that directly involves and invokes the sexuality of both the assailant and the victim, we can perceive the phenomenon as a threat to the possibility of embodied subjectivity, a threat to the victim's (sexually specific) personhood and intersubjectivity.

This articulation of the scope of rape corrects many of the major downfalls of other feminist theories of rape. MacKinnon's theory posited women as essentially victims and rested on an understanding of both rape and heterosexuality that necessitated women's lack of agency. Placing intersubjective embodiment at the center of a theory of rape allows us to understand the severe scope of the harms rape can impose without rendering women wholly passive. The intersubjectivity necessitated by a bodily existence includes a vulnerability that rape exploits, but it also includes an openness, an ongoing process of development that limits the power of the rapist. By understanding the rape victim as an embodied subject, we are able to take the crime and violence committed against her seriously without endowing her with an enduring helplessness. We therefore understand rape victims as victims, but not *merely* or *only* victims. The acts of the rapist will necessarily be integrated into a new bodily being, but they do not exhaust the rape victim's possibilities of being.

Brownmiller's thesis, by emphasizing power and violence to the exclusion of sexuality, defines rape in a way that does not allow for the inclusion of particularly sexual bodily meanings of such an attack. Understanding rape as an embodied experience allows for the recognition of the ways both sexuality and power are included in the phenomenon. From this perspective, the sexual aspect of rape does not threaten to place it in the realm of the purely "natural" (whereby the motivations of the rapist are ascribed to politically innocent drives), but rather demonstrates that both the social phenomenon and individual experiences of rape are qualitatively marked by sexual difference and sexual politics. Under the generic legal definition suggested by Brownmiller, a woman victim could articulate no sexual specificity to her experience. With an understanding of rape as embodied subjectivity, sexual difference becomes relevant without threatening to undermine the validity of the woman's perspective.

The sexual quality of the act of rape warrants further discussion. As argued above, any individual experience of rape is sexually differentiated, that is, characterized by the sex of both the assailant and the victim. Simultaneously, the social function of rape is one of sexual differentiation, in that it is a threat imposed disproportionately and specifically on women as a class. These factors alone are quite sufficient to preserve the importance of sexual difference with regard to rape. However, it is not insignificant that rape, as commonly understood, always involves at least one eroticized body part. A woman may be raped by an object other than a penis, and indeed the penetration may occur in an orifice other than the vagina; but in such examples of rape, those objects or orifices not always perceived as sexual *become sexualized* in the context of the assault. Rape is an assault on a person's embodied sexuality using eroticized weapons, whether or not they are bodily parts. To claim that rape is always sexual thus does not necessarily privilege the genitals as a site of sexuality (a concern of Michel Foucault's which will be explored in the following chapter). It rather recognizes sexuality itself as a means of power, domination, and the infliction of harm, to the extent that in the context of an example of rape, the particular weapon becomes eroticized by virtue of its purpose of sexual domination.

Feminist theories of rape emanating from the second wave of U.S. feminism resisted including sexuality as a defining element of rape in order to protect women from a discourse that always already defined their sexuality as guilty. Removing the element of sexuality and defining rape as a primarily violent act ensured that the female victim's sexual past, preferences, and tendencies would be considered irrelevant to the question of the accused's guilt. As long as the crime was considered in any part sexual, victims, particularly if they were female, could (and most likely would) be perceived as contributing to their own victimization. Unlike the crime of assault, to which the legal discourse rarely if ever poses the question of the participation or consent of the victim, a particularly sexual crime seems to invite interrogation as to whether the victim actually consented to, or even invited, the sexual encounter. It would appear that this current analysis of rape as an embodied experience, and thus as necessarily sexual, would risk the recurrence of this line of blaming the victim.

Such a recurrence, however, would be wholly contrary to the substance of this analysis. The assumed guilt of the rape victim is directly linked to a portrayal of feminine sexuality as both dangerous (such that it seeks to "trap" men, for example, by marriage or by false accusations of rape) and indecisive (such that women often say "no" when they mean "yes"). In this context, the claim that rape is a sexual act almost necessarily invokes the participation of the victim. The analysis of rape that emerges from the present discussion locates the sexuality of rape not in the participation of the victim—who is, by definition, at least temporarily denied subjectivity and selfhood—but in the sexually specific social, political, and bodily meanings of the assault as committed by the assailant, as well as the eroticized means by which the assault is committed. The mutuality that is implied by the previous descriptions of rape as sexual, and which thus led inevitably to questions of victim participation, is thus denied.

We are then led to a rather odd conclusion: while an experience of rape certainly has sexual significance to the victim and most likely significantly affects her sexuality, and while that experience is differentiated by the victim's sex and that of the assailant, we may perhaps aver that by the act of rape itself, the assailant has had sex with the victim, but the victim has not had sex with the assailant. One rape victim, describing the horrific physical trauma of forced sex, explains that such an assault is not, in fact, intercourse:

> Forcible rape is not in any normal sense intercourse. In most cases, the lubrication of the vagina required for normal completed intercourse does not exist, since petting has, more often than not, not occurred. As a result of this crucial aspect, as well as the fact that the victim is usually in a traumatized state immediately preceding the rape and, thus, the muscles at the entrance to the vagina are not relaxed, penetration cannot either easily or immediately occur. What does happen is that the rapist repeatedly batters with his penis in the very delicate and sensitive features lying *outside* the vagina, causing the tissues to tear and to bleed. When the force of the thrusting eventually results in the penis entering the vagina, it enters usually no more than a few inches, and again the tissues (this time, the lining of the vagina) are repeatedly, with each thrust, ripped and torn. (Quoted in Stanko 1985, 34)

The victim goes on to assert that in the crime as thus described there is no sex. In a profound sense, this is true; it is difficult to imagine the victim of such an assault describing the experience in terms of "having sex." Yet the category of violence does not sufficiently account for the particularity of the assault. In this sense, for the victim the experience is *sexual,* but it is not sex itself. It is difficult to imagine a victim of rape, for example, describing her assailant as a sexual partner, while one can easily imagine a rapist portraying the event as perhaps purely sexual.[13] If we describe the act of rape as sexual, but not as one wherein the victim actually had sex with the assailant, the question of victim culpability is sufficiently rendered moot, while the sexual significance of the crime is preserved.

This distinction—that rape is sexual but not sex, from the victim's perspective, although it very well may constitute sex from the perspective of the assailant—invokes the difficulty concerning women's agency in regard to their own sexuality. Rape is a sexual act that is foisted on the victim; it denies precisely as it destroys (at least temporarily, and perhaps in the long term) the possibility of sexual choice. MacKinnon's point was that it was a mistake to assume that women have any sexual choice in the first place, and that therefore rape was not qualitatively different from heterosexual intercourse in general. However, the analysis developed here regarding agency and embodiment asserts that a woman's sexuality, while no doubt formed in relation to discourses that are certainly detrimental to her interests, is not wholly determined by those discourses. Women have a (limited) degree of choice regarding their sexual experiences; moreover, different women have differing degrees of choice. Heterosexual activity is not by definition a violation of women's agency—a reassuring point that refuses to relegate to a patriarchal construction of heterosexuality an unlimited degree of power. Heterosexist, and sometimes racist, coercion (which is itself not omnipotent; after all, lesbians exist) limits the scope of available choices, but it is qualitatively different from the coercion present in the act of rape, which, in the short term, makes agency impossible.

Brownmiller's implicit point was that precisely because rape involves the absence of the victim's choice or agency, sexuality itself was not the primary element of rape. Sexuality here is (again, implicitly) understood as necessarily associated with agency, and so to remove the sexual aspect of rape is to free the victim from accusations of complicity. Yet it is possible to impose a sexual act on someone without that act losing its sexual quality. Given the nature of patriarchy, which serves to construct feminine sexuality in certain definable (although not exhaustive) ways, sexuality can be understood as deeply implicated with coercion. That an assault is sexual, then, does not necessarily mean that the victim was in any way a participant in that act.

MacKinnon asserts that consensual heterosexual intercourse is always in some way illusory, and that therefore rape is sexual precisely insofar as it disallows the possibility of the (usually female) victim's agency; Brownmiller asserts that the absence of consent necessarily privileges the violent aspect of rape over the sexual, and that therefore rape should be understood as primarily violent. Both fail to understand the significance of the fact that rape occurs to an embodied subject. The act of rape is a distinctly sexual attack on the possibility of embodied subjectivity. It is an act that at least temporarily denies the (bodily, and sexually differentiated) agency of the victim and that almost certainly involves a transformation of the victim's subjectivity, but which need not subsequently determine wholly the victim's personhood. It is a violent act indelibly marked by the presence of sexuality, an aspect which distinguishes it in important ways from other acts of violence.

Rape as an embodied experience defies the traditional distinctions of self/other, autonomy/dependence, body/mind, sexuality/violence. It speaks the vulnerability of an intersubjective embodiment, whereby the personhood of the bodily subject is necessarily connected to, and thus in some way dependent upon, the actions of other subjects. The bodily nature and aspects of rape constitute it as a threat to the possibility of the subjectivity of the victim.

A Phenomenology of Fear

The Threat of Rape and Feminine Bodily Comportment

The body of the embodied subject, as discussed in chapter 3, is not to be understood as a purely natural blank slate on which social forces inscribe their values, meanings, and narratives. Nevertheless, individual bodies develop their habits, tendencies, desires, and particularities in the context of a social immersion. Given that rape is a pervasive social phenomenon that affects all women, individual experiences of rape are imposed on an embodied subject who has already been influenced by that social phenomenon. We need to explore the significance rape has in forming the body, and specifically the feminine body, itself. As the ensuing analysis will demonstrate, the threat of rape is a formative moment in the construction of the distinctly feminine body, such that even bodies of women who have not been raped are likely to carry themselves in such a way as to express the truths and values of a rape culture.

During a 1977 roundtable discussion concerning, among other matters, his work that was later published in English as *Discipline and Punish* (1979), Michel Foucault commented on the problem of rape. His analysis was inspired by questions posed to him by a French commission concerned with the reform of the penal code:

One can always produce the theoretical discourse that amounts to saying: in any case, sexuality can in no circumstances be the object of punishment. And when one punishes rape one should be punishing physical violence and nothing but that. And to say that it is nothing more than an act of aggression: that there is no difference, in principle, between sticking one's fist into someone's face or one's penis into their sex. . . . [T]here are problems [if we are to say that rape is more serious than a punch in the face], because what we're saying amounts to this: sexuality as such, in the body, has a preponderant place, the sexual organ isn't like a hand, hair, or a nose. It therefore has to be protected, surrounded, invested in any case with legislation that isn't that pertaining to the rest of the body. . . . It isn't a matter of sexuality, it's the physical violence that would be punished, without bringing in the fact that sexuality was involved. (1988, 200–202)

At first glance, it would appear that Foucault's suggestion was remarkably in keeping with the current feminist wisdom, which sought to define rape solely as a violent crime. It is perhaps surprising, then, that both the women who were present at the discussion and subsequent feminist thinkers responded vehemently, and negatively, to his position. Yet the philosophical motivation behind Foucault's support of the desexualization of the crime of rape (and its legal redefinition as merely an example of assault) is significantly different from the impetus behind Brownmiller's (admittedly incomplete) solution of a "gender-free, non–activity-specific" law (Brownmiller 1975, 378). Whereas feminist thinkers were seeking to purge rape of its sexual content in order to render moot the legal question of victim (i.e., female) culpability, Foucault viewed the desexualization of rape as a liberating blow against the disciplining discourse that constructed sexuality as a means of social and political power.

Despite this difference in motivation, one could still expect Foucault's position to be largely in agreement with feminist theories that also located sexuality as one means by which a patriarchal culture maintained control over women. Judging by the response of various feminist theorists to his assertions, however, this was not the case. It is important to note at this juncture that Foucault's comments were relatively spontaneous and not fully developed; nevertheless, they at least appear to be generally consistent with his larger concern with the separation of sexuality from disciplinary power, and therefore cannot be dismissed out of hand. The challenge represented by his remarks was immediately taken up by Monique Plaza (1981), and later most directly by Winifred Woodhull (1988) and Vikki Bell (1991), although several other feminist works on Foucault (including Martin [1988]) have mentioned the problem in passing. Most recently, Laura Hengehold (1994) has attempted a new analysis by locating the crime of rape in the overall system of hysterization of women that Foucault himself posited. While her argument succeeds in doing just that, it and other feminist theories seem unable to answer the question posed by Foucault: why should an assault with a penis be distinguished legally from an assault with any other body part?

Even this particular posing of this question leads us to a distinction that will prove crucial to the following discussion. Foucault here is considering rape as something done by a penis, that is, accomplished by a distinctly male and masculinized body. Because Foucault's implied definition is centered around the male physiology, it does not include a consideration of the multiple ways a woman can be violated sexually (see Tong 1984, 92–94). To redefine rape not as something a man does, but something a woman experiences shifts the conversation in important ways. This provisional redefining of the act of rape also has its problems, for women are not the only beings who can be raped. Yet while men are capable of being raped, they are not subjected to the pervasive threat of rape that faces women in the present culture. Nor are they raped at the horrifying (if controversial) numbers that women are. The fact that men can be, but are not often, raped emphasizes the extent to which rape enforces a systematic (i.e., consistent, although not necessarily conscious), sexualized control of women. Thus Monique Plaza writes:

> Rape is an oppressive act exercised by a (social) man against a (social) woman, which can be carried out by the introduction of a bottle held by a man into the anus of a woman; in this case rape is not sexual, or rather it is not genital. It is very sexual in the sense that it is frequently a sexual activity, but above all in the sense that it opposes men and women: it is *social sexing* which underlies rape. (1981, 29; emphasis in the original)

Extending Plaza's logic to the phenomenon of male-on-male rape emphasizes the implicit womanizing that occurs on the victim, who is placed in the role of the sexually submissive and helpless. He is, at that moment, a "social woman."

To return to the question as formulated by Foucault: how is an assault with a penis different from an assault with a fist? The answer to this question, I will argue, is dependent not only on the bodily phenomenon of rape, as Foucault seems to assume, but also on the social production of the feminine body. Winifred Woodhull points to this necessity when she claims, "If we are seriously to come to terms with rape, we must explain

how the vagina becomes coded—and experienced—as a place of empti-
ness and vulnerability, the penis as a weapon, and intercourse as violation,
rather than naturalize these processes through references to 'basic' physiology" (1988, 171).

However, Woodhull here has neglected to consider seriously enough
Foucault's concern with the construction of the particularly sexual body, a
historical process he documents in his first volume of *The History of Sexuality* (1990). In that work, as well as its sequels, Foucault details the various
ways sexuality has been constructed in the context of other overarching
social demands, particularly the demand for self-mastery. The centrality
of sexual identity to the subject was a means of the exercise of power:

> [Sex] was at the pivot of the two axes along which developed the entire
> political technology of life. On the one hand it was tied to the disciplines
> of the body: the harnessing, intensification, and distribution of forces,
> the adjustment and economy of energies. On the other hand, it was
> applied to the regulation of populations, through all the far-reaching
> effects of its activity. It fitted in both categories at once, giving rise to
> infinitesimal surveillances, permanent controls, extremely meticulous
> orderings of space, indeterminate medical or psychological examina-
> tions, to an entire micro-power concerned with the body. (1990,
> 145–46)

Because the construction of the sexual body, whose sexuality was
grounded strictly in the genitals, was fundamental to the disciplines that
formed both the body and the subject's place in society, Foucault locates
one important possibility for resistance in a process of extricating sexuality both from its limited, genital definition and from direct, oppressive
legislation. In *Power/Knowledge,* Foucault praises feminist movements for
their attempt at desexualization:

> The real strength of the women's liberation movements is not that of hav-
> ing laid claim to the specificity of their sexuality and the rights pertaining
> to it, but that they have actually departed from the discourse conducted
> within the apparatuses of sexuality. . . . What has their outcome been? Ul-
> timately, a veritable movement of de-sexualisation, a displacement ef-
> fected in relation to the sexual centering of the problem, formulating the
> demand for forms of culture, discourse, language, and so on, which are
> no longer part of that rigid assignation and pinning-down to their sex
> which they had initially in some sense been politically obliged to accept
> in order to make themselves heard. (1980, 219–20)

Foucault questions the definition of rape as sexual because such a definition retains sexuality as an appropriate target and expression of disciplinary power. Resistance to that disciplinary power demands a desexualisation of rape, just as feminist movements have resisted the "sexual centering of the problem." Moreover, Foucault infers from the sexual definition of rape a continuation of the privileging of the genitals with regard to sexuality, a privileging that supports the "naturalness" of the sexual body and therefore serves to veil the intricate relation of sexuality and power. Foucault suggests the desexualization of rape on the basis of an analysis of the social construction of the sexual body, a construction that privileges the genitals and sexuality in general as a primary seat of identity.

A critique of this conclusion must begin with a more detailed consideration of the Foucauldian analysis of the body. From there, I shall argue that the act of rape is distinct from other types of assault not solely because of the body parts involved in the act, but more importantly, because of the role rape—or, more precisely, the threat of rape—plays in the production of the specifically (and socially recognizable) feminine body. Moreover, I will assert that the legal reform suggested by Foucault—that is, the redefinition of rape as assault and the eradication of rape as a distinctly sexual crime—would serve to veil aspects of the crime that impinge directly on women's experience and bodies and that constitute the current phenomenon of rape itself in important ways.

The Body for Foucault

Perhaps one of the most well-known aspects of Foucault's work is his compelling analysis of power.[1] Refusing the traditional description of power as primarily repressive and imposed solely from a position of authority, Foucault claims instead that power actually produces social bodies and realities, and does not emanate from one central source, but rather is diffused throughout the social structure:

[P]ower would be a fragile thing if its only function were to repress, if it worked only through the mode of censorship, exclusion, blockage and repression, in the manner of a great Superego, exercising itself only in a negative way. If, on the contrary, power is strong this is because, as we are beginning to realise, it produces effects at the level of desire—and also at the level of knowledge. Far from preventing knowledge, power produces it. If it has been possible to constitute a knowledge of the body, this has been by way of an ensemble of military and educational disciplines. It was on the basis of power over the body that a physiological, organic knowledge of it became possible. (1980, 59)

For Foucault, the structures and dynamics of power actually create the possibilities of various social discourses by constituting the subjects who will undertake them. In this model, what is significant is not merely, or perhaps even primarily, who has power over whom, but how power has produced the specific and characteristic moments of a discursive reality.

If power is not solely a punishing, authoritarian force that seeks to control the actions of subjects primarily by prohibiting certain ones, if instead it is a subtle, pervasive, creative force that seeks to influence actions on the level of desire and identity, then it is not surprising to find the body as its privileged site. Indeed, as Foucault claims, "[N]othing is more material, physical, corporal than the exercise of power" (1980, 57–58). The body, far from being in any sense natural or primary, is the location of the inscription of power discourses. Specifically, Foucault is concerned with the power dynamics that construct the body as sexual:

> What I want to show is how power relations can materially penetrate the body in depth, without depending even on the mediation of the subject's own representations. If power takes hold on the body, this isn't through its having first to be interiorised in people's consciousness. There is a network or circuit of bio-power, or somato-power, which acts as the formative matrix of sexuality itself as the historical and cultural phenomenon within which we seem at once to recognise and lose ourselves. (1980, 186)

As a theoretical moment in Foucault's analysis of power, the body and its corresponding abilities, desires, and habits are the results of the inscription of power dynamics that renders knowledge as well as agency possible. Through this inscription, individual bodies are produced with certain powers, capabilities, and expectations. As Jana Sawicki describes it, "Disciplinary power is exercised on the body and soul of individuals. It increases the power of individuals at the same time as it renders them more docile (for instance, basic training in the military)" (1991, 22). Any limitations imposed on the body are always concomitant with certain, delimited powers, but both the limitations and the endowed capabilities are directly related to and supportive of the overall power dynamic.

Moreover, the sexuality of the body is central to its construction and to its vulnerability to discursive power. Because power is not ultimately or merely repressive, but also productive, sexuality cannot be understood as

an innocent, underlying set of desires, dynamics, and practices that various power structures attempt to suppress or deny. Rather, sexuality is produced as a moment within a network of power itself.

> But I said to myself, basically, couldn't it be that sex—which seems to be
> an instance having its own laws and constraints, on the basis of which the
> masculine and feminine sexes are defined—be something which on the
> contrary is *produced* by the apparatus of sexuality? What the discourse of
> sexuality was initially applied to wasn't sex but the body, the sexual or-
> gans, pleasures, kinship relations, interpersonal relations, and so forth.
> (Foucault 1980, 210)

Foucault's *History of Sexuality* in its entirety is a historical exploration of
sexuality in relation to other workings of power, for example, in the construction of the self that is capable of self-mastery. However, given that the
diffuse, decentralized, productive power Foucault describes is particularly
bodily (one of its salient characteristics is its ability to produce bodies of
particular types, with particular abilities), sexuality is not just another site
of discursive power, but a particularly trenchant one. "I believe that the
political significance of the problem of sex is due to the fact that sex is located at the point of intersection of the discipline of the body and the
control of the population" (1980, 125). Not only is sexuality not a force
outside the realm of power that calls for its own liberation from oppressive
forces, but in fact, precisely because of its bodily significance and grounding, it is a major site for the expression and production of power itself. Resisting the norms that are imposed through and by power dynamics does
not demand sexual liberation, but a decentering of the significance of
sexuality with regard to pleasure and subjectivity:

> [I]n the West this systematisation of pleasure according to the "laws" of
> sex gave rise to the whole apparatus of sexuality. And it is this that makes
> us believe that we are "liberating" ourselves when we "decode" all plea-
> sure in terms of a sex shorn at last of disguise, whereas one should aim in-
> stead at a desexualisation, at a general economy of pleasure not based on
> sexual norms. (1980, 191)

The possibility of such a desexualization leads us to the question of resistance with regard to Foucault's theory of power. To a certain extent, the
concept that power is not only repressive but productive implies that the
produced or constructed (sexual) body of the subject is entirely reducible
to the purposes and values of that particular network of power. However,

that the body is the result of power dynamics does not necessarily imply
that the body is wholly or predictably determined. Even as Foucault terms
the body "docile," referring to its status as reflection or projection of the
dominant discourse, he insists that the body as constructed is not incapable of resisting or defying some (if not all) of the demands of that discourse. Because power is diffuse and lacking a single source as well as a
single object, its effects are scattered and uneven with regard to individual
bodies, even as its predominant claims may be coherent and consistent.
For Foucault, resistance is the necessary counterpart to power, for while
power produces bodies as subjects with certain and different capabilities,
it cannot always control the ways those abilities are utilized. As pervasive as
the play of power is, its control is not omnipotent. Excess persists.

> [T]here is always something in the social body, in classes, groups and in-
> dividuals themselves which in some sense escapes relations of power,
> something which is by no means a more or less docile or reactive primal
> matter, but rather a centrifugal removement, an inverse energy, a dis-
> charge. . . . This measure . . . is not so much what stands outside relations
> of power as their limit, their underside, their counter-stroke, that which
> responds to every advance of power by a movement of disengagement.
> (1980, 138)

The fact that the body is socially constructed by the play of power does
not necessitate its own powerlessness. Rather, its ability to resist certain expressions of power is itself related to the nature of power. Concomitantly,
just as the power that Foucault describes is not omnipotent, the resistance
that is possible is not limitless. No embodied subject is capable of resisting
any and all expressions of power, for the simple reason that to do so would
be to undermine that subject's ability to act at all.

The meanings and codings of the body differ radically in various historical and social situations, and indeed, Foucault's point is that the sole
commonly held characteristic or property of bodies of varying environments is that of effect-hood. The only stable point about the body is its relationship to power; in all other matters, it is necessarily in flux, subject to
change, lacking any ontological status (see McWhorter 1989).[2] Yet liberation *of a sort* is certainly possible. At any given moment, certain aspects of
the dominant discourse are vulnerable, and subjects are capable of questioning and undermining them. With regard to real, live bodies themselves, and the disciplinary power that shapes them and their possibilities,
the only hope of so-called liberation lies in our ability to see them precisely as a site of this inscription and production of power dynamics—as

long as we understand their inscribed status as not utterly determinative. An analysis of these dynamics can serve to loosen certain aspects of the discourses of power imposed upon actual bodily persons.

To complain that such bodies would then be reinscribed with different discourses is to forget Foucault's analysis of power, which insists that power involves not only oppression, but also production. If to "liberate" bodies is to render them wholly independent from the various discourses that exist in the particular historical and cultural context, then indeed such a goal is, within the context of Foucault's project, impossible. There is no purely "natural" or "free" body to reclaim. If, however, one seeks to liberate individual bodies from particular moments of the relevant dominant discourses, then precisely this type of analysis is necessary. To recognize that virtually no aspect of bodies can be described in terms of universally true, objective discourses (for example, the scientific discourse), that is, to recognize them as *fundamentally* nonnatural, does not weaken familiar feminist insights concerning various cultural and bodily methods of expressing and enforcing women's inferiority. It is rather to say that the effects of power do not stop at such blatant practices as corseting, foot binding, clitoridectomies, and forced sterilization, but that these are only the most obvious results of a discourse whose influence is far deeper and more subtle than originally thought. Whereas some early feminist thought relied on the objective and ostensibly value-free realm of the "natural" to serve as a contrast to the artificial aspects of femininity (Wollstonecraft [1792] 1983 is a prime example), Foucault's model allows no such easy opposition. In fact, it allows no totality of any sort, so that while resistance is possible (that is, while subjects can express and effect their objections to certain aspects of the dominant discourse, and can even eradicate some), *total* resistance, that is, a wholesale resistance to the power structure *as such,* is not. Because the body is always already implicated in the play of power, because the inscription of power occurs at the moment at which the body enters culture, the body never exists as a *tabula rasa.* For Foucault, the body only and always exists as a social and cultural entity.

If, as Foucault claims, individual bodies are produced with certain identifiable characteristics that relate directly to power dynamics, then bodies are texts that we may read in order to discern the (sometimes implicit) claims of the dominant discourse. Given the admittedly complex but always central role of the body in the political oppression of women, the feminine body is a particularly crucial text. Indeed, much feminist scholarship has been devoted to reading the details of the feminine body for precisely such purposes. The specifics of the feminine body, particularly feminine bodily comportment, reflect the power relations that have produced them and the myriad ways this production is accomplished. A closer look at the behavior and habits of bodies typically described and recognized as feminine is therefore warranted. The work of two feminist theorists is invaluable here: Iris Marion Young's "Throwing Like a Girl" (1990) and Sandra Lee Bartky's "Foucault, Femininity, and the Modernization of Patriarchal Power" (1988).[3]

The Feminine Body

Describing "the" feminine body in a distinctly phenomenological sense presents, of course, a host of difficulties. Strictly speaking, there is no one feminine body, no single incarnation that fulfills perfectly the ideal set up for it. Moreover, it would appear doubtful that even within the confines of a particular culture and a particular historical period, there is one static ideal of the feminine body. Femininity has never been that simple. Certainly in current times, the ideal is somewhat of a moving target, whereby women are at once exhorted to be thin but muscular, slender but buxom, fit but not overly strong. Definitions of "feminine" behavior, appearance, and character vary widely among classes and ethnicities, and gender is only one means by which bodies are constructed and categorized. Finally, each individual woman is affected differently by the demands of femininity. While a largely consistent definition of the elements of that femininity may be possible, there will always be individual women (and perhaps groups of women) for whom such definitions will not hold. Given these multiple and varied factors, phenomenological attempts to discern that which is feminine can run the risk of ignoring other factors in the construction of the feminine body, thus implicitly holding up one ideal of femininity to the exclusion of all others. Iris Marion Young defends against just this kind of criticism when she writes,

I take "femininity" to designate not a mysterious quality or essence that all women have by virtue of their being biologically female. It is, rather, a set of structures and conditions that delimit the typical *situation* of being a woman in a particular society, as well as the typical way in which this situation is lived by the women themselves. Defined as such, it is not necessary that *any* women be "feminine"—that is, it is not necessary that there be distinctive structures and behavior typical of the situation of women. This understanding of "feminine" existence makes it possible to say that some women escape or transcend the typical situation and definition of women in various degrees and respects. I mention this primarily to indicate that the account offered here of the modalities of feminine bodily existence is not to be falsified by referring to some individual women to whom aspects of the account do not apply, or even to some individual men to whom they do. (1990, 143–44)

Young is answering only one part of the problem (namely, that however femininity is articulated, there will be individual women whose experiences are not included within the stated parameters), and insofar as her argument is so limited, I find it a useful one. However, she does not address the alleged singularity of the femininity that she then proceeds to describe. Her description of the feminine body is notoriously unraced, which suggests that there is only one standard of femininity, which, however complex and contradictory, nevertheless provides a continuum upon which most, if not all, women can be placed. It may be argued that, to the contrary, there are many different standards of femininity that are particular to economic classes or ethnic groups, and that to assume that there is only one once again reinscribes the dominance of the European American in contemporary U.S. society by claiming that the experiences of that group are the parameters that "delineate the typical" (Huggins 1991; hooks 1981; Spelman 1988).

While I am sympathetic to such criticisms of Young's work—criticisms to which, it seems to me, most if not all phenomenological analyses are vulnerable—I do not consider them ultimately fatal. The femininity which Young (and Bartky too, for that matter) describes is a distinctly white one, and it should be delimited as such. However, in the context of a racist political structure, the construction of white femininity was, and in many ways still is, the construction of the ideal femininity. White femininity has held a privileged place in the construction of gender, and as such holds significance not only for those women it includes, but also for those whom it excludes. The significances, obviously, differ, and it is these differences that the theories of Young, at least those concerning typical feminine bodily comportment, are incapable of approaching. But it is precisely the dominance of a white femininity that has often served to define women of certain ethnicities or classes out of their femininity (and thus, importantly, out of their humanity); Barbara Smith notes that "when you read about Black women being lynched, they aren't thinking of us as females. The horrors that we have experienced have absolutely everything to do with them *not even viewing us as women*" (Smith quoted in Spelman 1988, 37). African American women have certainly not, historically, been accorded the chivalrous courtesy allegedly commanded by those of the fairer sex—hence the paradoxical and unanswerable question traditionally attributed to Sojourner Truth. Insofar as the particularities of the dominant white femininity have been utilized to construct women of color as not "really" women, they have constituted the standard of femininity itself and are significant (although in different ways) to women of all races.

That being said, any analysis that takes as its basis the racially limited work of Young will inevitably be similarly limited. While the ensuing discussion will concern itself with the construction of the typically or socially recognizable feminine body, it is important to keep in mind that this body is also, simultaneously, raced. Moreover, the raced quality of the recognizably feminine body has particular import for the matter of rape, in that women of color who do not exemplify the ideals of white femininity (passivity, submission, etc.) may have their status as "victim" doubted even more strenuously than white victims. It is quite possible, even likely, that the conclusions reached in this chapter apply not to women in general, but to a racially specific and dominant subset of women, a limitation that demonstrates the need for phenomenological analyses of feminine ways of being that are excluded by the distinctly white standards.

In her essay, Young is primarily concerned with the limited scope of feminine motility. Although she focuses her analysis on goal-oriented actions and therefore claims to avoid "sexual being" (1990, 143), her conclusions shed considerable light on the bodily fear that constricts the sphere of feminine physical experience. One of her central claims is that the feminine body is treated by the woman as an object, a thing that exists separate from (and often opposed to) the aims of the woman as subject. "[T]he modalities of feminine bodily existence have their root in the fact that feminine existence experiences the body as a mere thing—a fragile thing, which must be picked up and coaxed into movement, a thing that exists as *looked at and acted upon*" (Young 1990, 150; emphasis in the original). The woman experiences her body as an alien, unwieldy, weak object that, depending on the particular goal, needs either massive transformation or kid-glove treatment. As it stands, it seems, a woman's body is good for very little.

To experience the body as itself *essentially* weak is to necessitate placing it under constant surveillance. Dangers are rife, and the woman attempts to protect her appallingly vulnerable body by restricting its spatial scope. Limiting the area into which the body extends is a means of reducing possible risks, and thus "the space . . . that is *physically* available to the feminine body is frequently of greater radius than the space that she uses and inhabits" (1990, 151). Similarly, given the assumed fragility of the female bones, muscles, and tissues, the girl learns to throw not with her whole arm (an action that demands, after all, faith), but rather with a mere portion of it. Feminine bodily comportment is marked by an odd economy, where any given action is undertaken not by the entirety of physical capabilities that could be gathered, but rather only with the necessary minimum. "Women often do not perceive themselves as capable of lifting and carrying heavy things. . . . We frequently fail to summon the full possibilities of our muscular coordination, position, poise and bearing" (145).

Young emphasizes that this disciplining of the female body is not merely prohibitive, but also linked to the acquiring of positive habits and capacities (1990, 154). By constituting one's body as essentially and irrevocably weak and vulnerable, the person becomes a card-carrying woman, with all the rights and responsibilities assigned thereto. Her position in the larger society is established securely (although perhaps not as securely as may appear at first glance, for femininity, and masculinity too for that matter, demands constant maintenance). "The more a girl assumes her status as feminine, the more she takes herself to be fragile and immobile and the more she actively enacts her own body inhibition" (154).

Unlike Young, Bartky is working explicitly out of a Foucauldian analysis of the body, although she decries his failure, in *Discipline and Punish* (1979), to account sufficiently for the implications of sexual difference (Bartky 1988, 63). She attempts to answer this omission by examining "those disciplinary practices that produce a body which in gesture and appearance is recognizably feminine" (64). In her analysis of the social practices of dieting, exercise, and makeup, she reveals a systematic and simultaneous vilification and disempowering of the female body. In the case of makeup, the impetus to transform one's body into something beautiful by means of cosmetic force transforms the body into a hostile entity, constantly threatening to revert to its natural, that is to say, unbeautiful, state, and in so doing manifesting itself to be directly oppositional to the wishes of the woman. Note that while the *ideal* feminine body may be believed to be "naturally" beautiful, *individual* female bodies are subjected to a host of intrusive, expensive, and high-maintenance practices in order to be rendered beautiful. Left on its own, the female face is plain, common, unremarkable (and, perhaps worst of all, subject to the process of aging). In order to be femininely beautiful, it needs paint, if not surgery. The war against unwanted weight is an even more confrontational phenomenon. One's appetites and desires must be carefully guarded against, lest unwanted pounds find their way onto the hard-won slender frame. The body is constituted again, perhaps even more insidiously, as that which the woman needs to struggle against, to control, to whip into shape, in an effort to counteract its inherent tendencies to lapse into an unattractive appearance.

Bartky remarks that one crucial aspect of the ideal feminine body that inspires these social practices is precisely its unrealizability. Constant and inevitable failure is necessary to the perpetuation of the ideal. The power of the cosmetic, diet, and exercise industries lies precisely in their ability to promise beauty while always defining the horizon as just beyond reach. If the ideal were actually within the grasp of individual women, innovative techniques would be rendered unnecessary. The beautiful woman is never finished, but is constantly adapting to changing and sometimes contradictory definitions of attractiveness. Not only, in Simone de Beauvoir's (1974) famous formulation, does one become a woman, but one is *always* in a state of becoming.

One interesting point about this process of creating the beautifully feminine self that Bartky doesn't address directly is its significantly individualistic nature. Despite the fact that the project of beautification provides women with all-women or mostly-women spaces within which to achieve their goal (one thinks immediately of the intimacy of the beauty salon), the pervasive sense of having failed to achieve the desired image is relentlessly personalized. Even as women commiserate about the difficulty of weight loss, for example, each individual woman is more likely to recognize her own particular lack of thinness while assuring her friends that they are really quite all right. Not only is the woman's body vilified for failing to live up to the desired image (both of society and of the individual woman), but that failure is experienced as unique to that particular body. As long as the failure is personalized, as long as the enemy is *this particular body* with its particular faults, stubbornness, or weakness, the culture-wide "disciplinary project of femininity" that is at work is successfully concealed (Bartky 1988, 71). Yet if the body is the site of the failure to beautify, of alienation and hostility, it can also be experienced as the site for success, mutual admiration, and creativity. The creation of the beautiful feminine appearance has its poignant and self-affirming moments, and the process of getting "dressed up," especially if it is a communal, girls- or women-only undertaking, can be intensely pleasurable. In this case, the project of creating feminine beauty exists briefly as an artistic challenge, and it is the process of doing, rather than the result of being seen, that is momentarily emphasized.[4]

If the feminine body is constituted and experienced as the enemy of the womanly subject—not a docile body in relation to power dynamics, but a hostile one in relation to the social desires of the woman—it is also a paradoxically weak one. Bartky describes the limitations of feminine motility as the results of bodily fear. The woman experiences her body not as a means by which to accomplish a variety of physical tasks, but rather as a barrier to those accomplishments. In a point that Young takes up in greater detail, Bartky claims that "woman's space is not a field in which her bodily intentionality can be freely realized but an enclosure in which she feels herself positioned and by which she is confined" (1988, 66). Here the body is not so much an enemy as an assumed hindrance, plagued by weakness, uncertainty, and fragility. Of course, these two aspects of Bartky's analysis—body as enemy and body as hindrance—find a common source in the ideal feminine image. "An aesthetic of femininity, for example, that mandates fragility and a lack of muscular strength produces female bodies that can offer little resistance to physical abuse, and the physical abuse of women by men, as we know, is widespread" (1988, 72). To approach success in the realm of beauty is to abandon a degree of physical strength, and it is the mutual exclusiveness between beauty and strength that increases the vulnerability of women's bodies. The ideal feminine image is, of course, constantly shifting, and in its metamorphoses we occasionally encounter an image that is more muscular than its predecessor. However, it is safe to say that while images of contemporary Western beauty at times invoke physical strength, it is never beautiful for a woman to be as strong as she possibly can. A male bodybuilder is the epitome of masculinity, a female bodybuilder at best a borderline woman and at worst (i.e., at her most muscular), a monstrosity.[5]

Both Young's and Bartky's analyses describe a feminine bodily comportment that is marked by fear: fear of bodily desires (so strong they threaten to undo all the subject's best efforts) and fear of harm (so likely that the subject constructs a small "safety zone" around the body). What is significant about these analyses is that they stress the degree to which the woman experiences her own individual body as culpable for producing all these dangers. It appears that the feminine body is not only essentially weak, but also somehow accountable for its own vulnerability.

The feminine body that Young and Bartky describe is that of a previctim. If it attempts something beyond its highly limited capacities, if it wanders beyond its safety zone, it—*by virtue of its own characteristics*—can expect to be hurt. The woman who experiences her body in this way does not locate the dangers presented to her body as originating from outside her body. Rather, they have as their source the fact and nature of her body itself. If that body is hurt or violated, the blame must rest on the woman's failure to sufficiently limit its movements.[6]

This typically (white) feminine experience of the body, while not universally or similarly applicable to every individual woman, is related to the constitution of the feminine body as that which is alien to the female subject. Considering the body as a force or element somehow fundamentally separated from the wishes and desires of the female subject confirms its status as a source of impending danger. Likewise, perceiving the body as a liability positions it outside the female subjectivity in such a way as to endow it with a degree of ontological alienation. If the body is so distanced from the female subject, we may wonder whether that subject can be held at all responsible for the control of her charge. Who could hope to control this wild and weak mass of flesh? Yet insofar as it is able to be controlled at all, that responsibility rests squarely on the female subject. Only she can take that flesh, mold it in the image of the beautiful, and shelter it from the ramifications of its own countless failings. Even when a degree of the responsibility is abdicated to a man, still the (adult) woman bears the responsibility of finding a suitable protector. If control is lost and violence or harm ensues, she bears the blame.

Note too that this bodily alienation pits the female subject against her own body, such that her ability to be and move in the world is directly contingent on her successful control of that barbaric flesh. Women thus experience the "unbearable weight" (Bordo 1993) of their bodies, a weight that continually hampers their full and free inclusion in society.

Rape and Feminine Bodily Comportment

The feminine habits and motility described by Bartky and Young clearly imply a constant state of danger for the feminine body, and indeed find the source of the danger within the feminine body itself. But what specific dangers do all the hard-won feminine habits seek to counteract? In refusing to call on the totality of physical abilities present in the feminine body, the woman attempts to reduce the risk of self-inflicted bodily harm. To throw with her whole arm may cause her slender muscles to snap; to run fast, hard, for an extended period of time may overtax her tender heart.

However, woman's limitation of the space within which her body can move seems to gesture not toward self-inflicted harm, but rather toward harm inflicted by other bodies. Within the invisible wall she throws up around her, a woman may consider herself safe; in this space, she has maximum control over her body. To go beyond that space is to enter an arena where her body is in danger of being violated.[7] This limited, individual safety zone, which determines the smallness of a woman's step, the gathering-in of her sitting body, and the daintiness of her gestures, mirrors in fact the larger hampering of her mobility. For a woman, the travellable world is a small place. Entire portions of each twenty-four-hour day are deemed unsafe, and unless accompanied by a man (or, alternatively, many women), a woman should spend these hours in the safety of her own home. Geographical areas that may be considered completely accessible to men are, for women, sites of possible (even likely) harassment, molestation, or rape.

What is important in this comparison is that where women are encouraged or mandated to restrict their movement for safety's sake, the danger described is not to the body *in general*. That danger is almost always specifically sexualized. The reason that men can travel where women ought not to is only that women can be and are raped (whereas men can be, but are not often), not that women can be and are mugged or beaten up (as in fact men can be, and are). For the male subject, the threat presented is one of destruction of the body, whereas for the female subject, the trenchant harm concerns her sexual being and freedom. Women's individual restrictions of their bodily movements reflect an attempt to deny unwanted sexual access. Paradoxically, this denial serves to highlight their persistent vulnerability.

> In an extraordinary series of over two thousand photographs, many candid shots taken in the street, the German photographer Marianne Wex has documented differences in typical masculine and feminine body posture. Women sit waiting for trains with arms close to the body, hands folded together in their laps, toes pointing straight ahead or turned inward, and legs pressed together. The women in these photographs make themselves small and narrow, harmless; they seem tense; they take up little space. Men, on the other hand, expand into the available space; they sit with legs far apart and arms flung out at some distance from the body. Most common in these sitting male figures is what Wex calls the "proffering position": the men sit with legs thrown wide apart, crotch visible, feet pointing outward, often with an arm and a casually dangling hand resting comfortably on an open, spread thigh. (Bartky 1988, 67)

The men's sex is expressed freely, almost defiantly, while the women cover theirs, for fear of its being stolen, violated, consumed. The women, conscious of the sexual dangers that surround them, attempt to make themselves even tinier, as if the safest status they could hold would be invisibility. Not only is this self-protection illusory, but it actually serves to reiterate women's vulnerability. It produces and presents women as pre-victims expecting to be victimized (not because men are rapists, but because women's bodies are rapable). Even more worrisome, this attempt at invisibility is in direct contradiction to the importance of beautification to the distinctly feminine body. We have here a strange situation indeed, where women spend inordinate amounts of time and money on creating an image designed to attract male desire, and then, on entering the public world, find it necessary to protect themselves from that desire. Attracting the male gaze is, in the context of a patriarchal society, necessary to achieve social status and worth, yet that attraction is in itself a trenchant threat.[8]

The hesitancy with which women enter the bodily world, the assumption of responsibility regarding the behavior of men, the locating of danger within the facticity of the feminine body: all these express the power dynamic that blames women for the sexual assaults inflicted upon them. That rape is experienced as a fate as frightening as death demonstrates the privileged role which the threat of sexual violence plays in the production of the feminine body (according to a study performed by Mark Warr [1984], most women in most age groups fear rape significantly more than they fear death; see also Gordon and Riger [1989]). If we claimed previously that the socially produced feminine body is that of a pre-victim, we may also claim that it is the body of the *guilty* pre-victim. In the specific moments and movements of this body are written the defense of the sexual offender: she was somewhere she should not have been, moving her body in ways she should not have, carrying on in a manner so free and easy as to convey an utter abdication of her responsibilities of self-protection and self-surveillance.

Returning to our Foucauldian analysis of the body, we are compelled to ask, What power relations are inscribed on this feminine body? To what purpose has it been created, and whom does it serve? In feminine gestures and bodily comportment, we see the effects of a power dynamic that holds women responsible for their own physical, sexual victimization. Insofar as the assaults considered most dangerous and most pervasive are precisely sexual assaults, we may also recognize the production of culpable feminine sexuality, which by its existence alone incites men, who remain allegedly powerless in the presence of its overwhelming temptation, to violence. Hence Lynne Henderson writes:

> [A] primary impediment to recognition that rape is a real and frequent crime is a widely accepted cultural "story" of heterosexuality that results in an unspoken "rule" of male innocence and female guilt in law. By "male innocence and female guilt", I mean an unexamined belief that men are not morally responsible for their heterosexual conduct, while females are morally responsible both for their conduct and for the conduct of males. (1992, 130–31)

The "story" to which Henderson refers is not only believed, not only implied, not only stated, it is in fact lived in the bodily habits of feminine subjects.

Let us be exact about this process. In acquiring the bodily habits that render the subject "feminine," habits that are inculcated at a young age and then constantly redefined and maintained, the woman learns to accept her body as dangerous, willful, fragile, and hostile. *It* constantly poses the possibility of threat, and only persistent vigilance can limit the risk at which it places the woman. The production of such a body reflects and supports a status quo that refuses, in the particular case of sexual assault, to consider the victim innocent until proven guilty; rather, the opposite is assumed.

The threat of rape, then, is a constitutive and sustained moment in the production of the distinctly feminine body. It is the pervasive danger that renders so much public space off-limits, a danger so omnipresent, in fact, that the "safety zone" women attempt to create rarely exceeds the limits of their own limbs and quite often falls far short of that radius. Women consider their flesh not only weak and breakable, but also violable. The truth inscribed on the woman's body is not that, biologically, all men are potential rapists. It is rather that, biologically, all women are potential rape victims. Note, too, that this bodily inscription may take place without the explicit articulation of the concept of "rape" or the actual experience of sexual assault. Girls especially may know that their bodies are inherently dangerous without being clear as to the precise nature of the danger they present. They may only sense that something very bad and very hurtful will befall them should their surveillance falter, and, correspondingly, that all sorts of social opportunities will be open to them should their project of femininity be successful.[9]

The Problem of Resistance

With the feminine body described as the expression of a distinct power discourse that includes at a fundamental level the threat of rape, the question of resistance again becomes pertinent. Foucault, it will be remembered, insisted on both the constitutive role of power and the necessarily concurrent force of resistance. With regard to rape, Foucault's suggestions seem to imply that a legal redefinition of the crime would constitute a major change in the discourse, thus helping to free women's bodies from the defining elements that produce them as pre-victims.

Yet in this suggestion Foucault has seemed to forget, or perhaps underestimate, the force of his analysis of power. A mere change in the legal definition of rape is not nearly sufficient to answer the constitutive and productive effects of this particular discourse. To believe that such a change would have the desired result is to accept the legal realm as a privileged source of power with determinative effects. It is obvious that the legal world is a source of political and social power, as well as a reflection and extension of the dominant discourses that Foucault describes. However, it is but one node in a complex matrix of relationships and institutions. It not only expresses dominant discourses, but is subject to them.

Here we see one significant result of the differing motivations behind the similar claims of Foucault and feminist theorists. In seeking primarily to liberate sexuality from a disciplinary discourse, and doing so in a way that, as many feminist criticisms have stated, does not sufficiently take into consideration the differing power positions related to sex and gender, Foucault suggests that the legal discourse refrain from passing judgment on the sexual content of the act of rape. In making that suggestion, Foucault remains focused on the sexual content of an act that a man performs. His primary concern, with regard to rape, is in protecting a certain aspect of male sexuality from the disciplinary force of the law. Were rape to be redefined as primarily a crime of assault, the *sexual* behavior and meanings inherent in the crime would be legally invisible.

A significant element of the woman victim's experience of rape is directly related to the constitutive element of a power discourse that produces her body as violable, weak, and alien to her subjectivity. From the rape victim's perspective, although not necessarily consciously (in fact, precisely in a bodily way), these meanings too are part of the crime, insofar as that particular action is perceived as a threat fulfilled. To redefine the crime as primarily an assault would mask these meanings. Moreover, given the historical relationship of the law and women's bodies, it seems dubious (although not impossible) that the categories, language, and concepts found in the legal world could be effectively wielded to change significantly the character of the produced feminine body.

Foucault's suggested decriminalization of rape as a sexual crime underestimates the degree to which the bodies of rape *victims* (overwhelmingly feminine bodies) are themselves expressions of a given power discourse. It also fails to recognize that the act of rape itself, especially given its pervasive occurrence, is fundamental to the discourse that defines women as inferior and socially expendable. The real, live, living, breathing women who experience rape and the threat of rape on a daily basis, and whose bodily behavior and being are to a significant degree formed by the presence of the threat of rape, will not be liberated by a redefinition of rape that ignores its constitutive and oppressive effects on their existence.

Where, then, is resistance to be found against this pervasive and constitutive discourse of power? Given that rape is, among other things, a crime recognized by society (even as it is implicated in fundamental social dynamics and beliefs), it has a specific legal status that should be preserved. Regardless of how rape is defined or understood, it is widely recognized as a behavior worthy of legal recriminations, and despite feminist concerns with the means of law enforcement in the United States (especially its distinctly racist results), it would seem all but impossible to imagine a feminism that did not urge that serious legal action be taken against the rapist. Foucault, after all, does not wish to render rape itself legal, but merely wishes to punish only one particular aspect of rape, that pertaining to its status as assault. The analysis of rape's role with regard to women's bodily comportment and experience suggests that one way of resisting this particular discourse would be to urge the legal world to recognize not only the violence inherent in rape but also its sexually specific meanings insofar as it is a sexually differentiated enforcement of a set of patriarchal, misogynist values. The legal definition of rape should include, therefore, an understanding of the bodily and sexual meanings central to the action of rape, and should take those meanings into consideration when considering the appropriate legal response to a rapist.

Such an inclusion in the legal world constitutes resistance to the particular discourse of power that underscores rape by rendering that discourse visible. A great deal of the power behind the particular discourses that constitute and produce the feminine body is due to their allegedly biological and hence irrefutable claims. What is needed is an explicit recognition of the roles of those discourses within an overarching and markedly unnatural, system of oppression by which women were reduced to an inferior status. Such a recognition does not, importantly, deny the validity of women's experiences of such bodily comportment and behavior; the distinctly feminine body does not need to be wholly natural in order to be a valid source of knowledge. However, that recognition does render nonsensical any defensive invocation of a "natural"—and naturally culpable—women's sexuality (especially a sexuality oriented around the erotic appeal of being dominated). The sexual meanings of rape from the perspective of the victim have everything to do with the construction of the particularly feminine body, and as such are fundamental to the crime as experienced by the victim. An emphasis on the implication of the construction of the feminine body within a larger system of sexual hierarchization would account for women's feelings of shame and self-blame while refusing to hold the victim accountable for the assault. Foucault's strategy, on the other hand, by silencing any and all sexual meanings relating to rape, would allow assumptions concerning women's culpability to remain intact, if, perhaps, unsaid in the courtroom itself.

In other words, given that rape is a constitutive element of women's experience and that it is a social means of sexual differentiation (such that it has radically different meanings for men and women), it must be approached legally in such a way so that its sex-specific meanings may be articulated. Foucault's analysis of power, especially the way power discourses act on real, live, living bodies, should remind us that the individual women rape victims who prosecute their cases were marked by the threat of rape long before their bodies were actually violated, and that their experience of rape is not exhausted, although it is certainly dominated, by the particular incident that commands the court's attention.

The Act of Rape

The location of the threat of rape as a basic source of feminine bodily comportment has specific ramifications for the individual experience of being sexually assaulted. On a bodily level, a woman will be likely to experience a rape in some important sense as a threat fulfilled. The typical reactions of a rape victim, marked by overwhelming guilt and self-loathing, are the reactions of a person who should have known but temporarily forgot that she was constantly at risk. To have believed for even a moment that she was not in danger, for whatever reason, is felt to be the cause of the attack. Those assumptions that were prevalent in the production of her bodily comportment have been confirmed, and the attack itself may well be considered a reminder of the need for increased self-surveillance.

Why is an attack on a woman by a man with a penis (or its substitute) distinct from an attack with any other body part? Why is, in Foucault's terms, sticking one's fist into someone's face different from sticking one's penis into their sex? Precisely because the attack with the penis, the particularly sexual (and usually male) assault of and into one's (usually female) sex, is a danger that is fundamental to the specifics of feminine bodily comportment. To desexualize the act of rape, to consider it legally only as any other assault, would be to obfuscate—not weaken—its role in the production of the sexual hierarchy through the inscription of individual bodies. Rather than resisting the insistent process of sexualization that Foucault describes and decries, it would support the equally insistent process of sexual hierarchization which places women's bodies at such daily risk. As Teresa de Lauretis observes,

> In the terms of Foucault's theoretical analysis, his proposal may be understood as an effort to counter the technology of sex by breaking the bond between sexuality and crime; an effort to enfranchise sexual behaviors from legal punishments, and so to render the sexual sphere free from intervention by the state. Such a form of "local resistance" on behalf of the men imprisoned on, or subject to, charges of rape, however, would paradoxically but practically work to increase and further to legitimate the *sexual* oppression of women. (1987, 37)

Brownmiller's analysis of rape as primarily violent rather than sexual, that is, as a means of the expression of sheer power by which one group of people dominated another, failed to explicate sufficiently the ways rape was distinctly sexual and the ways sex and power were co-implicated. Although Foucault arrives at a similar conclusion as Brownmiller, his error lies not in a failure to consider the interplay between sex and power, but in his interpretation of rape only as something a man does, for which a man may be punished, and not as something experienced by a feminine body. His analysis remains solidly focused on the *masculine* body and its vulnerability to disciplinary discourses. However, in locating the man as central to the phenomenon, he has forgotten to ask the question of the bodily significance of the experience of being raped, an experience that occurs disproportionately to women. If we make the bodily experiences of women central to the question, it is possible to claim that an assault with a penis is distinct not because of what it claims about the masculine body, but rather because of what it claims about the feminine body, and how those claims are located in an overall power structure. To challenge that set of cultural assumptions, the discourse that produces the feminine body, necessitates not a desexualization of rape, but rather a recognition of its sexual meanings.

Interestingly enough, our analysis may lead us to quite the opposite conclusion than Foucault's in another way as well. While the threat of rape is, I have argued, the threat most feared by women, more compelling even than the threat of death, it is not the only threat. Other assaults, including those made with fists, and especially those that occur in the context of sexual relationships, may be experienced as sexual in nature precisely insofar as they confirm the assumptions about the feminine body discussed above. In some ways, these assaults may be perceived as precursors to the act of rape; if this is the case, then this analysis would call for a serious reconsideration of domestic violence not merely as an act of assault, but rather as an act with an underlying set of sexual meanings as well.

If the feminine body is a location whereon the tenets of a sexually hierarchical culture are written, it is also the site where they may be fought. Working out the Foucauldian notion of resistance, Lois McNay writes, "[T]he sexed body is to be understood not only as the primary target of the techniques of disciplinary power, but also as the point where these techniques are resisted and thwarted" (1992, 39). When women's bodies are constituted not as objects that incite other, more innocent bodies to violence, but rather as powerful means of counteracting that violence, the power structures that support the all too pervasive phenomenon of rape will be seriously undermined.

The Ethical Wrongs of Rape

Few people (even among philosophers) would claim that rape does not, in virtually all conceivable contexts, constitute a serious moral wrong. Yet determining the precise wrong or the various wrongs inherent in an act of rape proves to be a difficult proposition. The ethical dimensions of the crime of rape, insofar as they invoke standards of sexual appropriateness as well as models of personhood and consent, involve those aspects of social being that are at once among the most politically loaded, and hence the most public, *and* among the most personally invested, hence the most private. Indeed, the persistent attempts to define rape without reference to sexuality or sexual politics can be read as a defense mechanism against inappropriate and invasive legislation; according to this logic, sexuality is a private matter that should not be regulated by the body politic. In order to punish rape without overstepping its bounds, the law is from this perspective encouraged to eradicate or at least not consider the sexual meanings of the crime.

The problem of the sexual nature of rape is only one among many difficulties ethicists have faced in their attempts to delineate the precise wrong or wrongs of rape. Due to a host of factors—the historical oppression of women, the particular constructions of feminine sexuality, the imposition of a compulsory heterosexuality, the inherent contradiction between the ostensibly grave manner in which rape is considered ethically and the sheer prevalence with which it occurs—the determination of not only how, but also whether rape is wrong is fraught with uncertainties. The differing ways rape has been approached ethically are reflections of the social and political status of women as well as the underlying assumptions concerning sexual difference and sexual hierarchy. There is, however, no easy symmetry between the seriousness with which rape is perceived both legally and ethically and the social worth of the women subject to such a crime. Depending on how the crime or moral wrong of rape is determined, it is possible (and indeed logically consistent) to consider it a crime worthy of serious punishment, even though its direct target is a socially inferior being. For example, Ruth Kittel has noted that in the common law courts of thirteenth-century England, which accorded women few rights at all, the possible penalties for rape included death, castration, and blinding (perhaps, in some cases, meted out by the victim herself; see Kittel 1982, 101).

Traditional Western concepts of rape that define it primarily as a crime against (male) property also fit into this category. In this distinctly and blatantly patriarchal schema, the crime of rape is not, properly speaking, committed against the woman who is its direct victim, but against the man under whose social protection and identity the woman exists. The wrong committed here is not one of violence against the female victim, but of trespass on another man's property, which constitutes a threat to the rights, and therefore the political and social identity, of the owning male. This trespass (especially insofar as it represented a financial loss on the part of a father whose daughter was now damaged goods relative to the market of marriage) was perceived with social outrage and therefore punished severely. Nowhere in this model, however, need the female victim be represented as anything other than the property of the male under whose auspices she exists socially (the father, husband, or brother). Her social worth is persistently derivative, and as a derivative being, she does not hold any rights individually. The wrong cannot, therefore, be defined in terms of her personhood, because her full personhood was socially, politically, and legally nonexistent.

This definition of rape as trespass, as a crime against property, is defined by Keith Burgess-Jackson as the "conservative" theory of rape (1996, 44), which understands the crime as an unlawful use of another person's property. Burgess-Jackson notes that the crime as thus delimited is not, properly speaking, a theft, but more an unlawful borrowing or usage; nevertheless, it is clear that in certain cases, most notably if the victim was a virgin, rape could be understood as a theft of an irreplaceable piece of property for which the real victim (usually the father in this case) deserved financial compensation. The liberal critique of the conservative position is easy enough to predict. It will argue that the woman in question should be endowed with the same rights accorded to the men in society, and that therefore the crime of rape needs to be understood as an affront to those individually held rights. Since the liberal position remains committed to the basic concepts of rights and is in fact merely arguing against a particularly gendered organization of rights that serves to place women in a socially subservient role in relation to men, rape continues to be perceived as a threat to civil rights. In the context of this critique, Burgess-Jackson notes, rape appears as a type of battery (1996, 49), an assault more or less equal to any other physical assault against the body of a citizen. Since the liberal critique was grounded in an emphasis on the equality (that is, the political similarity or even identity) of the sexes, the moral wrong of which rape consists is defined without reference to sexual difference or sexual hierarchy. The violation is against that which every citizen, regardless of gender, depends on and holds dear, that is, personal autonomy.

Rape and the Problem of Consent

In this liberal theory of rape the problem of consent becomes paramount. Note that under the traditional, or conservative, theory of rape, the question of the victim's consent or lack of same was irrelevant. Because women were not the ultimate possessors of their sexuality or their sexual freedom, they were not in a position to allow or disallow any particular sexual interaction. Since the liberal theory now understands the crime as a violation of autonomy, as a failure to recognize the victim's civil rights of self-determination, consent becomes the standard that determines whether or not the crime occurred. If the woman consented to this particular sexual encounter, she was exercising her autonomy, and thus no rape was committed; if the sexual act was committed without her consent, then it constituted rape.

Many feminist theories of rape developed in the 1970s located the lack of consent as the source of the wrongness of rape. In their analysis of rape, Carolyn Shafer and Marilyn Frye write, "[W]e shall proceed to presume that rape is sexual intercourse performed without the consent of the woman. Since we share the public view that rape is morally wrong and gravely so, and since we would not want to say that there is anything morally wrong with sexual intercourse per se, we conclude that the wrongness of rape rests with the matter of the woman's consent" (1977, 334). Shafer and Frye share the liberal view that personhood is intricately tied to self-determination and autonomy, the loss of which in the context of rape results in a denial of the victim's personhood:

So to fail to defer to a person's rightful power of consent is to deny either
the actual extent of its personhood or its actual personal identity. Either
is flagrantly disrespectful, and thus grievously wrong. The closer the item
is to the center of the domain of the person whose rightful power of consent over it is not recognized, the more violent is the attack upon that
creature's personhood itself. To presume to wield an effective power of
consent over the personal properties and/or the body of that creature,
the center of its domain, is ipso facto to deny that there is a person there
at all. . . . The ultimate disrespect is, then, the exercise of the power of
consent over another *person*. And this is exactly what rape is. (340.)

Rape is wrong, therefore, because it undermines the integrity of the personhood of the victim by denying their right of consent over that property
that is most personally, most intensely held: the body.

In a similar vein, Stephen J. Schulhofer argues that lack of consent,
rather than the presence of force, be considered a sufficient criterion for
the determination of "sexual abuse" or "sexual misconduct" (1992, 67).
Although Schulhofer persists in including the use or threat of force as a
defining element of rape, he suggests a new category of sexual crime that
is related solely to consent, to be perceived as something perhaps less serious than rape, but nonetheless a serious infringement upon a person's
sexual autonomy. He asserts that "intercourse in the face of verbal objections, ambivalence, or silence is intercourse without consent, and it represents a clear offense against the physical autonomy of the person. Even
in the complete absence of force, such behavior is 'nonviolent sexual
misconduct' and should be treated as such" (77). Taking sexual autonomy seriously, Schulhofer claims, means questioning the context within
which consent was given or refused, and using the quality of the consent
or lack thereof as the yardstick by which the crime is measured. "The important questions for reform center not on how aberrant, egregious, or
potentially lethal the behavior of a man may be but rather on whether
the preconditions for meaningful choice are present and whether behavior that may interfere with meaningful choice has adequate social justification" (68).

It is important to note at this juncture that the liberal theory of rape
does not always highlight consent to the exclusion of other factors. J. H.
Bogart notes that rape can be understood as "forcible, coerced, nonvoluntary, or nonconsensual sex" (1991, 117), and that despite the apparent
similarity of the various adjectives, they actually denote quite different
sets of defining criteria. For example, understanding rape as forcible sex
prioritizes the use or threat of violence as a necessary element of the

crime. Coercion is constituted not only by physical threats but also by threats to other aspects of the victim's life (the safety of the victim's loved ones, for example). The scope of the criteria for rape as nonvoluntary sex is larger still, and includes all instances of sexual intercourse where the only alternatives come "at the cost of serious inconveniences or substantial harm . . . [for example,] such things as exchanges of sex for employment, or an exchange of sex for not being abandoned in a remote location" (Bogart 1991, 118).

While the liberal models of rape presented by Shafer and Frye, Schulhofer, and Bogart differ slightly, a model of consent remains central. Force, coercion, or seriously inconvenient or harmful alternatives are here presented as mitigating factors in the process of consent itself. The victim who is coerced into having sex with the assailant—who *chooses*, for example, to have sex rather than to placed a loved one at risk—does, strictly speaking, consent to the sexual encounter. However, because that consent was obtained not freely, but under a serious threat, it is understood legally and morally as not a full or valid consent. Even the criteria associated with rape as forcible sex do not distinguish between the actual use of violence (which may result in no kind of consent at all) and the threat of violence (which may produce a kind of consent). A real possibility accounted for by theories of rape as forcible sex is that the victim did consent, in some degree, to the encounter, but that that consent, because of the context in which it was obtained, does not indicate the absence of a crime against the victim's autonomy.

Liberal theories of rape depend on a certain understanding of consent that demands that it be freely given, that is, that the alternatives to the encounter in question are not so seriously inconvenient or harmful so as to be virtually unthinkable. Yet this conceptualization of consent, when taken against political and social structures that seriously limit women's agency and autonomy under many circumstances, proves problematic.

While not addressing solely the problem of rape, Carole Pateman's (1980) discussion of consent theory impinges directly on the role of consent as a defining element of rape as a crime. In tracing the history of the concept of consent, Pateman notes that modern political theorists relied on consent to solve a difficulty that arose from the assumed equality and freedom of each person, namely, the difficulty of authority. If all members of the society are born equal and free, how does one justify, or even account for, the authority of any one over the rest? Modern theorists, Pateman argues, answered the question by invoking the authority of individual consent:

If their freedom and equality is to be preserved, free and equal individuals must voluntarily commit themselves—for example, by consenting—
to enter into such a relationship. Consent theory is thus a specific example of a broader voluntarist theory of society which argues that
relationships of authority and obligation must be grounded in the voluntary acts or commitments of individuals. (1980, 151)

With regard to the consent necessary to the existing social contract, most
consent theorists argued that consent could be assumed as long as it was
not being actively or explicitly denied or withheld. So the consent that
provided the foundation for the enlightened political structure of democ-
racy did not need to be explicit, verbalized, or indeed consciously given in
any particular instance.

Historically, consent theory has consistently defined women as incapable of effecting true consent. "Women are not 'individuals' who own the
property they have in their persons and capacities, so the question of
their 'consent' to the authority of men never actually arises. Rather, their
apparent 'consent' to the authority of their husbands is only a formal
recognition of their 'natural' subordination" (Pateman 1980, 153). This
apparent or tacit consent that justifies the authority of men over women
was not the conscious act of a rational, fully free being, but was rather
rooted in women's natural lack of freedom and independence. It is difficult to imagine that this tacit consent, which is seemingly closer to resig-
nation or acceptance than choice, constitutes anything other than the
recognition of an imposed hierarchy. Indeed, one of Pateman's most
trenchant critiques of consent theory is that it fails to distinguish consent
"from habitual acquiescence, assent, silent dissent, submission, or even
enforced submission. Unless refusal of consent or withdrawal of consent
are real possibilities, we can no longer speak of 'consent' in any genuine
sense" (150).

While consent theory, then, relies on the participation of the citizen in
the authority structure to characterize that structure as other than oppressive, other than imposed by sheer force, it simultaneously defines
consent so loosely as to allow for the possibility of essentially coerced consent—which, properly speaking, is not consent at all. Pateman notes, for
example, that the consent represented in Hobbes's image of the body
politic is expressly obtained by the threat of violence and the use of intimidation. Not only has consent theory not consistently defined consent
as freely given, but it has often excluded large groups of persons from the
class of rational, equal, free beings. Such exclusions have served to justify
the inherent inequality of relationships traditionally defined by domina-

tion and submission (such as that between husband and wife) by invoking the "natural" inferiority of one party to the other.

Pateman asserts that those situations that demand women's consent in order to appear, in contemporary times, socially acceptable—marriage and sexual intercourse, for example—are structurally opposed to the possibility of that consent. As an institution that legally, socially, and historically endows the husband with greater authority than the wife, marriage demands from a woman a consent to limit her possibilities of consent. More exactly, the model of consent theory constructs marriage as that which benefits a man, but to which a woman must *consent*. To accede to the offer that a man makes, to accept a given situation, to consent to it, is strikingly different than to seek out a certain situation and to choose it for oneself. Implicit in this emphasis on a woman's consent are assumptions concerning the active, male role and the reactive, female role. To speak of a woman's consent in this context is to fail to recognize that women are not endowed with the power to construct their own desirable ends, but are expected to respond to situations constructed for them by others. A similar dynamic occurs with regard to sexual intercourse, although Pateman argues forcefully that with regard to sexuality, women's consent is subject to an entirely different set of standards than consent in any other arena. In legal criteria for demonstrating nonconsent to a sexual encounter, for example, words are not sufficient; women must express their nonconsent in every possible, bodily way in order to convince both the assailant and any judging body that consent was absent (Pateman 1980, 157). Nevertheless, underlying the emphasis on consent in sexual relations is the assumption that the proper place of women is essentially a reactionary one, where their participation is almost always reduced to a response to the offers (or demands) of a male.

Given these assumptions concerning the sexual aggressiveness of men and the sexual passivity of women, it is obvious why the issue of consent becomes increasingly murky:

> At present it is widely believed that a woman's "no" does *not* constitute a refusal, that it *is* "reasonable" for men to put a lesser or greater degree of pressure on unwilling women in sexual matters, and that it *is* "reasonable" for consent to be inferred from enforced submission. In short, unless accompanied by visible signs of severe physical violence, rape is not actually seen as a serious crime—or even a crime at all—despite its formal legal status. . . . Rape is conventionally presented as a unique act that stands in complete opposition to the consensual relations that ordinarily obtain between the sexes. The most tragic aspect of even a brief consid-

eration of the problem of women, rape, and consent is that rape is revealed as the extreme expression, or an extension of, the accepted and
"natural" relation between men and woman [*sic*]. (Pateman 1980, 161)

Pateman's analysis bears a striking similarity to that of Catharine MacKinnon. However, in rooting her analysis in the modern structure of consent
theory, rather than the assumption that women are fully constituted by
the patriarchal structure that surrounds them, Pateman is avoiding the totalizing definition of women that would render all agency impossible. It is
not the possibility of women's self-determination or movement that Pateman is denying; it is rather the worth of a model that inherently demands
that women consent to that which does not serve their purposes or interests, and that they perform that consent (usually implicitly) as a reaction
to their inferior status:

> Consent must always be given *to* something; in the relationship between
> the sexes, it is always women who are held to consent to men. The "natu-
> rally" superior, active, and sexually aggressive male makes an initiative, or
> offers a contract, to which a "naturally" subordinate, passive woman
> "consents." An egalitarian sexual relationship cannot rest on this basis; it
> cannot be grounded in "consent." Perhaps the most telling aspect of the
> problem of women and consent is that we lack a language through which
> to help constitute a form of personal life in which two equals freely agree
> to create a lasting association together. (164)

The failure of liberal consent theory rests in its simultaneous assumption
of gender neutrality and its distinctly gendered application. In valorizing
the ideology and action of consent, ostensibly in a gender-neutral fashion,
consent theory leaves unquestioned the genderedness of the structures
that individuals, allegedly, either accept or deny. Women throw a wrench
into this neat system by being constructed as something less than the generic person, and hence more likely to consent to unappealing offers;
feminists further complicate matters by revealing political institutions and
structures as dependent on that constructed inferiority. If marriage and
intercourse were clearly beneficial to women, if they were experiences
that women, as self-interested, autonomous, rational beings, perceived as
appealing and desirable, we would not speak of women's consent, but
rather of their desire.

Specifically with regard to rape, consent theory falters on locating the
ethical wrong of rape in the absence of the victim's consent. To approach
the wrong of rape as embedded in the nonconsensual nature of the act is

inevitably to place the ethical burden on the victim. The ethical question that courts must pursue becomes whether the victim sufficiently communicated her nonconsent, or whether that nonconsent was likely given the history of the victim. Moreover, given the loose definition of consent that is usually applied to matters sexual regarding women, courts have traditionally perceived a variety of behaviors and characteristics to be indicative of some form of consent. The issue of the clothing of the victim, for example, while no longer admissible evidence in some courts of law, was accepted as relevant because it was unthinkable that a woman would dress in a certain way except for the purpose of engaging in sexual activity. The specifics of that activity (the particular partner, the setting, etc.) were assumed to be irrelevant; if the woman was seeking sex (as her clothes, any "reasonable" man could tell, so clearly indicated) and she received it in some form, it was illogical to claim that she did not consent to it. In an astounding conflation of terms, the fact that the woman dressed in a particular way was immediately translated into her consent to virtually any and all sexual encounters.

Because consent is not itself ungendered, because it is an integral part of the modern political theory that, even as it professes equality and liberty, nevertheless endows women with an inferior social status, and because gender relations are structured such that the consent of women is called for in remarkably different situations than that of men and hence evaluated in substantially different ways, consent theory does not provide a stable basis for an understanding of the ethical wrongs of rape. It too easily dismisses the structural inequalities that are inherent in most gender relations, and in its attempt at gender neutrality it ignores the political and bodily significances of sexual difference. Joan McGregor implicitly invokes the relevance of sexual difference when she suggests "specific changes [in rape law] which include requiring affirmative consent and relying upon the standard of the *reasonable woman* as evidence in rape cases" (1994, 232). The implication here is that the perceptions of a reasonable woman may differ importantly from those of the reasonable man who has embodied legal standards of intelligence and common sense. Although McGregor retains the concept of consent as an important one when judging rape cases, her suggestions that consent be affirmative (rather than the mere lack of resistance) and that consent itself be approached as a gendered phenomenon mitigate the disadvantages described above. Whether the U.S. legal system is willing or capable of recognizing differing standards with regard to consent on the basis of sex is dubious; what is clear is that any analysis of the ethical wrongs inherent in the act of rape will fail without due consideration of the implications of sexual difference.

Other Models of the Ethical Wrongs of Rape

We have discussed so far two dominant models of the ethical dimensions of rape: the first, a traditionally patriarchal model that defines rape as the trespass of (male-owned) property, and the second, a traditionally liberal model that locates the absence of consent at the root of the crime. These models by no means exhaust the various theoretical approaches to the ethical wrong of rape, however.

To begin with, there are those theorists who suggest that while rape does in fact constitute a serious ethical wrong, it is not a *very* serious ethical wrong. In a rather astounding article, H. E. Baber argues that "while rape is very bad indeed, the work that most women employed outside the home are compelled to do is more seriously harmful insofar as doing such work damages the most fundamental interests of the victim, what Joel Feinburg called 'welfare interests,' whereas rape typically does not" (1987, 125). Baber rather simplistically locates the ethical wrongness of rape in the fact that it "constitutes a serious harm to the victim" (125), and that, specifically, "virtually everyone has an interest in avoiding involuntary contact with others, particularly unwanted contacts which are intimate or invasive" (126). Rape is here taken as merely another type of assault, essentially ethically similar to a mugging or a beating. In fact, Baber claims that "there is a tendency to exaggerate the *harmfulness* of rape, that is, to make much of the incapacitating psychological traumas that some victims suffer as a result of being raped" (126). Viewing rape as distinct from any other physical crime, however, Baber claims, is a mistake (perhaps because by exaggerating rape's harmfulness we risk becoming unable to analyze rape in a clearheaded, methodical way; or perhaps because by positing the experiences of some rape victims as generic or normal, we end up speaking not about rape in general, but only about some specific cases of rape). We need go no further than those aspects that rape does share with other kinds of assault to consider it a serious crime indeed. Baber also notes that approaching rape as the physical assault that it is will avoid the incriminating questions concerning past sexual history that victims have often faced in the courtroom (127). In general, Baber wishes to approach rape independently of the trauma that rape victims do or do not experience; the exploration of such psychological damage can only obfuscate the actual wrong of the crime while simultaneously unfairly placing the focus on the victim.

Having defined the harm of rape as the involuntary imposing of physical contact, Baber continues to argue that while the crime constitutes a serious harm to the victim's welfare interests (defined as "those which are typically most vital in a personal system of interests, e.g. interests in minimally decent health and the absence of chronic distracting pain, a tolerable environment, economic sufficiency, emotional stability, the absence of intolerable stress and minimal political liberty—all those things which are required for the 'standard person' to pursue any further projects effectively" [128]), it is "not among the most serious harms that can befall a person" (130). Baber defends this rather amazing claim by noting that while rape does diminish the victim's liberty to a certain extent, it does not completely incapacitate the victim. Moreover, the experience of rape does not permanently affect the life of the victim:

> No doubt most rape victims, like victims of violent crime generally, are traumatized. Some rape victims indeed may be so severely traumatized that they incur long-term, severe psychological injury and are rendered incapable of pursuing other projects. For the standard person however, for whom sexuality is a peripheral matter on which relatively little hangs, being raped, though it constitutes a serious assault on the person, does not violate a welfare interest. There is no evidence to suggest that most rape victims are permanently incapacitated by their experiences nor that in the long run their lives are much poorer than they otherwise would have been. (130)

One wonders at this point just who is this standard person for whom sexuality is such a trifling matter.[1]

While Baber's more general point (that there are ethical wrongs more serious and more harmful than rape) may be correct, the narrower claim (that the chronic, tedious work relegated disproportionately to women in the public sphere is a greater harm than rape) is dubious at best. Baber, whose gender is pointedly unspecified, arrives at this conclusion by willfully limiting the significant harmful effects of rape and by describing harms to one's body as essentially temporary. The harms of low-paying, repetitive work, by contrast, are constant, as is the sense that one is compelled by external forces to do such work. The analysis of rape as an embodied experience, however, indicates that the harms of rape are not in fact temporary, precisely because they are bodily; as such, they have enduring effects that extend well beyond the temporal limits of the rape itself. Indeed, the experience of having been raped and the wrongs such an experience includes affect the victim's personhood and agency at a profound level. Baber's analysis is a prime example of an approach to rape that explicitly denies the ethical relevance of the body (and hence of sexuality) and that therefore tends, despite the repeated protests to the contrary, to minimize the harms rape imposes.

The primary purpose of Baber's argument is not, in fact, to shed light on the problem of rape, but rather to demonstrate the severe harms represented by the imposition of tedious, undervalued work. By contrast, Michael Davis takes rape and the problem of imposing just legal punishment on rapists as his main foci. Yet his analysis too criticizes the exaggeration that surrounds ethical and legal approaches to rape. Rape is serious, Davis claims, but not *very* serious (1984, 62–63). Feminist analyses of rape are significantly lacking, according to this argument, in their failure to compare the seriousness of rape with the seriousness of other crimes. Davis is seeking to place the crime of rape in a legal context such that it takes its rightful place as a type of assault, so that just and effective penalties may be accorded to those who commit it.

The standard for "serious" in Davis's analysis is, apparently, the degree to which a given act is perceived as life-threatening, and he notes that crimes that may appear to be more serious than rape are in fact punished less severely than rape (67), a legal situation that, if his argument is tenable, is unjust. However, at several points in this article, Davis demonstrates a marked inability to comprehend the harms rape imposes on a victim. Regarding the loss of personal integrity a victim of rape may suffer, he claims that

> Sex is not the only attribute close to the center of the self. The rest of our physical integrity lies there too, as may some of our property. Even coming home to find one's house vandalized can be a personal affront so unnerving that for years afterward any strange noises around the house will arouse dread. The reaction of a man who has been badly beaten for no particular reason does not seem all that different from that of a woman who has been raped. Both will feel humiliated, frightened, violated. Perhaps there are differences in reaction. . . . Still, it is hard to see that the difference between a beaten man (or woman) and a raped women [*sic*] (or man) can be all that great. Most women would, I think, prefer to be raped if forced to choose between simply being raped and being very badly beaten (but not raped). So, on the personal integrity analysis, simple rape cannot, it seems, even be as severe an invasion of personal integrity as aggravated battery is. (78)

Much of Davis's argument relies heavily on a distinction between simple rape and aggravated rape, a distinction not often recognized in penal codes (although, as Susan Estrich has noted, it has perhaps been functioning implicitly; a study by Harry Kalven and Hans Zeisel "found that juries were four times as willing to convict in the aggravated rape as in the simple one" [Estrich 1987, 4–5]). Davis defines simple rape as being "compelled by brute force to have sexual intercourse (but be otherwise unharmed)," whereas aggravated rape includes the explicit threat and/or imposition of further violence (Davis 1984, 95). Moreover, because he is concerned that the "word 'rape' makes us think of the worst rape, not the typical," (97) most of his examples utilize simple rape as the model. The difficulty with this distinction, obviously, is the rather murky line between the application of "brute force" and the explicit and/or imposed act of violence. Here the ostensible sex neutrality of Davis's analysis serves to obfuscate the fact that, given the sexual hierarchies inherent in a patriarchal culture, the use of brute force by a man on a woman for the purposes of rape not only evokes the threat of further violence but also itself constitutes violence—whether additional violence, in the form of blows, and so forth, is committed. The brute force present in what Davis terms a simple rape occurs within a context where the female victim, justifiably so, can expect an escalation of violence should she choose to resist. Indeed, Davis's own description of the "typical" rape indicates that the submission of the victim is achieved by the recognition of the victim that increasing levels of violence are quite possible, and perhaps likely: "In the typical rape, a man overpowers a weaker woman or just makes it clear that he will do so if she does not do what he wants. The woman quickly gives in to avoid the mess, pain, and danger of a useless fight against superior force" (71). Ignoring for a moment the question of the degree to which this scenario is "typical," nevertheless it is difficult to imagine that the victim of such a serious violation would so quickly "give in" were she not aware of further threats to her safety. Davis's error is in emphasizing the necessity to make such further threats explicit, either verbally or by the disclosure of a weapon. Given dominant sexual dynamics, no such concretization is necessary for those threats to be made real for the victim.

Also problematic is Davis's idea that the degree to which a crime is comparatively serious is directly related to the degree to which it threatens the life of the victim. As chapter 4 demonstrated, understanding rape as an embodied experience and the body as central to personhood entails an acknowledgment of the profoundly intersubjective potential of rape. The social death a rape can impose can qualitatively transform the victim's being. While the strictly biological life of the victim may be continuous, the sense of personhood experienced by the victim may be so drastically changed that she quite literally feels herself to be different from the person who existed prior to the attack. When a person's "life" is understood in somewhat broader terms than Davis implicitly invokes, we may see that an act of rape certainly holds the potential to destroy a victim's life while leaving her strictly physical body more or less intact. Indeed, contrary to Davis's claim, it is not at all clear that most women would prefer "simple" rape to a severe beating; the mere differences between the strictly physical damages imposed by these two types of attack cannot, in and of themselves, account for the harms they are capable of inflicting.

For Davis, the ethical wrong of rape is no different from the ethical wrong of any other kind of assault; indeed, he claims that "rape differs from other violent crime in only two ways: The rape victim is less likely to have precipitated the offense than most victims of violent crime, and she is more likely than most to have her word doubted" (71–72). That is to say, ethically speaking, rape is merely a subset of violent crimes, and its place in any given penal code should represent this proper characterization. Davis does not consider that the social construction of rape (one facet of which is the persistent doubt with which an accusation of rape is greeted) is itself a constitutive element of the crime. He fails to take into account the role which rape plays in social sexual differentiation and the role of sexual difference in general. In arguing for lesser penalties for rape, he admits that "the typical rape does not look all that bad to most people" (108), so that imposing severe penalties would not only make convictions less likely, but would continue to contribute to the "mythology" (109) that inspires women's pervasive fear of rape. Finally, Davis rather improbably suggests that defining rape as a very serious crime may in fact increase the likelihood that it will be committed:

> But is it not at least possible that some men rape because the laws themselves help to maintain the myth that rape is somehow special, more like murder or some other great crime than like dishonorable bullying? To be a rapist, our laws now say, is to be very bad. Might there not be fewer rapes if the law made it clear that rape is just another battery, not a sex crime or a great crime, just another way to make a helpless victim suffer? (109)

To suggest that men rape because laws, in their categorization of rape as a very serious crime, encourage them to do so is to indicate an appalling lack of understanding concerning the political and social role of rape in a patriarchal political structure. It is also to demonstrate that Davis's perspective on the crime of rape focuses far more on the assailant than on the experience of the victim. Because Davis persistently excludes from his analysis the role of sexual difference, the political aspects of rape, and the considerable scope of the damage it can cause, he inevitably ends up comparing rape to experiences that, from the perspective of most women, are significantly and relevantly different. In other words, his analysis excludes from the ethical and legal consideration of rape anything that is specifically sexual and/or bodily, and in so doing achieves an understanding of rape that is markedly narrow and incomplete.

A Kantian approach to rape, such as that taken by Raymond Belliotti (1979), would argue that the crime constitutes a clear violation of the ethical principle that prohibits the use of another human being as a mere means to one's own ends. What is wrong in the case of rape is that the victim is utilized as a mere mechanism for the achievement of the assailant's sexual ends (or, it may be argued, for the achievement of the assailant's political ends, if by that term we mean a general desire for power over another person). Specifically, Belliotti describes all sexual relations as inherently contractual; rape, insofar as it constitutes the denial of reciprocity, involves the violation of a particular contract. Note that in this schema what has been violated, properly speaking, is not the body of the victim, but the victim's right to be a participating, effective, and respected partner in a particular kind of contract. Force, rather than the lack of consent, indicates the immorality of the act: "Since the basis of the sexual encounter is contractual it should be clear that any coercion or force renders the interaction immoral; contracts are not validly consummated if one of the parties is compelled to agree by force or fraud" (Belliotti 1979, 9). This contractual analysis, unlike the models of consent theory, presents the parties involved as equally self-interested beings, who arrive at a mutually beneficial contract that stipulates a set of rights and responsibilities that adhere to each.

The rather severe limitations of this ethical approach to rape are manifested by several of Belliotti's subarguments. In consideration of the "reasonable expectation" that should form the basis of the sexual contract, Belliotti adopts an obviously masculinist perspective:

> Although sexual contracts are not as formal or explicit as corporation agreements the rule of thumb should be the concept of reasonable expectation. If a woman smiles at me and agrees to have a drink I cannot reasonably assume, at least at this point, that she has agreed to spend the weekend with me. On the other hand if she did agree to share a room and bed with me for the weekend I could reasonably assume that she had agreed to have sexual intercourse with me. . . . If there is any doubt concerning whether or not someone has agreed to perform a certain sexual act with another, I would suggest that the doubting party simply ask the other and make the contract more explicit. (9)

The rule of thumb Belliotti invokes is clearly implicated in a socially and politically specific discourse concerning sexuality and sexual behavior, a discourse that may well produce expectations that differ significantly according to the sex of the holder. Although Belliotti accounts for the occurrence of some confusion, he does not impose on the persons involved a responsibility to gain explicitness regarding the contract. Indeed, like consent, the notion of contract grows so inexact as to include situations where the practices agreed to are never articulated. Certainly the agreement to share a bed for a weekend can produce a *hope* that sexual intercourse will follow; Belliotti, however, is inferring an *expectation* that is closely associated with a contractual obligation. A person who has assumed that the sharing of a bed includes sexual intercourse may be surprised to discover that this is not what the other person had in mind. Belliotti's model, however, indicates that the person who does not receive the particular sexual experience that was expected has in some way been wronged, cheated of a good to which he or she feels entitled. One major flaw in Belliotti's contractual model is that it constitutes sexual experiences as, given a certain set of conditions, that which a person may be owed. After all, if sexual encounters are essentially contractual, then it is conceivable to imagine a situation wherein one person, upon completing his or her side of the contract, reasonably demands the other to complete theirs.

Implicit in this model is an assumption that sexuality and its expressions are essentially possessions of subjects, to be doled out on appropriate occasions under appropriate conditions. The model of the contract implies that sexual encounters are, properly understood, exchanges, whereby one person agrees to perform certain acts in exchange for receiving similar acts by the other. To act in such a way that violates that contract is essentially to steal that which does not belong to you. While the victim's sexuality is now properly understood as her own, and not as the property of another person (the father or the husband), nevertheless, it remains understood as the property of an assumedly primarily nonphysical being. Sexuality is thus constructed as under the control of a rational, autonomous, and distinctly disembodied subject who, in order to be constituted as a full human being, must maintain its authoritative position over the body in its care.

An understanding of rape as an embodied experience, however, demonstrates that the contractual model of rape is severely lacking. In its definition of the subject as essentially rational and intellectual, and hence as properly "in charge" of matters bodily and sexual, it fails to recognize that persons are fundamentally, not peripherally, embodied. Sexuality is therefore not to be understood as a possession of an essentially intellectual, disembodied being, but rather as an ineluctable element of being, a facet of personhood no less relevant than one's capacity for rational thought. My sexuality is a central part of my being; it is not something that I "own" and can give away, because such a model of possession implies that "I" exist as myself separate from my sexuality.

Rather than subjecting sexual encounters to a discourse of property, and therefore to an economy of exchange, we should understand them as intersubjective engagements by which each involved person is simultaneously affecting the other's bodily personhood and in turn being affected. To interact with another person sexually is not to acquire a set of goods, nor is it to give a set of goods. It is to express and fulfill one's own sexual desires, needs, and beings while simultaneously engaging with those of one's partner. Moreover, the simultaneous expression and engagement allow one's sexuality to be deeply influenced by that of the other. In this intersubjective encounter, the distinction between the desires of the partners can become blurred, such that producing sexual pleasure for one's partner can itself become sexually pleasurable.

Because sexuality is central to one's subjectivity, it cannot be understood as a good to which another person, in any context, is owed. The degree to and manner in which each person can be affected by a sexual encounter differ radically among the contexts in which such an encounter may take place, as well as among differing subjects. All of this is to say that the meanings of a sexual encounter are significantly indeterminate. An invocation of a "reasonable expectation" fails to recognize this indeterminacy, and the invocation of any "expectation" at all implies that a person can have a "right" to the sexuality of another. Moreover, expectations that are constructed as reasonable under a political structure that insistently hierarchizes the sexes may not ultimately appear as reasonable (and certainly not as beneficial) to those consistently dominated by that structure, namely, women. In the light of the various differences that an emphasis on embodiment demonstrates to be fundamental, a Kantian approach, in its explicit or implicit dependence on a universal standard of reasonableness, is incapable of sufficiently accounting for the distinctly gendered (and otherwise differentiated) yet dominant harms an act of rape imposes.

Another perspective on the ethical wrongs of rape emphasizes its implication within a larger system of domination and oppression. Keith Burgess-Jackson distinguishes the radical feminist theory of rape from the liberal theory by an emphasis on the systematic nature of rape, that is, its role in a sexual hierarchy that renders women socially and politically inferior. Rape in this context is a form of degradation, by which other (perhaps less blatant) methods of control are strengthened and reinforced (Burgess-Jackson 1996, 53). Given the assumption of women's lesser status, questions of consent are rendered effectively moot; compulsory heterosexuality imposes sexual experiences on women constantly, and rape is but another example of such an imposition. It is not the case, then, that rape is distinct from other acts of heterosexual intercourse due to the lack of consent on the woman's part, but that heterosexuality itself (and, therefore, we must assume, virtually all heterosexual activity) is mutually exclusive of women's consent. The theories of Catharine MacKinnon, described in earlier chapters at some length, fall squarely within this category. Susan Rae Peterson, in arguing that the ethical wrong of rape lies not in the harms imposed by any one act, but rather in the social coercion that results from the constant threat of rape, notes that "[b]ecause of the practice of rape, women are denied not only their personal rights and liberties, but their political ones as well" (1977, 367). Rape is here understood as part of an interlocking set of practices, demands, and behaviors that serve to perpetuate the social and political domination of men over women. From this perspective, rape is constituted not as a horrific aberration from normal, healthy sexual encounters, but rather as a necessary element of a particular political structure. "What is wrong with rape, then, is that it is really not wrong at all" (367).

Pamela Foa offers another analysis of rape as an act of complicity with a fundamentally immoral system. "The special wrongness of rape is due to, and is only an exaggeration of, the wrongness of our sexual interactions in general" (1977, 347). Foa in particular notes that the wrong inherent in rape is (or at least appears to be) significantly different from the wrongs that accrue as a result of other types of physical attack. On this basis, she rejects any theories of rape that do not sufficiently account for the particularly sexual aspects of rape or reduce rape to a subset of assault. To articulate the wrongness of rape, then, we must explore its place on a sexual continuum, or, more exactly, on a continuum of sexual behavior ordered by standards of morality or ethical acceptability. On closer examination of standards of sexual ethics—which are, of course, founded on distinctly patriarchal values—Foa concludes that rape can only be understood not as an exception, but as a paradigm:

> In spite of the fact, I believe, that as a society we share the *belief* that sex is only justified in intimate relationships, we act to avoid real intimacy at almost any cost. We seem to be as baffled as our predecessors were about the place of intimacy in our sexual and social lives. And this is, I think,

because we are afraid that real intimacy creates or unleashes sexually wanton relationships, licentious lives—and this we view as morally repugnant. At the same time, we believe that sex in the absence of an intimate relationship is whoring and is therefore also morally repugnant. It is this impossible conflict which I think shows us that we will be able to make sense of our response to rape only if we look at rape as the model of all our sexual interactions, not as its antithesis. (355)

The dominant model for all sexual behavior is essentially one of violence, in that the social structure imposed upon sexual interactions demands that girls and women fend off the advances of sexually aggressive boys and men, who are in turn responding to social demands to enact such aggressive roles. The aggressive male attempts to achieve an end that the female (not acting out of self-interest or in response to her own organic needs, but rather engaging in behavior that she has been taught to be socially appropriate and responsible) attempts to foil or at least forestall. Neither party is motivated by authentic and mutual desires for pleasure. Instead, their sexualities are shaped by the mores of a social structure that views sexual desire with at the very least some ambivalence, such that sexual encounters become little more than a struggle for power.

[B]oys and girls have no way to tell each other what gives them pleasure and what not, what frightens them and what not; there are only violence, threats of violence, and appeals to informing on one or the other to some dreaded peer or parental group. This is a very high-risk, high-stake game, which women and girls, at least, often feel may easily become rape. (Foa 1977, 356)

Because we are taught that "sexual desires are desires women ought not to have and men must have" (357), sexuality itself is necessarily constructed as a battlefield. Rape is normal because feminine resistance and the masculine overcoming of that resistance are both structurally endemic to this model. Constructing women's sexuality and therefore their sexual behavior as necessarily separate from (in fact, opposed to) the possibility of sexual pleasure necessarily and simultaneously constructs men's sexuality and sexual behavior as, essentially, violence. Unless we understand sexual encounters as including the possibility of women's sexual pleasure as a motivating principle, then all heterosexual intercourse, including that which occurs in marriage, must necessarily occur over the protests of women. Hence, "Rape is only different in degree from the quintessential sexual relationship: marriage" (Foa 1977, 357).

The ethical wrong of rape, according to this model, is thus the same ethical wrong that is at the basis of such a model of sexual relationships, that is, the failure to understand sexual desire as belonging to both genders and as morally acceptable and even valuable. The ambivalence toward sexuality results in a translation of sorts; we cannot deal with the messiness and intensity of sexual desire, so we rewrite it as a power struggle. Violence is not only eroticized, but becomes the standard of eroticism.

Foa's analysis constitutes an understanding of rape that highlights its embodied elements to a far greater extent than the theories previously discussed. Her theory is admirably more focused on the sexual content of rape, rather than the strictly violent elements, and as such she approaches the ethical difficulties that the sexuality of rape presents. However, her solution to this ethical problem—that lovers treat each other as friends rather than as enemies—demonstrates its limitations. Foa defines the problem of rape in terms of society's difficulties with "the legitimacy of sexual pleasure" (357). Given that definition, she is able to claim that the answer is simply more honest, open talk among the sexes concerning sex and sexuality. In making such a claim, she underestimates both the scope and the ramifications of the sexual discourse she invokes (of which the ambivalence concerning sexual pleasure is only a part). That is, while her analysis emphasizes the bodily, sexual aspects of rape, ultimately she understands such bodily matters as relatively easily addressed by the speech of a rational subject. In other words, she does not question that the subjects developed in the context of such a discourse, as well as the sexualities about which she exhorts us to be more open, have themselves been qualitatively and profoundly shaped by those values. Foa assumes that there is some actual and true sexual desire that persists beneath the imposed narrative of violence and resistance; that women especially, when simply given the opportunity, will be capable of articulating authentic truths concerning their sexualities, truths which have simply been buried.

The analysis of the embodied subject, however, indicates that while sexuality is an integral and inherent facet of personhood, the nature of specific sexualities is indelibly marked by the surrounding political and social discourse. There is no truly authentic level of sexuality that can be exhumed by mere, even if sincere, honesty and openness. The subjects undertaking that project of openness remain as mired in the discourse as they ever were; while local and partial acts of resistance to that discourse are possible, the attempt to step outside the totality of the discourse is nothing short of hopeless. Foa's solution to the problem of rape and her analysis of its ethical wrongs assume that sexual subjects can stand outside the constituting discourses of sexuality by strategic use of language, an assumption that is untenable.

Foa's analysis is somewhat narrower than other theories that stress rape's political complicity in that she specifies a certain aspect of the discourse of sexual relations as particularly culpable. Peterson's analysis, for example, looks to the larger patriarchal motive of controlling women's mobility (and sexuality) as means of placing rape within a given continuum. One difficulty with all these attempts to articulate the ethical wrong of rape, however, is that they tend to be focused solely on rape as a larger social phenomenon, and not as an experience imposed on certain, and importantly differentiated, individuals. This is not to say that their analysis is not in some profound sense meaningful; rape does indeed have an important political and social function in the context of a patriarchal system. However, such an analysis proves less helpful when we aim to articulate the wrongs a particular act of rape confers on a victim.

Determining the precise ethical wrongs of rape demands a consideration of both the personal and the political harms it entails. Many of the ethical theories discussed above tend to emphasize one aspect of rape to the exclusion of the other. They understand rape either as an act committed against an (allegedly sex-neutral) individual, in which case the wrongs involved center around that individual's right to autonomy and self-determination, or as an act committed against a group, the class of women, in which case it is difficult to distinguish between the harms suffered by an actual victim of rape and those suffered by women in general due to the pervasive threat of rape. To arrive at a more comprehensive, complex understanding of the ethical wrongs of rape necessitates an acknowledgment of how these two differing levels of the effects of rape, the social and the individual, are co-constituted. In approaching rape as an embodied experience, we reject any easy distinction between the political realm and the personal, while simultaneously refusing to view individuals as merely and utterly obedient replications of models embedded in political discourse. From this perspective, because rape is both a political phenomenon and an individual experience of an embodied subject, the wrongs of rape have everything to do with the socially constituted body and everything to do with sexual difference and sexual politics.

The Ethics of Sexual Difference

The discussion in chapter 3 of the embodied subject produced an emphasis on the sexually differentiated nature of embodied persons. As embodied beings, subjects are differentiated from each other in a variety of ways, including sexual difference. Rosi Braidotti, for example, articulates sexual difference as a major axis of differentiation among subjects, and asserts that the thinking of sexual difference, insofar as it questions and undermines the allegedly sexually neuter category of "human" in masculinist thought, must remain primary to feminist questioning. It is important here to understand that while many of these thinkers emphasize sexual difference itself, they do not consider all differences among subjects to be reducible to that particular difference. Some consider sexual difference to be the most fundamental difference, given its strictly biological necessity (Irigaray, as we have seen, notes that the existence of human beings depends on this particular difference). However, the facticity of sexual difference is utilized theoretically to urge a consideration of difference in general. Sexual difference functions as a kind of lever of intervention that interrupts the assumptions of similarities and universals in order to allow all sorts of differences to be explored and recognized. To emphasize difference is to resist the adoption of singular, universal standards concerning personhood, and so to thwart the exclusionary effects of such generic models. Elizabeth Grosz eschews even the theoretical question of "the" body, insisting that bodies must be understood as essentially differentiated and multiple, and that sexual difference is one major means of such differentiation. The subject that emerges from this body of thought is thus an irreducibly, if indeterminately, *sexed* being, whose subjectivity is informed, influenced, and indeed limited by, among other factors, the play of sexual difference. With regard to the issues raised in this chapter, the questions then become, How is this factor of sexual difference relevant ethically? How does understanding rape as an embodied experience change our understanding of the ethical wrongs inherent in it?

In exploring the ways sexual difference affects the ethical wrongs of rape, this analysis will rely heavily on the theories of Luce Irigaray, whose thought represents the most considered articulation of the ethical dimensions of sexual difference. Her theories of difference constitute a direct challenge to the valorized unity of Western metaphysics, a unity that denies sexual difference while elevating the masculine to the status of the norm and the real. This masquerading of the masculine as the generic, as the sexually neutral norm, is *ethically* significant because it foists on an indelibly gendered world a demand of universalism that necessarily renders one aspect of human being lesser, weaker, more incomplete, and ultimately less valuable. For Irigaray, sexual difference is a necessary element to the human being: "The natural, aside from the diversity of its incarnations or ways of appearing, is at least *two:* male and female" (1996, 37).

The goal of sex-neutrality, particularly as a means of achieving liberation for women, is illusory and destructive, for it attempts to erase the significance of difference in the name of a false unity. Moreover, it is precisely difference that allows for alliance, love, connection. The logic of sameness and unity precludes the possibility of wonder (which, as Irigaray [1993a, 72–82] reminds us, Descartes names as the first philosophical passion). If each human being is fundamentally similar to every other, if we recognize no specificity to types of human beings and no relevance of the rather obvious ways we differ from each other, then we cannot view each other in wonder. If we are all of the same cloth, then we are all known; and so, under the logic of patriarchal unity, the scope of that which is feminine is clearly delineated, known, not wondrous, and in fact, not qualitatively (but only quantitatively) differentiated from that of the masculine. In order to make possible connections among differing types of people, connections that do not demand the domination of one person or type of person over another, we must not reduce difference to unity, but rather recognize it as untranscendable, fundamental, and primary. When we see the other merely as a reflection or reduction of that which is ourselves, we do not approach (and therefore cannot love) the other in his or her proper specificity. Only when we recognize the other *as profoundly other,* only where there is the abyss of difference that separates us from the other, can we truly love. Barring the recognition of difference, we are doomed to loving nothing but ourselves or replications of ourselves.

For Irigaray, it is not only the case that sexual difference is the most fundamental difference among human subjects, the difference that is a necessary condition of the existence of every human being; it is philosophically and ethically significant that it is this particular difference that has been denied by thousands of years of Western thought. In failing to acknowledge the significance of sexual difference, masculinist thought has presented the male not only as generic, not only as universal, but also as complete in and of itself, as holding within it all that is important and valuable for and about the human being. To claim that the "natural" for human being is always at least two is to understand that no one kind of being contains the entirety of human capabilities or experience. For Irigaray, recognizing difference entails recognizing the inherent limitations of any one sex, as well as of any one person:

Man is not, in fact, absolutely free. That is not to say that he is enslaved to a nature and he must overcome it. Nor does it mean he is a slave. He is *limited.* His natural completion lies in *two* humans. Man knows of only one part of human nature, yet this limit is the condition of becoming and of creation. . . . It is a mistake, therefore, to claim to be free and sovereign over nature. As I am only half of the world, I am not free in the way this is generally conceived. I am free, on the other hand, and as I should be, to be what or who I am: one half of human kind. (1996, 41)

The only thing that is universal is difference itself. Therefore, no one being or type of being can represent the whole of human being, experience, or capacity. To acknowledge the limitations that difference entails is necessarily to acknowledge a mutual and distinctively nonhierarchical interdependence. The projects properly belonging to human beings are never solitary ones: "To remember that we must go on living and creating worlds is our task. But it can be accomplished only through the combined efforts of the two halves of the world: the masculine and the feminine" (1993a, 127). The totality of that world remains beyond the capacity of one or the other sex. Indeed, Irigaray's work emphasizes that the wholeness of that totality is itself illusory, for the whole is irreducibly split by difference.

Because no humans exist who are neuter, unsexed, Irigaray asserts that any ethics, science, philosophy, or law based on such a model inevitably addresses a being that does not exist. This is especially true with regard to political structures that claim to endow individuals with civil rights. Because of the model of the individual with which these structures begin—the notoriously sexually neutral individual, whose bodily specificities are rendered irrelevant in the light of the universalism of his rational, autonomous capacities—they inevitably presuppose citizens not only to be male, but to be male *and* universal, masculine *and* generic, and indeed citizens who are universal and generic *because* they are male. Although such structures and such models benefit men at the cost of women's social and political status, nevertheless they also fail to approach men in their actual limitedness:

> There are still no civil rights proper to women and to men. This is particularly true for women, since existing law is better suited to men than women inasmuch as men have been the model for citizenship for centuries, the adult female citizen being poorly defined by rights to equality that do not meet her needs. Strictly speaking, there is still no civil law in our era that makes human persons of men and women. As sexed persons, they remain in natural immediacy. And this means that real persons still have no rights, since there are only men and women; there are no neuter individuals. (1996, 21)

As a remedy to this situation, Irigaray suggests the notion of sexed rights (1994, 67–87; 1993b, 81–92; 1993c, 1–5). While at first glance this suggestion may seem remarkably tame, especially insofar as it retains at least the language of rights, when understood against Irigaray's larger project of the recognition of sexual difference (and the depth of the political and philosophical ramifications of the denial of that difference) its truly radical nature becomes clear. In proposing that certain civil rights be extended to women qua women, and to men qua men, Irigaray is undermining the most basic assumption of modern political theory: namely, that all humans are fundamentally similar and therefore equal. Endowing sexed citizens with sexed rights would allow for the visibility of the political significances of sexual difference. No one kind of citizen would be the model citizen, and no types of citizens would be perceived as inferior or lesser than any other kind. All would be marked, all would be differentiated, and all would be recognized as limited and specific aspects of a totality that is not, fundamentally, a unity.

The Ethical Wrongs of Rape

Irigaray's emphasis on the fundamentally sexually differentiated nature of the human species—an emphasis both global (in its claims concerning the species as a whole, or rather not as a unified whole, but as a differentiated entity) and local (in its claims concerning each individual as irrevocably sexed)—holds a host of implications concerning the ethical problem of rape. Primarily, it insists that the consideration of any ethical problem must address the significance of sexual difference in particular, and difference in general. For Irigaray, it is difference that makes ethics both necessary and possible. Ethics are necessary because it is the other's otherness, the fact that the other is irreducible to myself, that calls me to recognize that my needs are not necessarily the needs of all, and only an ethics of otherness can inspire me to value and consider the needs of the other as significant. Ethics are possible because without the existence and recognition of difference, there can be no movement among persons, no speech, no love, no alliances. If the other is reducible to myself, then all love is self-love, all speech is monologue, all sex is masturbatory.[2]

With regard to rape, the ethical significance of sexual difference is at least twofold. On the one hand, as contemporary feminist theories of the body have already suggested, there should not be an assumption of a single, universally experienced and imposed wrong of rape. The phenomenon of rape will, it may be assumed, itself be differentiated not only by sex but by other factors of personhood. It is notable that many theoretical attempts to discern the ethical wrong of rape have explicitly sought a formulation that holds in any and all given cases of rape. In many cases, such as the definition of rape as primarily violence, this search for universalism has inspired, implicitly or explicitly, the denial of the relevance of the sexes of the persons involved. Irigaray's analysis would assert that the goal of universalism will doom the project to failure. To reduce the experience of rape, which occurs only to women and to men and never to some unsexed being, to a gender-neutral theory is necessarily to miss its most trenchant ethical meanings.

To say that any given experience of rape is differentiated by bodily differences such as sex, race, age, class, and so forth is not to claim that certain experiences of rape are by definition "worse" than others or constitute by definition graver ethical harms than others. Because we can understand embodiment as fundamental to all embodied subjects, and because sexuality is a significant element of embodiment, it is necessary to approach all rapes as serious, invasive attacks on the integrity of the victim's embodied subjectivity. It is impossible to claim that some women, due to their race, age, class, or other characteristic, are incapable of being severely harmed by rape. It is possible, however, to claim that such differentiations can and do give rise to different kinds of harms, and that those specified harms need to be approached in their specificity, and not with regard to a hierarchical standard of gravity that assumes a universal, normal, or generic experience of embodiment.

The second layer of ethical significance relates to the model of personhood and subjectivity that underlies Irigaray's ethical concerns. If an ethics of sexual difference demands a recognition of the inherent and distinct worth of the two sexes, such that each views the other with wonder and itself with an appropriate sense of limitation and discreteness, the act of rape can be understood as a violent destruction and denial of the difference that underlies the possibility of personhood. This destruction and denial are not to be understood in abstract or merely theoretical terms; rather, because the target of the assault is not only a body, but a sexed body, and because the differentiated nature of embodiment is the foundation of the integrity of personhood, rape constitutes a physical, sexual (and sexed) assault on the personhood of the victim.

In the act of rape, the assailant reduces the victim to a nonperson. He (for the overwhelming majority of rapists are male, another aspect of the sexually differentiated nature of the act) denies the victim the specificity of her (for the overwhelming majority of rape victims are female) own being, and constructs her sexuality as a mere means by which his own purposes, be they primarily sexual or primarily motivated by the need for power, are achieved. Because this assault is bodily, it is sexed; and because it is sexed, the scope of its harms includes the personhood of the victim. The dominance inherent in an act of rape, by which the assailant forces his incarnate will on the victim, is a hierarchical structure by whose unity and coherence the victim's difference from the assailant—her ontological, ethical, personal distinctness—is stamped out, erased, annihilated. One member of the roundtable that inspired Foucault's somewhat notorious comments concerning rape suggested that rape was "a sort of rapid masturbation in someone else's body" (Foucault 1988, 202). While this characterization was offered in demonstration of the allegedly nonsexual nature of rape (as if masturbation were not sexual), it more clearly illustrates the destruction of the other's subjectivity that rape represents. For in failing to recognize the difference that constitutes the possibility of personhood, the difference of the other, the rapist constructs his victim as a mere projection or reflection of his self. The domination inherent in the act of rape is now understood not as a statement of difference but rather as a production of identity, a destruction of difference whereby the woman becomes ontologically indistinct from her assailant. She is reduced to *nothing but* a means for the satisfaction of his desires for sexualized power; her embodied, sexually differentiated subjectivity is (temporarily, but destructively) nullified by his violent imposition of a sexual act.

The ethical wrongs of rape, its denial and destruction of full personhood for women, are mirrored in both the personal experiences of rape and the social and political functionings of the phenomenon of rape. Sharon Marcus analyzes the scripting function of rape, claiming insightfully that it actually produces the (passive) femininity of the victim (1992, 391). Note, however, that this femininity is not ontologically distinct from the identity of the masculine conqueror. The former exists to create and shore up the latter; similarly, the historical dominance of the male over the female has constituted not a project of differentiation that is remedied by the equality of identity, but rather as a refusal of true, that is, unhierarchicized, difference. The pervasive threat of rape constitutes an element of the overall social and political dominance of men, to such an extent that the threat literally shapes the details of feminine bodies. The beings produced in such a context are assumedly to be wholly derivative of the dominant beings. Their distinctness from the dominating class is both ignored and destroyed.

The actual experience of rape enacts a similar dynamic on a more individual level, as the rapist constrains the mobility of the victim, disregards or disbelieves her stated desires (or does not seek them out), and refuses to view her sexuality and her sex as anything other than tools for his use. In violating the sexed body of a woman, the rapist is undermining the possibility (at least temporarily, and more likely with significant subsequent ramifications) of the victim's personhood.

The general ethical wrong of rape, then, is to be located in its particularly sexual and sexed assault on the personal, subjective, and bodily integrity of the victim. It is a violent, sexual, bodily denial and destruction of a person's sexually specific intersubjective being. While there are other means, and even other physical means, of attack that undermine personal and bodily integrity, the sexual nature of rape can result in a differing set of harms. In a society where women are constantly threatened by the possibility of rape, an actual assault will lend the threat new credence, which may result in a heightened lack of mobility for the victim. In a case of a protracted series of rapes (that is, where a woman is raped continuously over a long period of time), harms may include the destruction of any sense of sexuality at all, or a sexuality that is centered around the familiarity of abuse and violence.

Not only can rape produce a different set of harms than other types of attacks, but different rapes can produce different types of harms. This does not contradict the general claim above, simply because there are many ways that undermining of a rape victim's personhood can be experienced and expressed. The wrongs that an act of rape can impose on a rape victim can all be linked to fundamental aspects of embodied subjectivity, but because embodiment is also the site of differentiation among subjects, those wrongs will vary from case to case.

What are some of the harms that can be imposed by an act of rape? In their groundbreaking articulation of rape trauma syndrome, Ann Wolbert Burgess and Lynda Lytle Holmstrom note the common occurrence of sleep and eating disorders, the development of phobias "specific to the circumstances of the rape" (1979, 41), and disruptions in the victim's social and sexual lifestyle. The authors describe two distinct phases to the syndrome: "the immediate or acute phase, in which the victim's lifestyle is completely disrupted by the rape crisis, and the long-term process, in which the victim must reorganize this disrupted lifestyle. The syndrome includes physical, emotional, and behavioral stress reactions which result from the person being faced with a life-threatening event" (35). Judith Lewis Herman argues that experiences of repeated trauma and assault result in a set of symptoms significantly different from those resulting from single experiences of trauma:

> People subjected to prolonged, repeated trauma develop an insidious, progressive form of post-traumatic stress disorder that invades and erodes the personality. While the victim of a single acute trauma may feel after the event that she is "not herself," the victim of chronic trauma may

feel herself to be changed irrevocably, or she may lose the sense that she has any self at all. (1992, 86)

As a means of recognizing these relevant differences, Herman proposes the diagnostic title of "complex post-traumatic stress disorder" (119).

The sexual nature of the crime of rape endows it with a set of potential harms that distinguishes it from other experiences of trauma. Rape victims must deal with the possibility of sexually transmitted diseases and pregnancy; although, in the case of a single experience of rape, the chances of being impregnated or infected are slim (Holmes 1999), nevertheless they present the victim with horrific prospects. Internal genital injuries, some of which are difficult to view by gross visualization (i.e., without additional technology; see Slaughter and Brown 1991), can include abrasions, tears, and cuts (Boyer and Dalton 1997). Beyond these effects, victims of sexual abuse also face the difficulty of rebuilding their sexual lives:

> Rebuilding a sense of control is especially problematic in sexual relations. In the aftermath of rape, survivors almost universally report disruption in their previously established sexual patterns. Most wish to withdraw entirely from sex for some period of time. Even after intimate relations are resumed, the disturbances in sexual life are slow to heal. In sexual intercourse, survivors frequently reencounter not only specific stimuli that produce flashbacks but also a more general feeling of being pressured or coerced. . . . Because of entrenched norms of male entitlement, many women are accustomed to accommodating their partners' desires and subordinating their own, even in consensual sex. In the aftermath of rape, however, many survivors find they can no longer tolerate this arrangement. (Herman 1992, 65)

A rape victim may find herself unable or unwilling to engage in those sexual activities which she enjoyed before the attack. The experience of being sexually assaulted may produce persistently negative reactions to any sexual experience, causing a profound strain on any relationship that included sexual activity. Linda E. Ledray writes that "approximately one-fourth of rape survivors decide to completely abstain from sex after the assault" (1986, 86) and notes, interestingly, that "while the frequency of sexual activity usually returns to normal after three to six months, it often takes longer for women to enjoy sex again" (87). The victim may find herself wary of any emotional intimacy, especially if the rape took place in the context of a relationship that demanded her trust and vulnerability; Deborah Rose notes that "victims are usually left with profound mistrust of others and themselves as a result of the rape" (1991, 87), and cites this mistrust as a hindrance to the victim's pursuit of psychotherapy or other forms of healing.

A rape victim may be robbed of her sense of mobility and freedom, hampered by a fear that has been proven to be justified. In such a case, the space in which her body may move may be severely restricted, resulting in a far narrower world than she lived in previously (Herman 1992, 46). A rape victim may react to the horrific experience of not having control over her own body by engaging in strict and sometimes dangerous dietary practices, or in self-mutilation, as if to solidify her own agency even at the risk of her health (108–9). Panic attacks may cause her to lose her job, and the weight of depression may keep her bedridden.[3] Rape victims are far more likely than non–rape victims to attempt or consider suicide, and are more likely to develop problems with substance abuse (National Victim Center and Crime Victims Research and Treatment Center 1992, 7).

All of these, and other, harms refer directly to the bodily and intersubjective aspects of rape. Moreover, they all result in a qualitative lessening of the joys and possibilities of intersubjective personhood. Nancy Venable Raine describes the oddly numbing and long-lasting effects of the posttraumatic stress disorder resulting from her rape:

> The numbness associated with PTSD seems to spread out over the entire emotional landscape, like fog. Not only is pain blunted, but pleasure as well. Of all the consequences of the rape, this was the hardest to perceive and the hardest to endure. It was living with novocaine in the heart, condemned to life on the glassy surface of the emotional horse latitudes. I felt cut off from everything and, as the years passed, even from the memory of emotional life as I had once experienced it. My capacity to feel deep concern about my feelings or the feelings of others seemed to have been freeze-dried, like instant coffee. The problem was, I didn't remember what brewed coffee tasted like. (Raine 1998, 61)

The bodily, sexually specific act of rape, in refusing and temporarily destroying the intersubjective being of the victim, in forcing on that victim an identity and being that are wholly derivative of the motives of the assailant, *makes the victim less of a person.* It can do so in many ways—by increasing fear, limiting mobility, tainting the meaning of touch, imposing mental and physical damage—but this threat against the personhood of the victim is always experienced on a visceral, bodily level.

To determine the harms imposed by any particular case of rape, we must make two presumptions. First, in keeping with the significance of difference in general, we must presume that different rapes committed in different contexts impose different harms. That is, we must resist the urge to recognize only those harms that are present in each and every case of rape as the "real" wrongs inherent in the crime. The multiplicity of rape as an embodied experience indicates that such ethical universalism is not only illusory but dangerous in that it could serve to define some rapes as less harmful, or perhaps not harmful at all, if they fail to incorporate those particular harms. Second, bodily harms (defined not as merely physical, but as all aspects of embodiment that are central to personhood) must be posited as central, not peripheral, to the determination of the particular ethical wrongs inherent in the crime. When we recognize that the victim is an embodied and therefore sexed subject and that different harms may accrue to differently sexed beings, we preserve the significance of sexual difference in respect to rape without necessarily invoking the feminine sexual culpability that has so often marked legal approaches to rape.

The loss of the universal promises an approach to feminine sexuality that is not by definition adversarial. By understanding feminine sexuality as significantly differentiated from male sexuality, while simultaneously understanding male sexuality not as a generic, but as limited by its own differentiation, we free women who are victims of rape from the assumption that they (contrary to their statements) actually desired the sexual encounter in question. They would no longer be assumed to be either lying or merely regretting that sexual encounter, nor would questions concerning clothes or past or present sexual behavior be automatically relevant. Feminine sexuality would be released from the assumptions concerning consent (i.e., that women said no when they meant yes) or complicity (that women somehow "asked for it"). These models present feminine sexuality as distinctively derivative, in that their approach is concerned solely with its effects on male sexuality; the implicit claim is that all of feminine sexuality is oriented ultimately around the specificities of male sexuality. Acknowledging and emphasizing sexual difference in such a way that refuses the attempt to hierarchize would render moot these questions while retaining the significance of sexuality in the crime of rape.

The integrity and identity of an embodied subject are intertwined necessarily with that subject's sexuality and gender. Rape, as a particularly sexual violation, is a bodily assault that particularly and blatantly invokes the sexuality of both the assailant and the victim. Because of the social and political functions of rape, as well as its focus on those bodily parts most invested with sexuality, it constitutes a wrong that is persistently and decidedly sexed. While the particular harms imposed on victims may differ from case to case, they are all linked to the bodily aspects of personhood, and especially those aspects related to the victim's sexuality.

Possibilities for Resistance

U nderstanding and approaching rape as the experience of an embodied subject allows for the avoidance of the dichotomies of sex/violence and self/society that have marked previous feminist theories of rape. Rape is not a mere act of violence, as Brownmiller suggests, but demonstrates the collusion of violence and sexual hierarchies. Nor is it, as MacKinnon claims, a mere extension of compulsory heterosexuality that writes large women's lack of agency under a patriarchal social structure. That social structure limits yet does not obviate the possibility of any feminine agency with regard to sexuality. Discourses of sexuality and discourses of violence are importantly and significantly related, but they are not symmetrically mapped. Rape as embodied experience accounts for both the distinguishing violence of rape and its sexual content. It thus appears as significantly distinct from other acts of heterosexual sex without being stripped of its sexual meaning.

What implications does the analysis of rape as an embodied experience hold for legal theory? Primarily, it questions the efficacy of legal reforms with regard to rape that utilize sex-neutral terms. To approach an instance of rape with the presumption of the irrelevance of the sexes of the parties involved is to render invisible a significant portion of the experience of the rape victim. As Drucilla Cornell writes, "the struggle against the enforcement of the gender divide in law or in other contexts cannot be separated from the affirmation of feminine sexual difference—which is not to be identified with the properties 'correlated' within current conventions with actual women—as a crucial movement in the displacement of gender hierarchy" (1991, 9). Cornell's later work on the imaginary do-main may be exceedingly helpful here, in that we can understand rape as an action that prohibits for women the right to "the moral space necessary for equivalent evaluation of our sexual difference as free and equal per-sons" (1998, 14). Although Cornell disagrees significantly with Irigaray on the point of sexed rights (30), she does insist that the law approach the individual as a sexual being without making assumptions as to the content of that individual's sexuality. This combination of assuming the relevance of sexed being without presuming the meaning of that sexed-ness is at the heart of the imaginary domain; it is also the direction in which legal re-form should move if it is to address rape in a more equitable and more feminist fashion.

Legal reforms need to be structured so that the embodied and sexual significances of rape are speakable and representable in the courtroom, without subjecting the victim to further traumatization. The ethical harms detailed in the previous chapter often relate directly to the sexual mean-ings of an act of rape, including its inherent refusal to acknowledge the embodied (and therefore differentiated) subjectivity of the victim. Those feminist theories that have encouraged a refusal of the sexual significance of rape—those that, in other words, suggested that it be seen as just another assault, with no more sexual meaning than other assaults—sought to put a stop to the persistent questioning of the victim's sexual past and behavior as well as her attire and justification for being in certain places at certain times. Yet rape is not just another type of assault. It differs in its explicitly sexualized method of violence, and thus imposes different types of harms upon a victim than other means of assault. Legal defini-tions of rape need to account for its particularly sexual content without exposing the victim to questions that assume her guilt or complicity. One way out of this conundrum, as I suggest in chapter 4, is to assume that rape is a sexual act, but not mutually so. From this perspective, it is possible to claim that rape as an embodied experience is sexual, but not sex, thus forestalling any questions concerning victim culpability.

Approaching rape as an embodied experience indicates that resistance to the phenomenon of rape is not to be limited to battles fought in the courtroom or the legislature. Much of feminist consciousness raising has depended on the speaking of women's stories, and indeed, it was only this speaking that allowed the phenomenon of rape to be acknowledged as a pervasive, society-wide problem. However, Renee Heberle (1996) has re-cently questioned the transformative possibilities inherent in such contin-uing discussions: "[W]hat if in emphasizing the strategy of piecing to-gether our reality as a rape culture through speakouts and detailed descriptions of experience, we participate in setting up the event of sexual violence as a defining moment of women's possibilities for being in the world? . . . Simply put, what if this strategy furthers the reification of masculinist dominance?" (1996, 65). My analysis of rape as an embodied experience and the role the threat of rape plays in the construction of a distinctly feminine bodily comportment indicates that sexual violence, at the present moment, is a defining element of women's experience, albeit not a determinative one. Nonetheless, Heberle's point is well taken. Stressing the pervasiveness of rape, the degree to which present-day culture is saturated in its meanings and occurrences, risks presenting and re-presenting women as the victims (or pre-victims) they have been constructed to be. Yet it cannot be denied that sexual violence is a persistent fact in most women's lives. How are we to balance these two insights? How can we account for the depth of the effects of rape on women's lives, indeed on their bodies, without reducing women to passive, helpless victims of constant sexual threats?

As I argued in chapter 5, the threat of rape is one that is found in the details of a particular but socially significant form of feminine bodily comportment. Claudia Card argues that the feminine body, as constructed by a patriarchal discourse, is a particularly "easy victim" for rapists:

> Women who lack martial training are an easy mark for those who would communicate the message of domination. Women in patriarchies are commonly unarmed and untrained for physical combat. Perpetrators need fear little direct reprisal. Where there is concern about reprisals, the only troublesome witness is easily eliminable. This suggests that strategies of resistance would have women become armed and skilled in the use of weapons and in other methods of defense and self-defense, not only by martial arts and other civilian classes (perhaps funded by the state) but also by infiltration of the military at every level. Not only do females need to be able to call on skills when attacked (for which conventional military weapons may not be helpful) but the social meaning of "female" needs to be changed so that it no longer connotes "victim." (1996, 11–12)

As women's bodies are constructed to be distinctly feminine, they are constructed to be vulnerable to particularly sexual attacks. Of course, women's socialized weakness also renders them vulnerable to attacks that are not sexual; but precisely because that weakness is deemed crucial to their femininity, which is crucial to their social acceptability, which is crucial to their "successful" interactions with men, women are *even less physically and psy-*

chically prepared to fend off sexual attacks than ones that are merely physical. In a sexual context, even if that context is a violent, imposed, hostile one, women can remain mired in social expectations of feminine kindness, passivity, and fragility. In other words, the instincts that are embedded in women, including the instincts not to fight back, not to resist, not to have faith in one's bodily strength, make them an easy target precisely as they render them feminine.

This point would seem to make the concern of constructing women as victims all the more acute. However, the body that adopts, internalizes, and habituates these assumptions of weakness, fragility, and passivity is never a finished product. The body of the embodied subject, as Elizabeth Grosz reminds us, is not merely the creation of the surrounding political discourses. Embodiment is not a matter of inertly soaking up the values of those surrounding discourses, reflecting and materializing them in straightforward faithfulness. The body is both active and passive, a site where those discourses are taken up in varying degrees of loyalty, a site that is always in a process of becoming. That women are constructed without the strong instinct of physical self-defense that is encouraged in men is not to say that that instinct cannot be cultivated. If women's bodies are the ground on which they are constructed as pre-victims, they are also the ground on which resistance to those embedded instincts can take place.

In her remarkable book *Real Knockouts: The Physical Feminism of Women's Self-Defense,* Martha McCaughey (1997) explores the political and theoretical aspects of a variety of self-defense methods, from the Model Mugging program to martial arts classes to instruction in the use of guns. She recognizes that many women are drawn to self-defense by dangers that are particular to women, specifically the threat of rape. Moreover, her descriptions of rape and the harms thereof emphasize the embodied effects of the assault as well as its implications for women's subjectivity and personhood:

> This is precisely why rape is harmful and worth fighting against: It reduces a woman's mode of being-in-the-world from an absorbed lived body to a broken body with a self somewhere else or a self reduced to a body-thing. Women are regarded by men who rape (and, regrettably, by many others) as things, void of a moral will or a body-self distinct from the rapist's, or they are reduced to his (mis)interpretation: "She really wants it." Rape is harmful because it imposes an "ownable" status, effectively construing woman as passive and as property. . . . Rape is harmful not only because a man claims sovereignty over that which belongs to a sovereign woman—the female body or female sexuality. The body in

feminist theory cannot stand simply as an appendage that women ideally own. Rape is a violation not simply because a woman lost sovereignty over this thing, but because the body is a form of social expression and rape makes the woman's body into an object or possession of the rapist rather than a lived body. Social identity is the body-self. A broken body is the collapse of one's social expressiveness. (McCaughey 1997, 171–73)

Because McCaughey approaches rape as the experience of an embodied subject, she can understand women's self-defense classes not merely as a social expression of women's victimization, but also as profound challenges to the political structure that shapes women in the form of victims. Taking feminist theory at its word—namely, assuming that the feminine body can be shaped into other, more empowered, forms than the ones imposed by patriarchy—women's self-defense seeks to transform women's bodies into defensive weapons. This bodily transformation necessarily constitutes a shift in the being of the woman who undergoes it, for to recognize and realize one's bodily strength and capability is to challenge a discourse of femininity that undermines women's physical abilities. Just as embodied subjectivity accounts for the profound harms rape can impose by stressing that an assault on one's body constitutes an assault on one's possibility for personhood, so it also accounts for the depth of the shift inspired by learning to defend one's self. To change the habits and abilities of one's body—as well as the assumptions and expectations one holds of one's body—is to change one's very self.

Women's self-defense, in all its various forms, is, for McCaughey, physical feminism. It is embodied resistance, which has the possibility of threatening the conditions that allow for a rape culture.

By requiring women to act in unfeminine ways, self-defense instruction makes possible the identification of not only some of the mechanisms that create and sustain gender inequality but also a means to subvert them. Self-defense is a counterdiscourse: It represents woman, man, and aggression in new ways that oppose those we take for granted. Women's new bodily comportment affects not only their confidence with respect to thwarting assaults; it proves highly consequential for many areas of their lives.

Gender is a lived ideology—a system of ideas about men and women with which we live our lives. As lived ideology, those ideas get transformed into specific bodily practices. . . . What feminists talk about interrupting—femininity—self-defensers practice interrupting: They enact the deconstruction of femininity. In the process, self-defense enables women to internalize a different kind of bodily knowledge. As such, self-defense is feminism in the flesh. (89–90)

Training women's bodies in various types of self-defense resists in a variety of ways the discourses that make sexual violence not only possible but likely. First, it locates the means of resistance squarely within the women themselves, thereby undermining the construction of women as (peculiarly culpable) victims. The sheer ability to fend off a male attacker and the knowledge that one is able to do so are themselves challenges to a discourse that assumes the physical weakness of women. Moreover, understanding one's body as capable of resisting such an attack contradicts the discourses that are embedded in typically feminine bodily comportment. If the typically feminine body as described in chapter 5 is inscribed with the assumption of female culpability (i.e., the assumption that the typically feminine body inspires the violence imposed on it, thus absolving the male agent, who is powerless in the presence of female sexuality, of any responsibility), the new body that emerges from self-defense training perceives dangers as worthy of retaliation and anger. To be willing and able to strike back is to acknowledge that the assault is unjust, unacceptable, and not the fault of the victim.

Locating the possibility of resistance in the facticity of one's own (female) body also lessens significantly the dependence of women on men. I am reminded again of the predominant advice given to me as a college student after a hallmate had been raped, advice that included the exhortation to be escorted by a male at all times while traversing the campus. Such advice, rather than making the women of the college feel safer, only underscored the assumption that they themselves were incapable of fending off any attack, and that as long as they were alone, they were at risk. Ensuring one's safety, according to the model presented by many college officials, consisted of limiting one's mobility and depending particularly on male friends or acquaintances (a paradoxical dependence, which assumed that the men of the college were not the ones likely to inflict sexual violence). Note that it was seen as perfectly acceptable to encourage the limitation of women's social mobility, while encouraging any changes in male behavior was virtually unthinkable. By contrast, had the college made available to the women a self-defense course, the message would have been very different. By being taught to defend ourselves, we would have little or no need for particularly male protection, and the blame for such assaults would have been squarely, explicitly, clearly placed on those who committed them, and not on the feminine bodies who had the audacity to walk alone at night.

Second, while self-defense training precludes the construction of women as passive victims, it does not underestimate the serious and pervasive threats that face women in contemporary society. Renee Heberle's (1996) concern that the repeated speaking of the violence imposed on women can serve to reify masculine dominance is a serious one—the mere re-presentation of sexual violence committed against women is an ambivalent accomplishment insofar as it merely makes such violence appear to be more present, more real, more pervasive. Self-defense training does not fall into this trap, because it consists not of a mere re-presentation of that violence but a powerful reaction against it. It confronts the reality of sexual violence and seeks to create an alternative discourse. It doesn't allow sexual violence to have the last word; instead, it writes an entirely new chapter. The bodily transformation that occurs through self-defense instruction results, as McCaughey notes, in a new bodily text:

> Thus it is not that self-defense inscribes a set of "unnatural" rules onto the naturally docile bodies of women. Nor is it that patriarchal culture has enforced a set of rules onto the bodies of women and self-defensers finally free themselves of any rules, disciplines, or ideologies. Nor is it that women in self-defense are unleashing a naturally aggressive instinct.
>
> Self-defensers replace an old embodied code with a new one—a more pleasurable one and a differently consequential one. (McCaughey 1997, 116)

This new embodied code acknowledges both the fact that women in present-day society are faced with the threat of sexual violence and the fact that such violence is not "natural," not necessary, not innate, but part and parcel of embodied gender hierarchies. It recognizes that women are often victimized without defining women as victims; it concedes the reality of sexual violence without further reifying it.

Third, and perhaps most important, self-defense training challenges the discourses of a rape culture by giving would-be rapists good reason to fear women. If women are constructed—if they construct themselves—as body-selves that are both capable and willing to defend themselves physically, to do serious bodily harm to an assailant, then the attempt to rape a woman becomes a dangerous proposition indeed. As long as women's embodied subjectivity is marked by physical frailty as well as the emotional hesitation to inflict harm on even an assailant, women are, as Claudia Card notes, easy targets. Not only is the act of rape a relatively easy one to accomplish, but the social and political environment in which it takes place (especially if it is an example of acquaintance or marital rape) gives the rapist fairly good assurance that his victim will not press charges against him. The woman who is able and willing to defend herself, who views sexual violence as an unjust expression of sexual dominance, is far less likely, should she experience such violence, to blame herself or feel shame. She has already embodied a critical perspective on the dominant assumptions concerning sexuality and violence by reorganizing her body such that it—that is, she—fights back. The would-be rapist should fear her not only because of the harm she can inflict upon him (although that's quite a powerful deterrent), but also because that willingness to inflict harm indicates that she is not a person who will honor the dominant assumptions concerning her own culpability.

Reorganizing women's bodies into self-defending beings makes sense as a strategy against rape because it is an embodied solution to an embodied problem. It contradicts the model of rape put forth by Brownmiller by refusing the definition of women's bodies as inherently rapable and men's bodies as inherently capable of rape. Rather, it approaches the bodies of subjects as products of certain discourses who are capable of representing other discourses, other sets of values. Likewise, where MacKinnon risked defining women by their status in patriarchy, by indicating that women's agency was rendered virtually impossible by their construction as inferior beings, self-defense training assumes that the body-self can be rewritten, that it is not doomed to perpetuate and replicate the existing power structures.

Women's self-defense exploits the gap between the dominant, oppressive discourses and the material iteration of those discourses performed by subjects (a dynamic best described in the work of Judith Butler). It recognizes the significance of embodied subjectivity and the degree to which embodied subjects are shaped and formed by their surrounding environments, but it also recognizes the possibility for disloyalty, for change, for transformation. If rape is to be understood as an embodied experience, if the harms it inflicts are directly related to embodied subjectivity, then a shift in the possibilities of feminine embodied subjectivity will constitute a significant shift in both the occurrence and the meaning of rape.

Indeed, the two—the occurrence and the meaning of rape—are intimately linked. We can imagine a world where women are able, and know themselves to be able, to fend off sexual attacks. This is, to me, a wholly feasible proposition. We can imagine that it may take some time, but that eventually men will learn that forcing sex on a woman can and often does result in severe physical and social harm to them. Just as individual men learn to rape from a culture that celebrates their sexual aggression and dominance, so can they learn not to rape from a culture that refuses to tolerate either. In such a world, women could roam the streets at any time at night. They could walk through bars alone or with each other without the fear or discomfort of being harassed by male strangers. They would not fear their husbands, boyfriends, lovers, brothers, or friends, as those relationships would be founded on a mutual recognition of physical and emotional strength. Knowing themselves, individually and collectively, in a distinctly embodied way, to be deserving of this kind of freedom and security would also result in a confidence that, were they to be attacked, their experience would not be met with suspicion or dismissal. Rape would be rare, and women's lives would not be shot through with an assumption of danger, victimization, and culpability.

Not only would rape be relatively rare in such a world, but its meaning as a phenomenon would undergo significant change. Given that embodied strength would no longer be understood solely as the domain of male persons, it may be that sexual violence itself would no longer be committed so disproportionately against women by men. Rape, then, would no longer be an expression of a sexual dominance that is exhibited by a variety of other means. The sexual differentiation that is part and parcel of rape as a social phenomenon at present—in that it is a threat which is disproportionately leveled against women as a class, and in that it is an act which is disproportionately committed by men—would no longer exist. Although rape would still be a horrific experience, women would no longer experience it as a confirmation of their inferior social status. Nor would it serve as a reminder of the culpability of their bodies. In other words, rape would not function as yet another tool in the patriarchal arsenal and would not gather its meaning from a political structure that accepted and imposed a sexual hierarchy.

What of sexual difference in such a world? Would the increased mobility and freedom accorded to women result in a social structure that did not distinguish between male and female? And would the phenomenon of rape therefore be significantly desexed? I would argue that the increased physical ability of women and their capability to defend themselves from sexual attacks would not constitute an "equalization" of the sexes in the sense of making them essentially similar. Rather, women's bodies would adopt habits and practices that would utilize their own potential for power. Many women's self-defense classes, such as Model Mugging, teach techniques that are based on the female body (such as kicking from the hips). They do not, in other words, teach means of self-defense predicated on a male body. The increased strength of women self-defensers cannot, therefore, be reduced to the same kind of strength found in male bodies, although the former is an effective tool against the latter.

Because the recodification of the female body would involve not an emulation of the male body, but rather the development of particularly feminine kinds of strength and power, the embodied subjects who undertake such recodification will be no less marked by sexual difference than previously. *Femininity* itself will be redefined, such that it no longer necessitates physical weakness and submissiveness, but women will not be subsumed into those models of subjectivity and political agency that are notoriously gendered male. The sexual difference that exists among embodied subjects will be recognized but not hierarchized, accepted but not exploited for the purposes of an oppressive political structure. With the possibility of defense lodged squarely within their own flesh and bones, women would be able to stand socially on their own, free from their dependence on men. They would be able to function socially and politically as beings complete unto themselves, and not as derivative reflections of the desires and needs of men.

Women's self-defense training is not, obviously, the only or sufficient means of dislodging the political structures of patriarchy. Nor is it the only tool of resistance against a rape culture—legal reform remains a powerful tool for political feminism. However, self-defense training does hold the potential to undermine some of the most crucial and embodied tenets of a rape culture, and as such it should become a central concern of feminist theory and practice.

Training women to defend themselves will not ensure that rape never happens. Even in the world described above, some women may find themselves sexually victimized. Regardless of the environment in which it takes place, rape will remain a violent assault on a person's embodied subjectivity. Whether that subjectivity is marked by an assumption of weakness or a recognition of its own bodily strength, whether it was constructed among a set of discourses that constitute a sexual hierarchy, the imposition of a sexual act, especially one that involves bodily penetration, will constitute a threat to and denial of the victim's bodily and therefore subjective integrity. Such an assault will indeed have different meanings and impose different harms in different social and political contexts; there are many ways a person's social being can be undermined, limited, endangered. The scope of the harms rape imposes, however, persists, and is directly related to the fact of embodied subjectivity. Rape is an experience imposed on an embodied subject, a violent sexual assault that in its corporal nature destabilizes the intersubjective personhood of the victim.

Notes

1. Feminist Theories of Rape

1. Spohn and Horney (1992) analyze the effects of rape law reform in several cities. One important reform undertaken by several jurisdictions that was clearly inspired by Brownmiller and others was definitional: "[M]any states replaced the crime of rape and other traditional sex crimes with a series of gender-neutral graded offenses with commensurate penalties. . . . [M]any states eliminated the term rape and substituted sexual assault, sexual battery, or criminal sexual content" (Spohn and Horney 1992, 22). In evaluating the effectiveness of these definitional changes, Spohn and Horney write:

> Changing the name of the crime from rape to sexual assault, criminal sexual conduct, or sexual battery also may have had unintended consequences. Reformers reasoned that the change would emphasize that rape is an assault and a crime of violence. Criminal justice officials in the three jurisdictions that changed the name of the crime disagreed. They pointed out that the term "rape" has a strong connotation and "conjures up a much more inflammatory image in the mind of the jury." A judge in Houston stated that changing the name of the offense from rape to sexual assault "sugarcoated" the offense. A prosecutor in Chicago charged that the new terminology was confusing to jurors, "who often wondered why we didn't just charge the guy with rape." (161).

In general, the authors find to their disappointment that the rape law reforms did not result an increase in convictions or in an increase in the reporting of rapes.

2. This statement is strikingly ambiguous. Brownmiller's analysis of rape, as discussed below, describes it as essentially a political means of the repression of one class (women) by another (men). In this sense, it makes sense that the threat of rape benefits all men. However, this does not necessarily entail that all men consciously participate in this process of intimidation, as the quote suggests. The distinction between men as a class and real, particular men (as well as that between women as a class and real, particular women) is difficult to trace in Brownmiller's thought, as exemplified by this quote.

3. For certain cultures and historical periods, of course, even the term "abdicates" is overly strong, as women, or usually young girls, are literally "given away" by their father to their husband, without any degree of consent or participation on the part of the bride. Brownmiller would link this type of extremely female social dependence with the possibility of rape and the need for constant male protection (not to mention the social currency of female virginity).

4. For surveys and comparative studies of various sociological theories (not always feminist) concerning the occurrence of rape, see Ellis (1989) and Baron and Strauss (1989). Sunday and Tobach (1985) provide a collection of essays criticizing the sociobiological theory of rape, which asserts that rape is the result of evolutionary selection and can therefore be understood as a reproductive strategy of men who would otherwise not reproduce.

5. Of course, women can and do retaliate physically against their attackers. Brownmiller does not explore the possibility of women's physical self-defense against rapists or abusers; however, her point here is that women cannot threaten men with a similar act (rape). Because Brownmiller is grounding her understanding of rape in "man's *structural* capacity to rape" and "women's corresponding *structural* vulnerability" (my emphasis), she cannot understand women's bodies as capable of physical self-defense. Nor can she account sufficiently for the phenomenon of homosexual rape.

6. For other feminist criticisms of science in general and biology in particular, see Anne Fausto-Sterling (1985); Evelyn Fox Keller (1985); Sandra Harding (1986, 1991); Ruth Berman (1989); and Ruth Bleier (1984).

7. Sanday considers rape in 95 "tribal" societies, and finds that in 47 percent of them "rape is reported as rare or absent," thereby leading Sanday to describe them as "rape free" (1981, 9). Sanday concludes that one of the indicators of a rape-prone society is a failure to recognize and respect particularly feminine capabilities and characteristics; "the one outstanding feature of these [rape free] societies is the ceremonial importance of women and the respect accorded the contribution women make to social continuity, a respect which places men and women in relatively balanced power spheres" (17).

8. See, for example, Beinen (1978) and Davis (1984).

9. A. Nicholas Groth, in support of just such an understanding of rape as primarily violent rather than sexual, claimed that "rape is in fact serving primarily nonsexual needs. It is the sexual expression of power and anger. . . . Rape is a pseudosexual act, complex and multidetermined, but addressing issues of hostility (anger) and control (power) more than passion (sexuality)" (1979, 2). However, it is worth noting that the rapists Groth studied were, by his own admission, representative only of those who "come to the attention of criminal justice and mental health agencies and with whom law enforcement officials and providers of social services are expected to deal in some effective manner" (xiii); not surprisingly, therefore, the anecdotal examples Groth quotes refer almost exclusively to stranger rape and do not address the phenomena of acquaintance rape and marital rape. Moreover, although Groth claims that only 25 percent of identified rapists experience no erective or ejaculatory dysfunction (88), the types of sexual dysfunction he does find prevalent do not indicate a complete lack of sexual arousal on the part of the rapist (for example, premature ejaculation, or temporary or conditional impotency, which refers to an inability to achieve an erection except by imposing a certain set of actions or scenarios).

10. For discussions of the role of the male generic in patriarchal logic, see Susan Moller Okin (1989), Joanna Hodge (1988), and Robin West (1991b). Okin argues that

allegedly sex-neutral theories of justice in fact depend on the existence of the sexually hierarchized family, which, insofar as it occurs within the sanctity of the private sphere, is perceived as outside of the realm of justice itself. The public/private split thus serves not only to erase the work that has been disproportionately performed by women, but also to produce a "citizen" who is remarkably, and inaccurately, free from the significance of gender. Hodge's analysis indicates that the very philosophical categories of subjectivity, rationality, and politics, are so indelibly marked by the masculine (despite their universal claims) that women's full inclusion demands a fundamental re-thinking of the terms themselves: "The very notions of the subject and of subjectivity are embedded in a system of distinctions, which must be challenged in order to reveal the way in which women and men do not enter into the domains of the political and the rational on the same terms" (Hodge 1988, 167). Finally, West claims that the field of modern legal theory is relentlessly masculinist in its approach to the (again, allegedly generic) person, and that therefore its assumptions concerning the generic human do not, in fact, hold true for female persons, especially insofar as they approach the individual human as profoundly separate from other individuals.

11. This is not to claim that feminist theorists are unanimous in their support of sexual differentiation as a means to justice for women; Wendy W. Williams (1991), for example, while noting some advantages to recognizing specific legal benefits for women, claims that such special protection will inevitably backfire by justifying the exclusion of women from certain social roles. Her point is that within a system of sexual hierarchization, the recognition of the relevance of sexual difference, however well-intentioned, can too easily be utilized against the very beings (women) such recognition intends to protect or benefit. For arguments against sex-neutral language and standards, especially in the legal discourse, see Fineman (1995) and Frug (1992); Weisberg (1993) includes several articles concerning the problem of difference as applied to law and policy.

12. Note that MacKinnon's argument differs here, albeit slightly, from Griffin's. Griffin reduced the sexuality in rape primarily to the eroticized violence inherent in heterosexuality, thus in general reducing the sex in rape to violence. MacKinnon, while recognizing the centrality of the eroticization of violence, is also stressing the violent imposition of heterosexuality, that is, its socially compulsory aspect, which limits or negates the possibility of feminine sexual autonomy, thus essentially reducing the violence in rape to sex.

13. See Barbara Ehrenreich and Deirdre English (1979) for a history of the medical institution's interpretation and treatment of women's bodies and women's health. Especially interesting is the discussion of the "rejection of the feminine" (270–74), a diagnosis that conveniently accounted for all aspects of that particularly feminine illness of hysteria—an illness that, Ehrenreich and English claim, utilized the feminine virtues of passivity and weakness to avoid the imposed duties of wifehood and motherhood (133–40). The real problem, as far as the medical institution was concerned, was not so much the suffering of the hysterical patient, but her failure to fulfill her various social duties.

2. Subjectivity and the Body

1. My mother told me once when I was in college that I would "go from your father's house to your husband's." The fear of that social and identity limbo that would otherwise exist between the roles of daughter and wife was, it is true, eventually and quietly outweighed by the realization that the presence of a loudly feminist daughter thwarted

from her own projects would hardly contribute to the workings of a harmonious house-hold. More to the point, however, I think that although my mother felt compelled to attempt an enforcement of a blatantly patriarchal lifestyle, she could not ultimately accept the imposition of limitations on her daughters' explorations of their impressive and varying talents. Such baldly conservative statements were more than drowned out by my mother's support of my intellectual endeavors, as well as her persistent and explicit refusal to judge the value of my life in terms of my relationships with men. All of this is to gesture toward the complicated relationships individual women have with a discursive regime that not only seeks to produce them in certain, pregiven models, but also demands that they in turn impose these models on others.

2. This is generally the case until such tasks become elevated to the level of expertise, at which point it becomes common wisdom that the best advice one can get regarding child rearing is from a childless male doctor (the famous Dr. Spock), and that the finest chefs are always male.

3. Feminist Theories of the Body

1. Braidotti is not, of course, suggesting that the medical practice of organ transference, a practice responsible for saving countless individual lives, be halted. Her concern on this point is strictly theoretical, as she is questioning the assumptions that make the practice, aside from its medical benefits, acceptable.

2. In using the phrase "the/a woman," Irigaray is grammatically challenging the distinction between women as a class and women as individuals. More exactly, she is complicating the distinction, for her analysis suggests that it is only in adopting a universal, though not determinative, sense of women as a class that individual women can act and be perceived as distinct individuals.

3. Irigaray's emphasis on the doubleness of human being, the distinction between the male and the female, often appears to have a distinctly heterosexist slant. However, given how difference functions in her thought to challenge the definition of the female as derivative of the male, I would argue that her theory presents a significant challenge to the assumption that the feminine is necessarily heterosexual. Not only does she emphasize the need for an ontology of the feminine that is wholly distinct from the masculine (a necessary heterosexuality would define the two in terms of each other), but the difference she describes is not, properly understood, a complementary difference. The male and the female do not combine to produce a unified whole; they are not parts of one complete entity. They are irreducible elements of a scope of possibilities that does not exist as a oneness. In a more practical and political vein, and contrary to some criticisms of Irigaray's thought, it seems clear to me that an emphasis on sexual difference is not necessarily essentializing, either in terms of sexual orientation or otherwise. To claim that the male is different from the female is not to claim that there are no significant differences within the category of female. In fact, Irigaray urges us to accept just the opposite conclusion: that the significance of sexual difference should indicate the significance of other types of difference as well. This seems to me to be intuitively true in the sense that a single-sex environment is a better means of exploring the differences within that sex than a mixed-sex environment. When women gather together as women, the differences among them (of race, sexual orientation, class, age, etc.) become more apparent, more open to discussion, more relevant—not less. Recognizing sexual difference, far from ignoring other differences, actually highlights them.

4. Rape as Embodied Experience

1. The traditional criticism of overly broad definitions of rape have been that they fail to protect men against false accusations. This is not my concern, for while false accusations are certainly possible, they do not constitute the pervasive danger with which they are often associated. Rather, I question definitions so broad so that they (implicitly or explicitly) deny the possibility of female agency, choice, or responsibility. Definitions that include, for example, any intercourse with a woman who has clearly consented although she is slightly or quite inebriated or under the influence of drugs risk adopting a seriously paternalistic attitude. Robin Morgan's (1977, 165; 1980, 136) insistence that any sexual activity not initiated by the woman be considered rape also overstates the case; for surely a woman can appropriately accept the advances of a given man (Morgan is obviously limiting her comments to heterosexual sex) without consenting to rape.

An example of an overly narrow definition is one that does not include rapes whose tool of penetration was other than a penis; note that these definitions look to the male body for the defining elements.

2. Bureau of Justice statistics indicate that 99.6 percent of imprisoned rape offenders are male, and 94.5 percent of the victims of those offenders are female (Greenfeld 1997, 21, 24).

3. Following the familial scenario, for example, different siblings experience similar family dynamics from distinct perspectives, due to age, personality, differing relationships to other family members, and so forth.

4. Rape is, by and large, an intraracial crime. See LaFree (1982).

5. Cleaver goes on to describe his eventual regret over his acts, claiming that they inherently degraded him.

6. Interracial rapes are relatively rare, but LaFree (1982) notes that among interracial rapes, there are "substantially higher rates of black offender–white victim than white offender–black victim rape" (LaFree 1982, 311). LaFree accounts for the disproportionality as follows:

> If we assume that America is characterized by race-specific rules of sexual access, then white fear about the rape of white women by black men and the greater frequency of BW [i.e., black offender/white victim] than WB [i.e., white offender/ black victim] rape become two different aspects of the same phenomenon. White males set this sexual stratification system in place by promoting the white female as the standard of sexual desirability. . . . Fundamentally the struggle between black and white males represents an age-old conflict where men from dominant groups attempt to protect their sexual property from subordinate-group men, while simultaneously ignoring the victimization of subordinate-group women. Women, black and white, have historically been the victims of this struggle. (325–26)

Although I disagree with the model of power that LaFree invokes—power is not a coherent system set firmly in place by any one group of individuals—this analysis does point to the co-constitution of race and gender by which the ideal femininity is raced white and the construction of an inferior race is supported by lack of sexual access.

7. While riding on a bus, I overheard a conversation between two women, one a mother of a troubled teenage girl. In the course of listing the various self-destructive

activities of her daughter, including taking drugs, engaging in criminal activity, and physically assaulting her parents, the mother mentioned rather parenthetically that the girl had been raped a couple of years earlier. "It wasn't her fault," she said rather lamely, then, much more emphatically, "but she put herself into that position." Clearly the mother had learned that to blame the victim was inappropriate, yet her dominant emotional reaction remained one of assigning blame to her daughter. Rather than viewing the daughter's self-destructive behavior as somehow linked to an experience of sexual assault, the mother placed the fact that she had been raped within the context of other socially unacceptable activities.

8. A possible exception to this general rule is the phenomenon of rape in all-male prisons. In this environment, certain men (although not all men, which again differentiates this situation from that facing virtually all women in contemporary U.S. society, of course to differing degrees) may be constantly under the threat of rape. The prevalence of homosexual rape in prisons can be understood as a societal attempt to re-create a sexual hierarchy without the presence of a strictly bodily sexual difference; in the absence of sexual difference itself (in the absence of otherly sexed persons, namely, women), a type of sexual difference is socially produced, whereby some men become "girls" and as such are either subject to the constant threat of rape or protected from same by an exclusive relationship with one inmate or guard. Scacco notes that homosexual rape in prison is not due to a lack of sexual outlet, but is rather "an act whereby one male (or group of males) seek testimony to what he considers is an outward validation of his masculinity" (1975, 3). Similarly, Buffum claims that prison rape is not reducible to the social dynamics of prison itself but an extension and adaptation of social and political values of the "outside" community: "[T]he prison provides a situation to which prior sexual and social styles and motives must be adapted and shaped" (1972, 9). See also Lockwood (1980), who argues that prison rape significantly mirrors the phenomenon of rape in larger society.

9. Statistics from the U.S. Bureau of Justice indicate that 75.6 percent of rapes were committed by persons known to the victim (Greenfeld 1997, 4); in addition, "nearly 6 out of 10 rape/sexual assault incidents were reported by victims to have occurred in their own home or at the home of a friend, relative, or neighbor" (3).

10. It is difficult to know, of course, whether men would be likely to report experiences of rape. The point is, however, that extremely few men in contemporary Western society face this choice, as opposed to a considerable number of women. The differences in the sexual threats posed to men and women are so great as to be not merely quantitative, but qualitative. Perhaps one reason my male relative was able to assume the masculine perspective of a rape victim so blithely is that it is, in fact, a fairly far-fetched example. Such an experience remained for him, despite his own argument, wholly theoretical.

11. The person with whom I was arguing was not basing his argument on any empirical data concerning male victims of rape; the most trenchant point of his argument, as he perceived it, was that some men are raped, and therefore to describe it as a crime against women was inaccurate.

12. With regard to Freud's work, Cathy Caruth describes trauma not as something that is actually experienced by the subject, but as that which the conscious subject cannot fully or immediately experience, and must therefore reconstruct by means of recollection:

Yet what is truly striking about the accident victim's experience of the event . . . is not so much the period of forgetting that occurs after the accident, but rather the fact that the victim of the crash was never fully conscious during the accident itself. . . . The experience of trauma, the fact of latency, would thus seem to consist, not in the forgetting of a reality that can hence never be fully known, but in an inherent latency within the experience itself. The historical power of the trauma is not just that the experience is repeated after its forgetting, but that it is only in and through its inherent forgetting that it is first experienced at all (Caruth 1996, 17).

With regard to rape, I read this lack of immediate experience of trauma, which many victims of sexual assault describe as dissociation, as a break in the victim's subjectivity and personhood, a break that must be addressed by the process of recollection, but that constitutes a fundamental shift in the victim's subjectivity. The process of healing, that is, of recollection and integration of that experience within the victim's personhood, is one that does not reconstruct the pre-rape person, but rather creates significantly new ways and modes of being.

13. This particular difference can illuminate cases of rape, which I believe exist, wherein the assailant himself does not recognize that a crime has been committed. In my belief, given the sexist assumptions concerning feminine sexuality, it is distinctly possible for a man to commit rape without knowing it (for example, by sincerely, if mistakenly and male chauvinistically, interpreting a woman's cries and protests as evidence of sexual excitement). This does not, however, relieve the assailant of any responsibility. Especially in these days of growing awareness of sexual violence, individual men have the responsibility, as well as the means, to respond critically to sexist portrayals of women. More importantly, however, I choose to privilege the fact of the crime perpetuated against the victim over the intent of the accused. Whether he meant to or not, he imposed upon the victim a serious threat to her personhood, for which he must be held responsible.

5. A Phenomenology of Fear

1. For three particularly interesting discussions of the role of power in Foucault's thought, see Ladelle McWhorter (1990), Annie Bunting (1992), and Mary Rawlinson (1987). Judith Butler (1987) briefly considers some of Foucault's assertions regarding power and the body specifically in relation to the theories of Simone de Beauvoir and Monique Wittig.

2. Ladelle McWhorter (1989), Lois McNay (1991; 1992, 11–47), and Judith Butler (1989) have challenged this concept of the body. For McWhorter, it leaves moot the possibility of liberty; if the body is marked only by its function to be formed according to power relations, "he leaves us with nothing to liberate" (1989, 608), and surely, as Foucault's emphasis on the project of desexualization implies, liberation seems fundamental to his purposes. McNay, while for the most part accepting Foucault's theory of the "docile" body, also argues that it fails to account sufficiently for a variety of experiences central not only to women's experience, but also to the development of a feminist consciousness. Butler takes Foucault to task because his analysis seems to imply, contrary to his asserted purpose, that the body does in fact exist prior to power's inscription, precisely as a blank surface—for, after all, power must have something to

write on, and thus "it would appear that 'the body,' which is the object or surface on which construction occurs, is itself prior to construction" (1989, 601). McNay and McWhorter, I would argue, fail to acknowledge sufficiently the deeply implicated relationship between power and resistance that I discuss above; Butler overemphasizes the inscriptive capabilities of power, which do not contradict, but coexist with, its productive abilities.

3. For a compelling Foucauldian analysis of a group of disorders usually associated with the female body and/or psyche, see Bordo (1991).

4. I thank Mary Rawlinson for this telling insight.

5. In contemporary U.S. society, there is much pressure on women to exercise and get "in shape"; however, the purpose of such exercise is not so much to build muscle and strength, but to lose weight and inches. One reason the female bodybuilder is so monstrous is that her muscles are so big (and her breasts, assuming they have not been surgically enlarged, so small). It is interesting to note that while female bodybuilding is suspect, cosmetic plastic surgery is not, and in fact is often praised by women as being a way of raising self-esteem. See Kathy Davis (1995) for an exploration of why women, even feminists, seek cosmetic surgery to mold their bodies to a more appealing shape; see also Kathryn Pauly Morgan (1991). Susan Bordo (1993, 245–75) notes that the postmodern emphasis on the plasticity of bodies, especially the ability of the (often female) subject to willfully shape one's body into a preferred shape, obscures the political content of the norms that are idealized. As Bordo points out, despite the promises and exhortations of choice, "one cannot have any body that one wants—for not every body will do" (230).

6. As an aside, we may note that this description of feminine bodily being provides a direct challenge to the Merleau-Pontian notion of the lived body on the basis of sexual difference. The body Merleau-Ponty (1981) describes as an openness to the surrounding world, a means not only of achieving certain projects but also, and more importantly, of perceiving those projects as feasible and attainable, seems distinctly male. The analyses of Young and Bartky suggest that the feminine lived body speaks more of limitation, failure, and harm than of achievement.

7. Over 88 percent of people who suffer from agoraphobia are women (Thorpe and Burns 1983, 20). Robert Seidenberg and Karen DeCrow write:

> We believe that in a culture that has consistently doled out punishment to women who travel away from home (from unequal pay in the workplace to blame for children who turn to drugs to actual physical assault on the streets), it is no surprise that certain women, sensing the existential irony of their situation, refuse to leave the home. We see agoraphobia as a paradigm for the historical intimidation and oppression of women. The self-hate, self-limitation, self-abnegation, and self-punishment of agoraphobia is a caricature of centuries of childhood instructions to women. . . . Only when society gives just value to the work women do at home, and makes it easier for them to leave the home to do fully accepted and compensated work, will women no longer need to be agoraphobic. (1983, 6)

8. I thank Eva Feder Kittay for the formulation of this particular contradiction.

9. Mary Pipher has explored the traumatic transformation which many adolescent girls undergo, and has located the difficulty of the transition within the demands of a patriarchal culture:

Something dramatic happens to girls in early adolescence. Just as planes and ships disappear mysteriously into the Bermuda Triangle, so do the selves of girls go down in droves. They crash and burn in a social and developmental Bermuda Triangle. In early adolescence, studies show that girls' IQ scores drop and their math and science scores plummet. They lose their resiliency and optimism and become less curious and inclined to take risks. They lose their assertive, energetic and "tomboyish" personalities and become more deferential, self-critical and depressed. They report great unhappiness with their own bodies. (Pipher 1994, 19)

6. The Ethical Wrongs of Rape

1. Baber defends this claim in a footnote that at once dismisses the relevance of Freudian theory, admits that the assertion is based on a male generic, and notes that to assume that women differ from this generic is "a manifestation of the sexist assumption that women are primarily sexual beings" (1987, 138 n. 3).

2. Irigaray's thought does not, necessarily, demand that we are capable of knowing ourselves in any absolute sense. Whether our self-knowledge is complete or accurate is, to a certain extent, irrelevant when we use it as a basis for constructing the other. The move is still the same: to assume that the other is fundamentally similar to myself is to fail to recognize the other's specificity (even if I am wrong about what "myself" is).

3. For a detailed discussion of the symptoms of rape trauma syndrome, see Burgess and Holmstrom (1979). While articulating a particular syndrome related to the experience of being raped is certainly useful, insofar as it groups together various emotional, psychological, and physical reactions to such an attack, it would tend to apply only to experiences of single rapes. Women who suffer from repeated rapes may have significantly different responses.

Bibliography

Baber, H. E. 1987. "How Bad Is Rape?" *Hypatia* 2 (2): 125–38.

Baron, Larry, and Murray A. Strauss. 1989. *Four Theories of Rape in American Society*. New Haven: Yale University Press.

Bartky, Sandra Lee. 1988. "Foucault, Femininity, and the Modernization of Patriarchal Power." In *Feminism and Foucault*, ed. Irene Diamond and Lee Quinby, 61–86. Boston: Northeastern University Press.

Beauvoir, Simone de. 1974. *The Second Sex*. New York: Vintage Books.

Beinen, Leigh. 1978. "Mistakes." *Philosophy and Public Affairs* 7 (spring): 224–45.

Bell, Vikki. 1991. " 'Beyond the "Thorny Question" ': Feminism, Foucault, and the Desexualisation of Rape." *International Journal of the Sociology of Law* 19 (Feb.): 83–100.

Belliotti, Raymond. 1979. "A Philosophical Analysis of Sexual Ethics." *Journal of Social Philosophy* 10 (3): 8–11.

Berger, Ronald J., Patricia Searles, and W. Lawrence Neuman. 1995. "Rape-Law Reform: Its Nature, Origins, and Impact." In *Rape and Society: Readings on the Problem of Sexual Assault*, ed. Patricia Searles and Ronald J. Berger, 223–32. Boulder: Westview.

Berman, Ruth. 1989. "From Aristotle's Dualism to Materialist Dialectics: Feminist Transformation of Science and Society." In *Gender/Body/Knowledge: Feminist Reconstructions of Being and Knowing*, ed. Alison M. Jaggar and Susan R. Bordo, 224–55. New Brunswick, N.J.: Rutgers University Press.

Bigwood, Carol. 1991. "Renaturalizing the Body (With a Little Help from Merleau-Ponty)." *Hypatia* 6 (3): 54–73.

Blackstone, William. [1765] 1979. *Commentaries on the Laws of England*. Vol. 1, *Of the Rights of Persons*. Chicago: University of Chicago Press.

Bleier, Ruth. 1984. *Science and Gender: A Critique of Biology and Its Theories on Women*. New York: Pergamon Press.

Bogart, J. H. 1991. "On the Nature of Rape." *Public Affairs Quarterly* 5 (2): 117–36.

Bordo, Susan. 1991. "Docile Bodies, Rebellious Bodies: Foucauldian Perspectives on Female Psychopathology." In *Writing the Politics of Difference*, ed. Hugh J. Silverman, 203–15. Albany: State University of New York Press.

———. 1993. *Unbearable Weight: Feminism, Western Culture, and the Body*. Berkeley: University of California Press.

Boston Women's Health Collective. 1973. *Our Bodies, Ourselves*. New York: Simon and Schuster.

Bourque, Linda Brookover. 1989. *Defining Rape*. Durham: Duke University Press.

Boyer, Lucy, and Maureen E. Dalton. 1997. "Female Victims of Rape and Their Genital Injuries." *British Journal of Obstetrics and Gynaecology* 104 (May): 617–20.

Braidotti, Rosi. 1994. *Nomadic Subjects: Embodiment and Sexual Difference in Contemporary Feminist Theory*. New York: Columbia University Press.

Brison, Susan J. 1993. "Surviving Sexual Violence." *Journal of Social Philosophy* 24 (1): 5–22.

———. 1997. "Outliving Oneself: Trauma, Memory, and Personal Identity." In *Feminists Rethink the Self*, ed. Diana Tietjens Meyers, 12–39. Boulder: Westview.

Brownmiller, Susan. 1975. *Against Our Will: Men, Women, and Rape*. New York: Penguin Books.

Buchwald, Emilie, Pamela Fletcher, and Martha Roth, eds. 1993. *Transforming a Rape Culture*. Minneapolis: Milkweed Editions.

Buffum, Peter C. 1972. *Homosexuality in Prisons*. Washington, D.C.: U.S. Department of Justice.

Bunting, Annie. 1992. "Feminism, Foucault, and Law as Power/Knowledge." *Alberta Law Review* 30: 829–42.

Burgess, Ann Wolbert, and Lynda Lytle Holmstrom. 1979. *Rape: Crisis and Recovery*. Bowie, Md.: Robert J. Brady.

Burgess-Jackson, Keith. 1994. "Justice and the Distribution of Fear." *Southern Journal of Philosophy* 32 (4): 367–91.

———. 1996. *Rape: A Philosophical Investigation*. Brookfield, Vt.: Dartmouth Publishing.

Butler, Judith. 1987. "Variations on Sex and Gender: Beauvoir, Wittig, and Foucault." In *Feminism as Critique: On the Politics of Gender*, ed. Seyla Benhabib and Drucilla Cornell, 128–42. Minneapolis: University of Minnesota Press.

———. 1989. "Foucault and the Paradox of Bodily Inscriptions." *Journal of Philosophy* 86 (Nov.): 601–607.

———. 1990. *Gender Trouble: Feminism and the Subversion of Identity*. New York: Routledge.

———. 1993. *Bodies That Matter: On the Discursive Limits of "Sex."* New York: Routledge.

Campbell, Alastair. 1991. "Dependency Revisited: The Limits of Autonomy in Medical Ethics." In *Protecting the Vulnerable: Autonomy and Consent in Health Care*, ed. Margaret Brazier and Mary Lobjoit, 101–12. New York: Routledge.

Card, Claudia. 1996. "Rape as a Weapon of War." *Hypatia* 11 (4): 5–18.

Caruth, Cathy. 1996. *Unclaimed Experience: Trauma, Narrative, and History*. Baltimore: Johns Hopkins University Press.

Castro, Ginette. 1990. *American Feminism: A Contemporary History*. New York: New York University Press.

Clark, Lorenne M. G., and Debra J. Lewis. 1977. *Rape: The Price of Coercive Sexuality*. Toronto: Woman's Press.

Cleaver, Eldridge. 1968. *Soul on Ice*. New York: McGraw-Hill.

Cornell, Drucilla. 1991. *Beyond Accommodation: Ethical Feminism, Deconstruction, and the Law*. New York: Routledge.

———. 1995. *The Imaginary Domain: Abortion, Pornography and Sexual Harassment*. New York: Routledge.

———. 1998. *At the Heart of Freedom: Feminism, Sex, and Equality*. Princeton: Princeton University Press.

Davis, Kathy. 1995. *Reshaping the Female Body: The Dilemma of Cosmetic Surgery*. New York: Routledge.

Davis, Michael. 1984. "Setting Penalties: What Does Rape Deserve?" *Law and Philosophy* 3 (April): 61–110.

de Lauretis, Teresa. 1987. *Technologies of Gender*. Bloomington: Indiana University Press.

Descartes, René. [1641] 1984. "Meditations on First Philosophy." In *The Philosophical Writings of Descartes*, vol. 2, trans. John Cottingham, Robert Stoothoff, and Dugald Murdoch. Cambridge: Cambridge University Press.

Di Stefano, Christine. 1990. "Dilemmas of Difference: Feminism, Modernity, and Postmodernism." In *Feminism/Postmodernism*, ed. Linda J. Nicholson, 63–82. New York: Routledge.

Dumaresq, Delia. 1981. "Rape-Sexuality in the Law." *m/f* 5–6:41–59.

Dworkin, Andrea. 1989. *Pornography: Men Possessing Women*. New York: E. P. Dutton.

Ehrenreich, Barbara, and Deirdre English. 1979. *For Her Own Good: 150 Years of the Experts' Advice to Women*. New York: Anchor Books.

Eisenstein, Zillah R. 1988. *The Female Body and the Law*. Berkeley: University of California Press.

Ellis, Lee. 1989. *Theories of Rape: Inquiries into the Causes of Sexual Aggression*. New York: Hemisphere Publishing.

Estlund, David M. 1997. "Shaping and Sex: Commentary on Parts I and II." In *Sex, Preference, and Family: Essays on Law and Nature*, ed. David M. Estlund and Martha C. Nussbaum, 149–70. New York: Oxford University Press.

Estrich, Susan. 1987. *Real Rape: How the Legal System Victimizes Women Who Say No*. Cambridge: Harvard University Press.

Fausto-Sterling, Anne. 1985. *Myths of Gender: Biological Theories about Women and Men*. New York: Basic Books.

Fineman, Martha Albertson. 1995. *The Neutered Mother, the Sexual Family, and Other Twentieth-Century Tragedies*. New York: Routledge.

Foa, Pamela. 1977. "What's Wrong with Rape." In *Feminism and Philosophy*, ed. Mary Vetterling-Braggin, Frederick A. Elliston, and Jane English, 347–59. Totowa, N.J.: Littlefield, Adams.

Foucault, Michel. 1979. *Discipline and Punish: The Birth of the Prison*. New York: Vintage Books.

———. 1980. *Power/Knowledge: Selected Interviews and Other Writings, 1972–1977*. Ed. C. Gordon. New York: Pantheon.

———. 1988. *Politics, Philosophy, Culture: Interviews and Other Writings, 1977–1984*. Ed. L. D. Kritzman. New York: Routledge.

———. 1990. *The History of Sexuality.* Vol. 1, *An Introduction.* New York: Vintage Books.

Frug, Mary Joe. 1992. *Postmodern Legal Feminism.* New York: Routledge.

Frye, Marilyn. 1983. *The Politics of Reality: Essays in Feminist Theory.* Freedom, Calif.: Crossing Press.

Gatens, Moira. 1996. *Imaginary Bodies: Ethics, Power, and Corporeality.* New York: Routledge.

Gordon, Linda, and Ellen DuBois. 1983. "Seeking Ecstasy on the Battlefield: Danger and Pleasure in Nineteenth-Century Feminist Sexual Thought." *Feminist Studies* 9 (1): 7–25.

Gordon, Margaret T., and Stephanie Riger. 1989. *The Female Fear.* New York: Free Press.

Greenfeld, Lawrence A. 1997. *Sex Offenses and Offenders: An Analysis of Data on Rape and Sexual Assault.* Washington, D.C.: U.S. Department of Justice, Office of Justice Programs.

Griffin, Susan. 1977. "Rape: The All-American Crime." In *Feminism and Philosophy*, ed. Mary Vetterling-Braggin, Frederick A. Elliston, and Jane English, 313–32. Totowa, N.J.: Littlefield, Adams.

Grosz, Elizabeth. 1994. *Volatile Bodes: Toward a Corporeal Feminism.* Bloomington: Indiana University Press.

Groth, A. Nicholas. 1979. *Men Who Rape: The Psychology of the Offender.* New York: Plenum Press.

Harding, Sandra. 1986. *The Science Question in Feminism.* Ithaca: Cornell University Press.

———. 1991. *Whose Science? Whose Knowledge?* Ithaca: Cornell University Press.

Heberle, Renee. 1996. "Deconstructive Strategies and the Movement against Sexual Violence." *Hypatia* 11 (4): 63–76.

Hegel, G. W. F. [1807] 1977. *The Phenomenology of Mind.* Trans. J. B. Baillie. New York: Humanities Press.

Henderson, Lynne. 1992. "Rape and Responsibility." *Law and Philosophy* 11: 127–78.

Hengehold, Laura. 1994. "An Immodest Proposal: Foucault, Hysterization, and the 'Second Rape.'" *Hypatia* 9 (3): 89–107.

Herman, Judith Lewis. 1992. *Trauma and Recovery.* New York: Basic Books.

Hobbes, Thomas. [1651] 1996. *Leviathan.* Oxford: Oxford University Press.

Hodge, Joanna. 1988. "Subject, Body, and the Exclusion of Women from Philosophy." In *Feminist Perspectives in Philosophy*, ed. Morwenna Griffiths and Margaret Whitford, 152–168. London: Macmillan Press.

Holmes, Melisa. 1999. "Sexually Transmitted Infections in Female Rape Victims." *AIDS Patient Care and STDs* 13 (12): 703–8.

hooks, bell. 1981. *Ain't I a Woman: Black Women and Feminism.* Boston: South End Press.

Huggins, Jackie. 1991. "Black Women and Women's Liberation." In *A Reader in Feminist Knowledge*, ed. Sneja Gunew, 6–12. New York: Routledge.

Irigaray, Luce. 1985a. *Speculum of the Other Woman.* Trans. Gillian C. Gill. Ithaca: Cornell University Press.

———. 1985b. *This Sex Which Is Not One.* Trans. Catherine Porter with Carolyn Burke. Ithaca: Cornell University Press.

———. 1993a. *An Ethics of Sexual Difference.* Trans. Carolyn Burke and Gillian C. Gill. Ithaca: Cornell University Press.

———. 1993b. *Je, Tu, Nous: Toward a Culture of Difference.* Trans. Alison Martin. New York: Routledge.

———. 1993c. *Sexes and Genealogies.* Trans. Gillian C. Gill. New York: Columbia University Press.

———. 1994. *Thinking the Difference: For a Peaceful Revolution.* Trans. Karin Montin. New York: Routledge.

———. 1996. *I Love to You: Sketch for a Felicity within History.* Trans. Alison Martin. New York: Routledge.

Jaggar, Alison M. 1987. "Sex Inequality and Bias in Sex Differences Research." In *Science, Morality, and Feminist Theory,* ed. Marsha Hanen and Kai Nielsen, 25–39. Supplementary volume 13 of the *Canadian Journal of Philosophy.* Calgary: University of Calgary Press.

Kant, Immanuel. [1763] 1965. *Observations on the Feeling of the Beautiful and Sublime.* Trans. John T. Goldthwait. Berkeley: University of California Press.

———. [1784] 1949. "What Is Enlightenment?" In *The Philosophy of Kant,* ed. Carl J. Friedrich. New York: Modern Library.

Keller, Evelyn Fox. 1985. *Reflections on Gender and Science.* New Haven: Yale University Press.

Kelly, Liz. 1987. "The Continuum of Sexual Violence." In *Women, Violence, and Social Control,* ed. Jalna Hanmer and Mary Maynard, 46–60. London: Macmillan.

Kittel, Ruth. 1982. "Rape in Thirteenth-Century England: A Study of the Common Law Courts." In *Women and the Law.* Vol. 2, *Property, Family and the Legal Profession,* ed. D. Kelly Weisberg, 101–15. Cambridge: Schenkman Publishing.

Komesaroff, Paul A., ed. 1995. *Troubled Bodies: Critical Perspectives on Postmodernism, Medical Ethics, and the Body.* Durham: Duke University Press.

LaFree, Gary D. 1982. "Male Power and Female Victimization: Toward a Theory of Interracial Rape." *American Journal of Sociology* 88 (2): 311–28.

Ledray, Linda E. 1986. *Recovering from Rape.* New York: Henry Holt.

Lloyd, Genevieve. 1993. *The Man of Reason: "Male" and "Female" in Western Philosophy.* Minneapolis: University of Minnesota Press.

Locke, John. [1690] 1980. *Second Treatise of Government.* Indianapolis: Hackett Publishing.

Lockwood, Daniel. 1980. *Prison Sexual Violence.* New York: Elsevier.

Los, Maria. 1994. "Feminism and Rape Law Reform." In *Feminist Perspectives in Criminology,* ed. Loraine Gelsthorpe and Allison Morris, 160–172. Philadelphia: Open University Press.

MacKinnon, Catharine A. 1989. *Toward a Feminist Theory of the State.* Cambridge: Harvard University Press.

———. 1997. "Pornography Left and Right." In *Sex, Preference, and Family: Essays on Law and Nature,* ed. David M. Estlund and Martha C. Nussbaum, 102–25. New York: Oxford University Press.

Mahowald, Mary Briody, ed. 1983. *Philosophy of Woman: An Anthology of Classic and Current Concepts.* Indianapolis: Hackett Publishing.

Marcus, Sharon. 1992. "Fighting Bodies, Fighting Words." In *Feminists Theorize the Political,* ed. Judith Butler and Joan W. Scott, 385–403. New York: Routledge.

Martin, Biddy. 1988. "Feminism, Criticism, and Foucault." In *Feminism and Foucault: Reflections on Resistance,* ed. Irene Diamond and Lee Quinby, 3–19. Boston: Northeastern University Press.

McCaughey, Martha. 1997. *Real Knockouts: The Physical Feminism of Women's Self-Defense.* New York: New York University Press.

McGregor, Joan. 1994. "Force, Consent, and the Reasonable Woman." In *In Harm's Way: Essays in Honor of Joel Feinburg,* ed. Jules L. Coleman and Allen Buchanan, 231–54. New York: Cambridge University Press.

McNay, Lois. 1991. "The Foucauldian Body and the Exclusion of Experience." *Hypatia* 6 (3): 125–39.

———. 1992. *Foucault and Feminism.* Boston: Northeastern University Press.

McWhorter, Ladelle. 1989. "Culture or Nature? The Function of the Term 'Body' in the Work of Michel Foucault." *Journal of Philosophy* 86 (Nov.): 608–614.

———. 1990. "Foucault's Analytics of Power." In *Crises in Continental Philosophy,* ed. A. B. Dallery and C. E. Scott, 119–26. Albany: State University of New York Press.

Merleau-Ponty, Maurice. 1981. *The Phenomenology of Perception.* London: Routledge.

Mill, John Stuart. [1869] 1911. *The Subjection of Women.* New York: Frederick A. Stokes.

Morgan, Kathryn Pauly. 1991. "Women and the Knife: Cosmetic Surgery and the Colonization of Women's Bodies." *Hypatia* 6 (3): 25–53.

Morgan, Robin. 1977. *Going Too Far: The Personal Chronicle of a Feminist.* New York: Random House.

———. 1980. "Theory and Practice: Pornography and Rape." In *Take Back the Night: Women on Pornography,* ed. Laura Lederer, 134–47. New York: William Morrow.

National Victim Center and Crime Victims Research and Treatment Center. 1992. *Rape in America: A Report to the Nation.*

Okin, Susan Moller. 1989. *Justice, Gender, and the Family.* New York: Basic Books.

Paglia, Camille. 1992. *Sex, Art, and American Culture.* New York: Vintage Books.

Pateman, Carole. 1980. "Women and Consent." *Political Theory* 8 (2): 149–68.

Peterson, Susan Rae. 1977. "Coercion and Rape: The State as a Male Protection Racket." In *Feminism and Philosophy,* ed. Mary Vetterling-Braggin, Frederick A. Elliston, and Jane English, 360–71. Totowa, N.J.: Littlefield, Adams.

Pipher, Mary. 1994. *Reviving Ophelia: Saving the Selves of Adolescent Girls.* New York: G. P. Putnam's Sons.

Plaza, Monique. 1981. "Our Damages and Their Compensation: Rape: The Will Not to Know of Michel Foucault." *Feminist Issues* 1:25–35.

Raine, Nancy Venable. 1998. *After Silence: Rape and My Journey Back.* New York: Crown Publishers.

Rawlinson, Mary. 1987. "Foucault's Strategy: Knowledge, Power, and the Specificity of Truth." *Journal of Medicine and Philosophy* 12: 371–95.

Rhode, Deborah. 1989. *Justice and Gender: Sex Discrimination and the Law.* Cambridge: Harvard University Press.

Roiphe, Katie. 1994. *The Morning After: Sex, Fear, and Feminism*. Boston: Little, Brown.

Rose, Deborah S. 1991. "A Model for Psychodynamic Psychotherapy with the Rape Victim." *Psychotherapy* 28 (1): 85–95.

Rousseau, Jean-Jacques. [1755] 1984. *A Discourse on the Origins and Foundations of Inequality among Men*. New York: Penguin Books.

———. [1762] 1968. *The Social Contract*. New York: Penguin Books.

———. [1762] 1979. *Emile, or On Education*. Trans. Allan Bloom. New York: Basic Books.

Sanday, Peggy Reeves. 1981. "The Socio-Cultural Context of Rape: A Cross-Cultural Study." *Journal of Social Issues* 37 (4): 5–27.

Sawicki, Jana. 1991. *Disciplining Foucault: Feminism, Power, and the Body*. New York: Routledge.

Scacco, Anthony M., Jr. 1975. *Rape in Prison*. Springfield, Ill.: Charles C. Thomas.

Schulhofer, Stephen J. 1992. "Taking Sexual Autonomy Seriously: Rape Law and Beyond." *Law and Philosophy* 11:35–94.

Schwendinger, Julia R., and Herman Schwendinger. 1983. *Rape and Inequality*. Beverly Hills: Sage Publications.

Seidenberg, Robert, and Karen DeCrow. 1983. *Women Who Marry Houses: Panic and Protest in Agoraphobia*. New York: McGraw-Hill.

Shafer, Carolyn M., and Marilyn Frye. 1977. "Rape and Respect." In *Feminism and Philosophy*, ed. Mary Vetterling-Braggin, Frederick A. Elliston, and Jane English, 333–46. Totowa, N.J.: Littlefield, Adams.

Slaughter, Laura, and Carl R. V. Brown. 1991. "Cervical Findings in Rape Victims." *American Journal of Obstetrics and Gynecology* 164 (2): 528–529.

Smart, Carol. 1989. *Feminism and the Power of Law*. New York: Routledge.

Smith, Valerie. 1994. "Split Affinities: The Case of Interracial Rape." In *Theorizing Feminism: Parallel Trends in the Humanities and Social Sciences*, ed. Anne C. Hermann and Abigail J. Stewart, 155–70. Boulder: Westview Press.

Sommers, Christina Hoff. 1994. *Who Stole Feminism? How Women Have Betrayed Women*. New York: Simon and Schuster.

Spelman, Elizabeth V. 1988. *Inessential Woman: Problems of Exclusion in Feminist Thought*. Boston: Beacon Press.

Spohn, Cassia, and Julie Horney. 1992. *Rape Law Reform: A Grassroots Revolution and Its Impact*. New York: Plenum Press.

Stanko, Elizabeth A. 1985. *Intimate Intrusions: Women's Experience of Male Violence*. London: Routledge and Kegan Paul.

Sunday, Suzanne R., and Ethel Tobach, eds. 1985. *Violence against Women: A Critique of the Sociobiology of Rape*. New York: Gordian Press.

Thorpe, Geoffrey L., and Laurence E. Burns. 1983. *The Agoraphobic Syndrome*. New York: John Wiley and Sons.

Tong, Rosemarie. 1984. *Women, Sex, and the Law*. Totowa, N.J.: Rowman and Allanheld.

Vetterling-Braggin, Mary, Frederick A. Elliston, and Jane English, eds. 1977. *Feminism and Philosophy*. Totowa, N.J.: Littlefield, Adams.

Warr, Mark. 1984. "Fear of Victimization: Why Are Women and the Elderly More Afraid?" *Social Science Quarterly* 65:681–702.

Weisburg, D. Kelly, ed. 1993. *Feminist Legal Theory: Foundations*. Philadelphia: Temple University Press.

West, Robin L. 1991a. "The Difference in Women's Hedonic Lives: A Phenomenological Critique of Feminist Legal Theory." In *At the Boundaries of Law: Feminism and Legal Theory*, ed. Martha Albertson Fineman and Nancy Sweet Thomadsen, 115–34. New York: Routledge.

———. 1991b. "Jurisprudence and Gender." In *Feminist Legal Theory: Readings in Law and Gender*, ed. Katharine T. Bartlett and Rosanne Kennedy, 201–34. Boulder: Westview.

Williams, Wendy W. 1991. "The Equality Crisis." In *Feminist Legal Theory: Readings in Law and Gender*, ed. Katharine T. Bartlett and Rosanne Kennedy, 15–34. Boulder: Westview.

Winkler, Cathy. 1991. "Rape as Social Murder." *Anthropology Today* 7 (3): 12–14.

Wollstonecraft, Mary. [1792] 1983. *A Vindication of the Rights of Woman*. New York: Penguin Books.

Woodhull, Winifred. 1988. "Sexuality, Power, and the Question of Rape." In *Feminism and Foucault: Reflections on Resistance*, ed. Irene Diamond and Lee Quinby, 167–176. Boston: Northeastern University Press.

Young, Iris Marion. 1990. "Throwing Like a Girl: A Phenomenology of Feminine Body Comportment, Motility, and Spatiality." In *Throwing Like a Girl and Other Essays in Feminist Philosophy and Social Theory*, 141–59. Bloomington: Indiana University Press.

Index